a boy named trout

mercy strongheart

Auctus Publishers

Havertown, Pennsylvania, United States

a boy named trout

mercy strongheart

Published by Auctus Publishers, LLC
606 Merion Avenue, First Floor
Havertown, PA 19083, USA

Softcover Edition: ISBN: 978-0-9979607-0-9
Electronic Edition: ISBN: 978-0-9979607-1-6

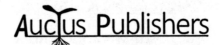

a boy named trout

For my sisters Lake, Faith, Lulu, Beth, and my brother Hickory.
And for the children of the flower children, wherever you are.

Acknowledgments

This book would never have made it into your hands if it weren't for my wonderful publisher Shrikrishna (Krish) Singh. His vision, dedication, and passion pushed this book from the back of a file cabinet to where it is now. Krish, thank you for pulling me along and believing in this story. Krish and I would not have met without Alison Gregg, our lovely friend who saw what could be and made it happen. Many thanks, Alison, for getting the pieces in place. And thank you to the team of folks who dressed this book up and shimmied it onto the dance floor.

I feel huge gratitude to all the readers who gave generously of their time and feedback throughout my rewrites, especially Stephen Pozgay, Rachel Lively, Karin Salzmann, Katharine Salzmann, Joe Lerro, and Beth Valdez. My sister Beth called me after I'd written the first section and begged to know what was going to happen. She became my muse henceforth. If my voracious, picky reader of a sister likes what I write, I feel I've done my job. Fellow writer Benjamin Parzybok helped me navigate the business end of things (not always the most intuitive thing for creative types). Thank you for that hand holding, Ben.

So many thanks are due to my late aunt Karin Salzmann, my great cheerleader since my fledgling attempts at writing. She would be thrilled to see this book in print, and ready with her red pen to help me with the next thing. Karin, I hope you are drinking heavenly lattes and entertaining all your favorite writers with your wit and charm.

Thank you to my parents and siblings for giving me the belief that art is a worthy pursuit in life. And to my little Elinor, thank you for putting up with your mama's unorthodox lifestyle so she can write. I hope I do good by you.

PART I

1

May 18, 1976

Tuesday

Trout wasn't sure what woke him. He lay in the dark, eyes searching the ceiling. It had been a sound, he remembered. A crash, like glass breaking. He blinked and woke, blinked and woke. Fire. It hit him all at once. The smell, the sound, the panic. He sprang up from his bed on the floor and to his parents' bed, a few feet away.

"Gordon, wake up! Wake up! Gordon!"

The twelve-year-old boy stood in the small, dark loft and shook his father furiously. Smoke drifted up from downstairs. Trout heard the fierce snapping of fire on wood. Gordon moaned and swiped his son's hand from his chest. Trout turned and saw his little sister, Precious Heaven, sitting upright in bed, her wide, blue eyes fixed on him without expression.

Jade, the oldest of the three children, rolled over on his wilted mattress on the floor and yelled, "What the fuck, Trout?"

Jade's body tensed as he sensed the fire, and then he sprang out of bed. "Gordon!" he yelled. "Shit! Gordon! Lotus! Wake up!" He quickly pulled his jeans on and leapt to his parents' bed. He wrapped his arms around his father and tried to pull him out of bed. When that failed, he shook him and yelled in his face, which still didn't wake the drunken man.

Their mother climbed out of bed and felt around on the dark floor for her nightgown, muttering, "Okay! Okay!"

Gordon opened his eyes, propped himself up on his elbows, and looked blearily about the room from beneath whiskey-soaked lids. His eyes fell on Trout, and he blinked slowly. A drunken grin spread over his face, and he laughed for a moment before his head fell back on the pillow, and he was out again. Trout stared at the stupid grin. He felt a hand on his leg and looked down to see Heaven, wide-eyed and clutching his thigh.

Trout realized that he suddenly didn't care all that much if his father made it out of the burning house. He grabbed Heaven in his arms and ran to the wooden ladder that led out of the loft. He had carried Heaven down this ladder since she was a baby. He knelt down, and she wordlessly climbed onto his back. His bare feet gripped the familiar knobby rungs, and in a matter of seconds, he was running across the dirt living room floor, his heart hammering in his chest.

The front door had become a mass of red flame. Black smoke poured into the tiny house. Trout ran for the back door. As he turned the rusted knob, he could hear the others upstairs, still trying to rouse Gordon. He carried Heaven outside into the crisp mountain air, her hands gripping his neck tightly. An instant later, Jade came flying through the window next to the back door. He rolled to a stop and picked himself up, laughing, bits of glass stuck in his skin. "OWOOO!" he howled. "I've always wanted to do that!"

Lotus appeared at the back door, framed in orange light from the fire behind her, frail and ghostlike in her nightgown, and yelled, "Jade! Get water from the creek! Trout! Go get Forest! I've gotta get your father!"

Trout set Heaven down on the damp ground. She clung to him for a moment and then released her hands as he set out running toward their neighbor's house on the other side of the field. Tall, yellow grass whipped at his naked legs, and tender spring thorns bounced off his tough feet. He began to call Forest's name as he pounded across the footbridge that led over the creek. Forest, who never slept as far as Trout could tell, was standing at his door, fully clothed, when Trout came running up the flagstone path yelling about the fire. Forest set out at a sprint, and Trout did a quick turn and followed him. As they tore across the field, Trout saw several figures in the light of the fire. More neighbors were helping carry water from the creek to the smoking house.

Forest grabbed Lotus's arm and yelled, "Where's Gordon?" Lotus motioned toward the creek and continued scooping water. Trout could see Gordon standing in the creek, swaying back and forth as water laced about his ankles, depositing a long arc of piss into the stream. Forest handed Trout a pail, and they set to work putting out the flames. They could not expect help to arrive anytime soon. The nearest fire department was thirty miles down the road. There were no phones and no other neighbors nearby. Trout heaved bucket after bucket of water onto the flames. The adobe house burned slowly. They had the fire out in less than an hour.

As the last wisps of smoke floated from the charred house, the adults gathered around Gordon near the creek. The children walked through the house to assess the damage.

"Check it out," Trout said to the neighbor boy, fingering the soaked, black door-frame. The front door had been devoured along with part of the front wall.

The neighbor boy kicked at two charred bottles on the floor. "Molotov cocktails."

Trout nodded solemnly.

"What's a malted cockball?" asked another kid.

"Molotov cocktail," the boys said in unison.

"It's how they set the house on fire."

Trout looked over at the creek where Jade stood with the adults. They were arguing. Trout couldn't make out what any of them were saying except Gordon, whose drunken voice boomed through the night. "Fuck! Those fuckers are gonna *pay*, man! Nobody fucks with me! Fuck!" Trout shuddered, remembering what he had thought to himself in the loft. He pushed the thought away and continued to examine the battered house.

The arguing by the creek continued until the neighbor whistled for his children, then he turned to Gordon and said, "Don't do anything stupid." Trout wondered what that meant as he watched the neighbors walk slowly back to their trailer on the other side of the barbed wire fence.

"Bullshit!" Gordon yelled. "That's bullshit! What kind a man are you! Huh?" Trout turned away, embarrassed. The neighbor kept walking as though he hadn't heard.

"Well," said Forest, pulling his long, brown hair back from his thin face, "you guys should probably sleep at my house tonight. Get away from all that smoke." They nodded, but nobody moved.

Gordon glared accusingly at them, his angry eyes drifting from one person to the next. Trout hated this mood: the mean drunk. He went into the house and began to gather up blankets and pillows. The sour smell of smoke pinched at his nostrils. Jade joined him, and then the family of five traipsed across the moonlit field to Forest's.

2

Wednesday

The next day was Wednesday, though only Trout kept track of the days, for school. Lotus had instructed him to stay home so he could help clean up after the fire. Jade had dropped out of school the year before, and Heaven, who spoke less and less the older she got, had been sent home from first grade after one week with a note that said she was "not learnable." Gordon, Lotus, and Forest had no regular jobs. They spoke in terms of "tomorrow," or "the day after tomorrow," or "sometime soon."

Back at the burned house, Lotus made coffee and oatmeal pancakes on the wood stove while Gordon set up two rickety sawhorses in the front yard. He stood in the bright morning sun, hungover and shirtless. His curly brown hair, sprinkled with gray, glinted in the sun. The skin on his freckled shoulders peeled from early spring sunburns. Across his golden back, a tattoo of a six-armed, green Hindu goddess bent and twisted as he worked. Nearby, Forest set about making *adobe*, mud bricks, in a rusted wheelbarrow. He had Trout and Jade bring water from the creek, which he stirred into the clay and dirt. Tall and lean with taut, ropy muscles that were deceptively strong, Forest used the wooden handle from a shovel to stir the mud with smooth, steady strokes. He showed the boys how to sprinkle yellow hay into the mud to bind it.

"What are we making adobe for?" Trout asked.

"We're gonna build a new house," answered Gordon, pounding long nails into a board.

Jade reached out and took the shovel handle. "Lemme try."

Trout watched his brother struggle against the thick mud. Jade's shaggy, brown hair fell into his eyes. His skin browned easily and was always several shades darker than anyone's in the family. Trout grabbed the handle to help, but Jade pushed him out of the way, intent on doing it alone. He wrestled the stick with his brown arms that were speckled with tiny cuts from crashing through the window the night before. Forest wordlessly took the handle from Jade and continued stirring.

When the mud was thoroughly mixed to the right consistency, Forest and Gordon laid out large sheets of plywood on the south side of the house. "Watch closely, boys," said Gordon, scooping mud onto a shovel with a thick, schlooping sound. He carried it over to the plywood, dumped the mud onto the board, and then took a one-by-four in each hand. "What we wanna do is make this mud into squares, see?" He pressed the mound of mud on each side with the boards. "Nice and flat, see?"

Trout, who thought his father's mound looked neither flat nor square, grabbed two pieces of wood. Jade carried chunks of mud over with the shovel while Trout helped the men shape it into bricks.

"We should have a mold," said Jade as he thunked mud down.

They worked until they had covered eight sheets of plywood with wet bricks, and the sun blazed high above them. Forest's squares were perfectly symmetrical. Trout had tried to imitate him and thought his squares at least looked better than Gordon's. They traipsed to the creek to wash the mud off their hands and arms, and then Gordon and Forest settled themselves against the charred wall of the house.

"You boys go into town," Gordon said. "I need nails, whiskey, and cigarettes. Ask your Mama what she wants."

Lotus needed cigarettes and a new broom, since the old one had been leaning against the front of the house and was devoured by the fire. She gave the boys food stamps and tried to get them to search for Precious Heaven so they could take her along, but Jade insisted that she was too slow and would only hold them up. Trout and Jade set out, leaving the men basking in the sun, rolling cigarettes and passing a bottle of tequila between them.

Town was several miles away. Some of the neighbors owned horses and often made the trip on horseback, but Jade and Trout were used to the walk and could do it in less than an hour if they didn't get hung up talking to somebody or find something interesting to examine. They pulled wild grass from the side of the road and sucked the milky sap from the stems as they walked.

"So, who do you think set the house on fire?" Trout asked, hooking his thumbs through his belt loops. It had been the topic of conversation all morning. Everybody had agreed that it was most definitely a local. No one in Trout's family even considered that it might have been a hippie. Torching the properties of undesirable hippies was not an unheard of practice in northern New Mexico. There was so much animosity between the locals and the hippies that even hippies who didn't like each other banded together for protection.

Jade kicked a bottle in front of him. "I don't know. I think it was probably Lucio." Lucio was the son of Mr. Garcia, who owned Cielo's only grocery store. He was a troublemaker and was often involved in acts against the hippies.

"Do you think Gordon did something?" Torchings were not random; they were almost always preceded by an argument or a bad deal.

"No! What the hell would Gordon do? Lucio just hates us for no reason."

Trout kicked the bottle. It rolled into the creek. He didn't believe that Gordon hadn't done something to anger whoever torched the house. He couldn't believe it; it made no sense. Trout liked things to make sense. Dust rose around their feet in pillowy clouds. It hadn't rained in weeks, and the land was parched and pale. The only sounds were the tinkling of the shallow creek and the occasional bumblebee cruising the rose hips. They passed Bob's trailer and his three horses grazing in the field. They passed the old barn that was sinking slowly into the ground and stopped to pitch a few rocks at it, as they always did, enjoying the satisfying thunks and cracks the stones made as they hit the rotting wood.

The boys rounded a turn in the road. Jade picked up his pace as a squat adobe house came into view.

"Jade, no," said Trout as Jade veered off the road and into Esperanza's driveway.

Esperanza was Jade's girlfriend and lived with her mother, Cookie, and younger brother, Joaquin. Trout was accustomed to Jade stopping off here, but he usually did not come back out, and Trout was left to go into town alone.

"Just a sec," Jade said and disappeared through the front door.

Trout waited for a few minutes, carving triangles into a fence post with a stick, and then he sighed and set off. His anger was short lived, though. Soon, the fever of high spring buzzing all around took hold of him, and he hummed as he walked, chucking stones into the creek and dragging his feet to create interesting patterns in the dirt.

The town of Cielo sat at 10,000 feet. Heading west into town, the only visible mountains were behind him, so Trout felt he was on top of the world. He waved to Ruth as he passed her house high on a hill where she was brushing her goats, their fine white hair drifting in the breeze. The air was spiced with rosehips and the woody smell of the wild willow that grew along the creek in long, red stalks.

More houses began to appear, at first cushioned comfortably in several acres of rolling grassland, but gradually crowding closer together until the dirt road gave way to asphalt, and the houses sprang to the side of the road where they stood, neatly, side by side. They were low houses, none higher than one story, many of them mobile homes. Chained-up dogs slept in the sun, and Mexican music drifted from tinny radios. Cars were propped up and open in various stages of repair. Trucks and lowriders sat up on blocks, engines exposed and parts scattered about them like knocked-out teeth. In the tidy gardens out front, daffodils and tulips squared off with purple and white irises. Some people stared as he passed. Most ignored him; a few waved.

The road snaked through town, following the curve of a ridge that dropped straight down into a steep ravine. Trout passed the green church and the daycare center, more houses, and then he saw Lucinda's gas pumps ahead. The town center, less than one block long, was comprised of Mr. Garcia's grocery store, Lucinda's convenience store with the two pumps out front that only sometimes had gas, and a tiny bakery that was just opening where there had once been a hardware store. Trout stopped at Lucinda's first. Though his parents never told him to, he always bought himself candy or a soda when he ran errands in town. He figured it was his reward.

Lucinda was an old, Hispanic woman with thick streaks of gray running through her black hair. A bit on the plump side, she shuffled behind her counter in house slippers and floral-print polyester dresses. She was nice to Trout and would give him candy after running her fingers through his blond hair a few times, sighing loudly. Her husband, Ben, sat in an adjoining room, out of sight. Trout had never seen him but could hear his radio rattling on in Spanish. Every once in a while, Ben would cough wretchedly which would start Lucinda humming to herself.

Trout stepped into the cool, dark store. It smelled of Pine-Sol and Popsicles. His feet carried him across the black-and-white linoleum floor to a refrigerator, which he opened and took out a bottle of orange soda. Lucinda stood talking to a tall woman, the two of them leaning on the counter and speaking fast Spanish. Trout liked listening to Spanish. It bubbled and flowed like the creek in front of his house. The woman talking to Lucinda spotted Trout and moved away. She scowled at his feet.

"*Qué niño sucio*," she said to Lucinda. "*Mira sus pies.*"

Trout translated in his head. Dirty boy. Look at his feet.

Lucinda slapped the woman's hands and worked her wrinkled lips into a frown. "*No puede ayudarle*," she said and reached a crony hand out to Trout. He can't help it. Trout handed her a crumpled food stamp. The tall woman stared at Trout as if he were an insect that had just crawled out of a turd.

"Hey! Hippie boy! Why are you so filthy? Huh? Can't you wash your feet? You stink!"

"*¡Cállate!*" snapped Lucinda, trying to quiet the woman.

"Well, his house was torched last night! Didn't you hear?"

Lucinda waved her hand dismissively toward the woman and turned away to rummage through some boxes behind the counter.

"It's true!" the woman said. She turned to Trout, who stepped back. Her eyes were rimmed in heavy, black liner and her dark lashes reached out to him like stiff, dead spiders. "Gringo, tell your family to go home! Tell them we don't like you!"

Trout felt his throat closing up, and tears pushed against the backs of his eyes. He looked down at the floor and saw that his feet really were filthy. He hadn't realized it until now, standing on Lucinda's sparkling black-and-white linoleum. They were coated in dirt and tar from the hot asphalt. He suddenly saw how he must look to this woman with the spider eyes. His thick, blond hair had grown to the middle of his back and hadn't been brushed in days. His skin was mottled with patches of soot, mud, dirt, and sap. He wasn't sure when his last bath had been. His once-white t-shirt had grown yellow and threadbare with age, and his blue jeans had holes in the knees and the bottoms of the pockets from collecting rocks. If he could just explain to this woman that all his friends had long hair, that the only place to bathe at his house was in the cold creek fed by snow runoff, that he wore Jade's hand-me-downs, and Jade wore other people's hand-me-downs. But he just stood there staring at his dirty feet and trying not to cry.

"Here, Troutcito," Lucinda said. She reached a plump fist out to him. "You don't listen to anything this woman tells to you."

Trout held out his hand, and Lucinda pressed a wad of wrapped candies into his palm along with the crumpled food stamp. Trout closed his fingers around the candy and walked wordlessly out of the store and into the bright sun. He tried to scrape his feet clean on the brittle grass beside the gas pumps. Trout knew who the woman was. She lived in a blue house near the church. She was married to Lucio, Mr. Garcia's son. Trout made a mental note to walk as quickly as possible past her house on his way home. He never wanted to see her again. He crossed the street to Mr. Garcia's grocery store. Several old men sat on the low wall in front, sipping Cokes and watching the road through crinkled brown slits. They watched Trout cross the street, and one of them spat near his feet as he entered the store.

Mr. Garcia sat in a rocking chair behind a glass counter, listening to the same radio station as Ben across the street. He had a handful of peanuts in one hand and a bottle of Coke in the other. He slowly cracked the shells off the peanuts and dropped the nuts into his soda.

Trout approached the counter and nodded his head. *"Buenos días."*

Mr. Garcia continued to stare out the window and crack peanuts, giving no sign that he had heard Trout say hello. Most of the merchandise was kept behind the counter, so customers had to ask Mr. Garcia to get up and bring what they wanted to the counter. Unlike Lucinda, Mr. Garcia was not very friendly. He didn't speak English, and with Trout's limited Spanish vocabulary, it was always a struggle to get what he needed from the store. It could have been his imagination, but it seemed to Trout that Mr. Garcia purposely made it difficult for him to shop there.

"Necesito cigarros, Johnny Walker Black, uno, clavas, y ..." Trout didn't know the word for broom. His eyes scanned the shelves that zigzagged toward the back wall. He did not see a broom to point to. Mr. Garcia rocked back and forth, chewing on

the Coke-softened peanuts. Trout walked over into Mr. Garcia's line of sight, but the old man's eyes immediately shifted to gaze over Trout's shoulder. Trout pantomimed sweeping with a broom. "*Cómo se llama?*" he asked, fishing for the word in Spanish.

Mr. Garcia pushed air loudly through his nostrils, and Trout saw that he had offended him. He scanned the counter for a pen and paper so he could draw a broom. Just then, somebody walked through the door, and he turned to see Jade with his best friend, Boonray. They swaggered to the refrigerator and took out two six-packs of beer.

"Trout!" Jade said, catching sight of his brother. "Where'd you go, man?"

"Hey, Trout," said Boonray, setting the beer on the counter. "What are you doing in here on a school day? Shouldn't you be fighting at Cielo Elementary? *¡Hola, Mr. Garcia! ¿Cómo estás?*"

Mr. Garcia slowly rose to his feet and shuffled over to collect Boonray's money.

"*Y dos cajas de Lucky Strikes, por favor. No, tres. Tres.*"

Mr. Garcia set the cigarettes on the counter. "Twelve dollars." Boonray counted the money out, waving Jade's wallet away.

"Hey, Boonray, how do you say broom in Spanish?" Trout asked.

"Broom? *¡Mujer! ¡Esposa!*" Boonray chuckled loudly at his joke. "I don't know, Trout! How the hell am I supposed to know how to say broom? That's women's work!" He smiled conspiratorially at Mr. Garcia. Mr. Garcia handed Boonray his change without looking at him.

Trout spied a pen behind a can of beef jerky and began to draw a broom on his hand.

"What the hell is that, Trout?" chided Boonray. "It looks like a rocket ship. Or a giant squid."

"Lemme see." Jade grabbed Trout's hand. "No, you're right, Boonray. It's a woman! Bent over in a fringed skirt!" Boonray and Jade practically fell over each other laughing. Then Jade took the pen and drew a broom on his own hand. He showed it to Mr. Garcia.

"*Necesito uno de éstos.*" I need one of those.

Mr. Garcia shook his head.

"*¡Una ... una escoba!*" Jade shouted. "Man, I can't believe I knew that! How the hell did I know that word?"

Mr. Garcia shuffled off toward the back of the store.

"Let's go, Jade, my man!" said Boonray, heading toward the door with the cigarettes and beer.

"Wait!" said Trout. "Give me a ride back home."

"Aw, Trout. We're headed in the other direction."

"No fair! You left me to walk into town by myself, and I don't wanna carry everything home by myself!"

"He's got a point," said Boonray.

Mr. Garcia was tapping the counter with the pen.

"Just wait for me, guys, okay?" Trout paid Mr. Garcia and trotted out the door with his arms full.

Trout threw his things into the back of Boonray's beat-up truck and started to climb in after Jade. Boonray whistled, his eyes staring across the street. Trout turned to see the object of his admiration: a black convertible Mercedes-Benz parked in front of Lucinda's, gleaming in the sun.

"Whoa, baby!" said Boonray, slamming the truck door closed before walking across the street to have a closer look.

Trout and Jade followed. The three of them leaned on the car and peered inside. It was spotless with immaculate beige leather seats. Walnut panels shone in the sun.

Boonray reached inside and opened the glove compartment. Just a few gum wrappers and a map of New Mexico. "Bummer," he said as his eyes scanned the seat and floors.

"Good afternoon, boys," said a voice behind them. They turned to see a short, clean-cut man in a tan sport coat and jeans walking toward them.

"This your car?" Boonray asked.

"It sure is."

Boonray whistled again, his eyes rolling all over the shining paint.

"450 SL?" Jade asked.

"You know your cars," the man said, planting his hand on the driver's door.

Jade grinned sheepishly and removed his body from the fender.

"Say, I'm looking for some waterfalls that are supposed to be around here. Would you boys know how I could get there?" The man jingled his keys around his index finger. His smile revealed a row of perfect, white teeth.

"You mean the Dixon falls?" asked Boonray.

"Well, I'm not sure what they're called. I just know they're nearby."

"Sure," Jade said. "We could tell you. But you don't plan on going in this do you?" he gestured toward the Mercedes, which looked ready to pounce onto the road and drive itself away.

"Why not?"

Jade chuckled. "I don't think that'd be a good idea. The road's pretty rough. She'll bottom out for sure."

The man smiled and jingled his keys. "I'll manage."

"All right," said Jade, raising his eyebrows skeptically. He gave the man directions while Trout and Boonray ran their hands over the velvety paint.

"Got it." The man put his hand on the door handle and raised his eyebrows at Trout and Boonray, who slid reluctantly away from the car.

"Hey, what are you going to the falls for, anyway?" Boonray asked.

The man smiled widely and started the engine. "I'm making a movie. I need to scope out locations."

"No way!" said Jade. "Got any parts for us?"

"Sure, sure. You boys can be the runaway outlaws." He waved his hand jauntily and drove smoothly off.

"That guy's awesome," Jade said as they walked back to Boonray's truck.

Boonray started his Ford with a bang and a shudder. "He seemed like a prick to me."

"We *are* runaway outlaws!" Jade's enthusiasm caused him to knock the beer he had just opened against the gearshift. Foam poured from the top, and he slurped it loudly.

Boonray laughed. "Boonray the Kid and Wild Jade." He pried the top off a beer with his lighter and pulled the truck onto the road.

"Where are we going, Boonray?" asked Trout. "Our house is the other way."

"Don't spawn out on me, Troutcito. We're just going for a little spin."

As usual, Trout felt uneasy around Boonray. He could never be sure if Boonray was going to be nice or mean, and his behavior could change suddenly. He had a hard glint in the corners of his eyes. His voice oozed sarcasm, and he walked around with his chest puffed out like a cock looking for a fight. Trout watched Boonray drive, his left hand drooped lazily over the steering wheel, his right holding the beer while grinding the truck's gears. His unwashed, brown hair hung to his shoulders. He wore a yellow t-shirt with the words EAT SHIT printed across the front of it, and a strand of ivory beads hung about his neck. His brown bell-bottoms flared around a pair of dusty cowboy boots.

Jade sat next to him, his long, brown hair pulled back into a ponytail. Jade was a few years younger than Boonray, and he periodically glanced over at the older boy. He tried to swig his beer the same way as Boonray and laughed loudly at his jokes. Trout wondered what it was that his brother admired so much. He often thought his brother was crazy—the way he did things suddenly and impulsively, his abhorrence for all rules—but next to Boonray, Jade seemed tame and well mannered.

Trout needed rules to feel safe. In every situation, he was constantly trying to figure out what the rules were and how he needed to behave in order to avoid getting into trouble. This wasn't an easy thing to do in his family, where the rules were vague and often in flux. What was okay one day was frowned upon the next. What could win his parents' approval in one situation brought punishment in another. For this reason, Trout watched everything closely, ready to pick up on the subtle clues that signaled things were changing, the atmosphere loosening or tightening, and he changed his behavior in accordance.

The truck headed down the highway toward Boonray's house. It jerked about on worn shocks, creaking and swaying. Boonray had found the truck on the side of the highway, its tires stolen and the windshield smashed. With Gordon's help, he got it running and had since rolled it three times, tearing drunk along the mountain roads. Trout was surprised every time he saw Boonray still alive. Trout knew three people who had died on the treacherous roads that lead to Cielo. He couldn't figure out how Boonray had escaped the same fate for so long. The truck passed the turnoff to Boonray's house.

"Where we going?" asked Jade. Boonray didn't answer, but a moment later, the truck slowed, and Boonray steered onto the road that led to the falls. "Boonray, no," said Jade.

The truck galloped and rocked over the pits and bumps of the dirt road. Trout felt a sickening clench in his stomach as he realized where they were headed. His hands gripped the weathered handle of the door. A plastic, naked man and woman hung from the rearview mirror. With each bounce of the truck, they knocked into each other, the man's stiff erection sometimes making it into one of the woman's several large, plastic orifices. At the top of the long hill before the falls, Boonray rolled the truck to a stop and shut off the engine. They waited in silence. Trout thought about protesting. He thought about jumping out of the truck. He cursed himself for being stupid enough to climb into Boonray's four-wheeled coffin in the first place. He looked over at his brother. Jade clenched his beer bottle tightly to his chest and glanced back and forth between the cracked windshield and Boonray's taut, feverish face. Boonray shifted into neutral, and the truck glided quietly down the hill.

"Okay," said Boonray as he steered the truck around the sharp turn. "If we see Mr. Hollywood, we tell him we came out to make sure he got here okay. Like we were worried." He snickered at the thought. "Jade, come on."

They had pulled up behind the parked Mercedes. Boonray climbed out of the truck, and Jade followed. Trout slid down in his seat, dreading what was coming. Thankfully, Boonray slammed the truck door and walked away without any effort to enlist Trout's help. Trout peered over the dashboard. The two boys were standing by the Mercedes and looking about for signs of the owner. In a flash, Boonray jumped into the driver's seat, and his head ducked beneath the steering wheel. A few moments later, Trout heard the Mercedes start up. Jade came running back to the truck chanting, "Oh, shit! Oh, shit! Oh, shit!" He climbed behind the wheel and started the truck with a roar. Boonray had swung the Mercedes around and was speeding up the hill. Jade turned the truck around with considerably less grace and followed Boonray, the truck's bald tires skidding beneath them.

Jade hunched over the steering wheel, gripping it tightly with both hands. "Fuck!" he screamed. "Mother fucker!" He looked over at Trout, whose hands were planted on the dashboard. "Fuck, Trout! What the fuck are we gonna do?"

Trout looked wide-eyed at his brother, who was grinning from ear to ear. The truck lurched from side to side.

"Look out!" yelled Trout, and Jade swerved to avoid a post they had nearly run into. They pulled onto the highway behind the Mercedes, Boonray's hair flying out behind him. They followed him onto the dirt road that led to his house. Trout watched the Mercedes, feeling strangely disconnected from himself, as though he were watching this happen in a dream. Boonray pulled into his driveway and parked the Mercedes in the field beside his gray house. He jumped out and started whooping loudly. Jade parked behind him and climbed out of the truck.

"We did it, Wild Jade!" Boonray whooped, his eyes bulging, a grin as wide as Jade's stretching across his face. Trout stepped onto the grass, feeling suddenly ill. Boonray began to strut around the Mercedes, bobbing his head back and forth like a rooster.

"Shit!" Jade yelled.

The back door of Boonray's house swung open, and a short, hunched woman came storming across the dry field in a gray dress, her weathered face puckered into a scowl. "What the hell is going on out here?" she demanded.

Boonray stepped toward her with his arms outstretched. "I bought you a Mercedes, Ma!"

She glared at the shiny car, which looked very out of place in the tangled weeds next to a pile of cinder blocks. "Where'd you get this car, Boonray?" She was in her son's face like an agitated yellow jacket.

"What, Ma? Don't you like it? I bought it for you 'cause it's purty, and you're so purty!"

"I won't be havin' the cops comin' 'round here no more, Boonray! I ain't coverin' your sorry ass no more!" She spoke with the generic accent of mountain dwellers, the same inflection that could be found from the Cascades to the Appalachians.

"So don't!" retorted Boonray, turning his back on her to pull two beers from the truck. She stood for a moment scowling at Boonray, then the Mercedes, then Jade and Trout, before she turned and stormed back into the house, slamming the door behind her.

"She's just pissed because she's afraid the cops'll find her crop," Boonray said and handed an open beer to Jade. They climbed into the Mercedes. Trout leaned on the side of the truck.

"Get in here, Trout!" Jade ordered. Against his better judgment, Trout climbed into the back seat. Boonray sat behind the wheel, running his rough hands over the smooth leather. "What are we gonna do?" asked Jade.

Boonray flicked at a few switches on the dash. "Let's take it out tonight!"

"Naw, I don't think that's a good idea," Jade said.

Trout thought of the Hollywood producer walking along the road in his shiny, brown boots and tan sport coat, jingling his useless keys around his index finger.

"I don't think so, Boonray," Jade said, but he was running his own hands along the gleaming walnut panels. "We should probably cover it up."

They sipped their beers in silence, caressing the car and raising their eyebrows at each other. Trout sat stiffly in the back seat. His idea was to turn around and take the car right back, but he didn't think he should mention it.

The boys climbed out and covered the Mercedes with a green tarp, which they weighted down with cinder blocks so the wind couldn't blow it off.

"Don't say anything to Lotus and Gordon," Jade instructed his brother. Trout nodded dumbly.

Boonray drove them to Esperanza's house. Jade clambered out of the truck, anxious to tell his girlfriend of his recent heroics. Esperanza came to the door wearing a white dress, an indigo scarf tied around her head. Her small, round, freckled face burst into a grin when she saw Jade. "I thought you weren't coming back!" she squealed.

They went inside, and Jade and Boonray recounted the car theft to her while Trout played with the two old dogs that lived on the sagging sofas. The house smelled of incense and patchouli. Scarves of every possible color and pattern hung from the ceiling, in the doorways, and were draped on the furniture. Like Jade, Esperanza had dropped out of school. She spent her days beading earrings and bracelets at home while her mother, Cookie, worked for a candle-maker in Taos. At night, Esperanza had a waitressing job in Dixon. She was saving money to go to Mexico.

"Oh my God," Esperanza said and shook her head, "you guys are crazy." Jade and Boonray laughed proudly, obviously taking this as a compliment.

Esperanza rolled a joint and passed it around. Trout considered it briefly but shook his head, his stomach still rolling uneasily from the truck ride.

"Well," Trout said and stood up, "I should probably get that stuff back home." He waited for an offer for a lift. When none came, he patted the sleeping dogs and headed for the door.

"Hey, no word to the folks," said Jade.

Trout nodded and stepped out into the afternoon. He took the stuff from the back of Boonray's truck. The whiskey bottle was miraculously unbroken, but the nails were scattered about. He gathered them up and headed home.

The house was empty except for Gordon, who snored loudly from the loft. Trout placed the things on the table and walked to the outhouse. The house sat on five acres made up mostly of pasture. They had owned horses at one point, but now the fields sat empty, and the grass had grown long and yellow. The property was bordered by a creek on the north side and by an *acequia*, a little irrigation canal that ran all the way through town, on the south, which fed the farms and houses that sat along the road. To the west stretched a falling-down barbed wire fence, on the other side of which sat Bob's trailer. The east side of the property disappeared into a tangle of willow and oak trees, beyond which Truchas Peak rose majestically. Trout was named after that mountain. His stomach rumbled, and he suddenly realized he was starving. He thought longingly of breakfast and decided to collect some eggs from Forest's chicken coop so he could make himself another batch of oatmeal pancakes.

The path that led to Forest's was well-worn from years of use. Trout's family had been in Cielo for seven years, and Forest had lived behind their property the whole time. More often than not, somebody from Trout's family was over at Forest's house, or else Forest was at theirs. The path led over the back creek that Trout's family used for bathing, wound through a patch of willow, and then met up with the flagstone path Forest had laid. The chicken coop sat off to the left. Forest was a vegetarian, but he kept the chickens for eggs. He didn't like killing the baby chicks, so the chickens continued multiplying. Every once in a while, he'd give a few away to people who promised they weren't going to kill them. Even so, the coop was overflowing with brown and white birds.

Trout decided he would stop in first to say hello to Forest. Forest and Trout got along well, and Forest often invited Trout to help with some project he was working on, such as adding onto his house or building furniture from the willow that grew by the river. Trout stepped in through the open door, the cool darkness of the house swallowing him. He was about to call hello when he heard strange sounds coming from upstairs. A woman was moaning. Trout's cheeks flushed as he realized what the sound was. He had seen adults having sex on several occasions, at parties or when visitors stayed at his house. His family slept together in the loft, and the night sounds of his parents were familiar to him. Trout turned and walked quietly back to the chicken coop. The eggs were not as plentiful today since Lotus had already taken some for the pancakes. He found one and then decided he would make an omelet instead, so he had to hunt for several more minutes through the jumble of nests and feathers before he found a few more. He gathered the brown eggs to his chest. They felt like warm stones.

As he emerged from the coop, Trout looked up and stopped in his tracks. Lotus was leaving Forest's house. Her hair was mussed up, and she wore blue jeans but no shirt. He watched as she walked barefoot down the flagstone path and disappeared into the willow. He dropped the eggs, and they cracked wetly on the ground. He caught up with Lotus at the bridge and followed quietly in her tracks. She hummed to herself and brushed the long grass with the tips of her fingers. Strands of her long, blonde hair caught in the grass and tickled Trout as he passed.

"Lotus," Trout said suddenly, his heart hammering in his chest.

He didn't know why he called out to her. There was no doubt in his mind that Gordon knew about her and Forest, and he guessed that Gordon didn't care. But Trout cared. He didn't know why, exactly, but he didn't want his mother over there, in Forest's bed. Lotus turned to face Trout. For a moment, she looked almost afraid. Trout glared into her eyes, his hands knotted into fists. She stared back and laughed a quick, nervous laugh, not like her usual one.

"What's the matter with you?" she asked, one eyebrow cocked up.

Trout stared into her eyes and watched them grow hard.

"Grow up," she said and turned away.

"You grow up!" Trout spat back.

With one quick step, Lotus was in front of Trout. She slapped him hard across his left cheek. "Don't you ever, EVER speak to me that way again! You hear me?"

Before Trout could answer, she was gone. He touched his stinging cheek and felt tears. He opened his mouth to the place where the grass had closed behind her.

"I HATE YOU!" he screamed from the bottom of his chest.

A rabbit bolted through the brush nearby, and a family of sparrows lifted from the ground, their wings beating furiously against the empty air.

3

Wednesday

Trout returned home to find the chairs had been moved outside. Heaven lay sleeping in one of them, her head sagging onto her shoulder. Lotus was inside sweeping. She had put a shirt on, and a cigarette dangled from the corner of her mouth. She didn't look up when he came in. Trout had forgotten all about his hunger. He looked at the scorched walls and thought about a new coat of paint. He fetched a bucket of water from the acequia and began scrubbing the black grime from the walls.

Heaven awoke and came wandering into the house. She stood silently in the doorway until Lotus looked up from her sweeping.

"Are you hungry?" asked Lotus. After several moments, Heaven nodded. "Trout, go get some eggs from Forest's."

"There are no eggs," said Trout.

"Yes, there are. I saw them this morning."

"But I was just there, and there aren't anymore." He thought of the eggs he had left smashed on the ground. He hoped Forest wouldn't be mad.

"Fine," Lotus snapped. She rummaged through her purse and produced a five-dollar bill which she held out to Trout. "Go to town for me. We need groceries."

"No." Trout dropped the black rag he was holding into the bucket of water. "I've been to town once already. You should have told me to get groceries then instead of just whiskey and cigarettes."

Lotus slammed her purse down on the wood stove. "Trout, goddammit! Don't fuck around with me! Your sister needs to eat!"

"I'll get her something to eat, then!" He grabbed Heaven's hand and strode toward the door. "You go fuck the neighbor or something!"

Lotus lunged at him. Her nails caught the back of his neck and raked through his skin. Trout broke into a run, grasping Heaven by the wrist. She ran stiffly beside him, trusting him more than their mother. They ran over the bridge and onto the road, leaving Lotus cursing at them from the doorway.

Trout wasn't sure where they would go. He remembered the candy in his pockets and shared it with Heaven. They chewed Tootsie Rolls and sucked on butterscotch. Trout looked up and saw that his feet had led him onto the road to Ruth's house. They passed Cookie's, and Trout looked over to see Jade and Esperanza cuddled in a hammock in the front yard, passing a joint between them. They didn't look up as Trout and Heaven walked by.

Ruth lived with her husband, Mark, in a small, gray house on top of a hill that looked out over Cielo and the valley to the west. Ruth had once pointed to a distant band of blue in the sky and told Trout that it was Colorado. Mark and Ruth were retired schoolteachers. They had built the house themselves, and they kept goats and chickens and grew most of their food in a large garden. Their only child, James, was grown and lived in Santa Fe. Trout had met him several times, and once, James had unrolled a bundle of large sheets of white paper with blue lines on them and showed Trout how the lines made a house. At that moment, when the blue lines sprang together and Trout could see the house James had designed, he decided he wanted be an architect, too. It sounded sophisticated and mysterious, and like it could get him far away from Lotus and Gordon.

When Trout's family first moved to Cielo, Ruth had come down to greet them, carrying an apple pie and wearing a plain dress. Trout and Heaven had taken an immediate liking to her, but after she left, Lotus closed the door and called her a "frumpy old hillbilly," which had set Jade and Gordon laughing. Ruth continued her house visits for a while, but Lotus's cold shoulder soon kept her away. After she stopped coming around, Trout began walking up the hill to see her, and ever since, he and Heaven had been regular visitors. She always gave them something to eat and let them help with the chores. Mark would teach Trout chords on the guitar while Ruth braided Heaven's hair and hummed softly, saying, "Nice, Trout. Very well done," even when Trout's fingers fumbled all over the place.

Ruth was squatting in the garden when Trout and Heaven approached. She looked up and smiled. Chavo, the baby goat, came running over and butted Trout playfully on the leg.

"Well, hello there!" Ruth beamed. "If it isn't my two favorite mountain goats!" She stood and brushed strands of silver hair away from her face.

Trout and Heaven walked gingerly through the garden rows. A pile of uprooted dandelions lay at Ruth's feet.

"I hate to kill these, but they will just take over the whole garden if I let them. Are you two hungry?"

Trout nodded. Heaven squatted down to examine the yellow flowers.

"Well," said Ruth, brushing off her hands, "I have just the thing for you two." They followed her out of the garden to the house. "I made some green chile stew this morning. I was hoping you two would come by to help us eat some of it! I was just telling Chavo, 'Why don't you run on down the hill and fetch my little *gueritos* for me, so they can eat some of this stew. Actually, Chavo, take the car so you can stop in town and pick up some flour and chocolate.'" She grinned mischievously at the children and led them through the front door.

The house was cozy and bright. The south-facing living room wall was comprised almost entirely of glass. Large, green plants spread their leaves to the windows, and several gray kittens chased each other on the plush rug.

Ruth poured two glasses of goat's milk and handed them to Trout. "It'll take just a minute to heat up. Why don't you two give those crazy kittens a little attention?"

Trout and Heaven sprawled themselves happily on the woven rug in a large patch of sunlight and sipped the milk. Heaven giggled as the kittens crawled on her lap and batted at her hair. Trout felt overcome with joy. He always felt this way at Ruth's. Her house was warm and tidy. Things were ordered, and every beautiful object had its special home, unlike his house where junk was scattered about, and you could lose your own feet if you weren't careful. At Ruth's, the rooms smelled of drying herbs and wood smoke. Everywhere he looked, living things beamed down on him, from the nodding plants to the kittens, to Ruth and her old dog, Bess, who slept by the door, groaning contentedly now and then. Trout never spent time relaxing in his house.

"How's your mom?" Ruth asked as she set the table.

Trout shrugged. His neck still stung from where her nails had scratched him. "Crabby."

Ruth said nothing as she dished two bowls from a pot on the stove, then called Trout and Heaven to the table. The children sat down to find two large bowls of stew with steam rising off the top. Chunks of beef, potatoes, carrots, and green chiles floated in the thick broth along with pinto beans and tomatoes. A loaf of warm, homemade bread was sliced onto a plate. Eagerly, Trout and Heaven dug in. Ruth sat between them peering at her knitting through silver-rimmed reading glasses.

"Do you like goat's milk?" she asked Heaven, who nodded and smiled.

Trout vaguely registered his sister's smile as he stuffed his mouth with meat. It showed up less and less often lately. He sneezed.

"Bless you," said Ruth.

He looked up at her. Suddenly, he felt as if he'd stuck his eyes in a cactus. He sneezed again.

"Are you okay?" Ruth asked.

Trout sneezed again. His nose was stuffed up, and it was harder to breathe than it had been a minute earlier.

"Holy smokes!" Ruth exclaimed. "I think you're having an allergic reaction! Are you allergic to cats?"

Trout shrugged. "I dunno."

"Come here. Let's wash your hands at the sink."

He followed her to the sink and washed his hands.

"You'd better stay away from those kittens for the rest of the day, and see if you feel better by this evening. Next time you come over, we can see if the same thing happens."

"Okay," said Trout, returning to his stew. Before long, the heat of the green chile was helping him breathe easier.

For a while, there was just the click of Ruth's needles and the sounds of the children eating. Trout finished, and Ruth motioned with her head to the pot. He served himself another bowl. The heat from the chile blazed deliciously through his skull.

"All we ever used to drink was goat's milk," said Trout, "back when we had goats. Now we get powdered milk, and it's gross if you ask me."

Ruth smiled and clicked away.

"Our house was torched last night," Trout said casually.

Ruth put down her needles and stared intently at Trout. "How do you know it was torched?"

Trout shrugged. "It caught on fire."

"And you think somebody set it on fire on purpose?"

"Uh-huh. I heard the bottles smash into the house, and then I heard a car drive off. Plus, there was a lady at Lucinda's today who said it was torched. She told me to tell my family to go home. She said we aren't wanted around here."

Trout had forgotten all about the woman with the scary eyelashes. He felt a surprising lump rise in his throat, and suddenly there were tears in his eyes. Ruth held her arms out to him, and he slid onto her lap. Ruth wrapped her arms around him, and he laid his head on the warm skin below her neck. She caressed his hair with smooth fingers.

"What's this, Trout?" she asked, her fingers on the place where Lotus had grabbed him.

For some reason, the concern in her voice made his throat feel tight and fiery. He pressed his face into her dress and sobbed. Heaven came over and placed a hand on his leg. Ruth enveloped Heaven in her other arm, and the three of them sat and rocked until Trout's sobs began to slow. Eventually the tears gave way to a feeling of relief, and he sat calmly, all traces of sadness lifted like low clouds from the morning fields. He grinned at Ruth sheepishly, feeling a little silly after his outburst.

"All better now?" Ruth asked. "Feels good to cry, doesn't it?"

Trout nodded.

"Tears are good, Trout. Don't ever be ashamed to cry."

Trout slid off her lap onto his chair and resumed eating. Heaven stared long-ingly at the kittens tumbling on the rug.

"Would you like some more stew, Heaven?" Ruth asked.

Heaven shrugged.

"That means no," Trout interpreted.

"Well, then would you like to give the kittens their evening dose of playtime?"

Heaven nodded eagerly and settled herself on the rug again. Trout was a little envious that he hadn't been chosen to give the kittens their playtime dose, but Ruth, it turned out, had other plans for him.

"Let's you and I have a talk, Trout," said Ruth as she unraveled a row of stitches. "How old are you now? Twelve?"

Trout nodded.

"Well, that's plenty old. Let's you and I have a grown-up talk." She looked Trout squarely in the eyes. Her eyes were like silver planets spinning behind her spectacle lenses. "For starters, who do you think this land we're sitting on belongs to?"

"You and Mark."

"And what makes you think it belongs to me and Mark?"

Trout shrugged. "'Cause you live on it."

"Right. Well, not that long ago, this land we're sitting on was inhabited by Indians. They lived on it, hunted on it, fished in its streams, and they died on it. They also took care of it. So, essentially it was their land, even though they didn't see it that way. The way they saw it, it was them that belonged to the land, and the land that took care of them."

Trout tried to picture Cielo empty of houses and cars. Teepees sprung up in his mind, and Indians walked about with feathers in their hair. He knew one Indian, Guapito, who came to some of the parties his parents went to. Guapito dressed like most people in Cielo, and Trout only knew he was an Indian because once, late in a party when everybody was drunk and sitting around a fire, Guapito had begun singing a soft, sad song in a language Trout had never heard. "I'm Apache!" Guapito had yelled, pulling his shirtsleeve up to reveal a bloody scrape on his forearm. His smoky eyes fell on Trout. "We are brothers. We belong nowhere." Several people had laughed, and somebody muttered, "Awesome."

Ruth stood and put a kettle on the wood stove. Then she bent down to stoke the fire inside. "One day, the Spanish arrived. First the explorers, then the settlers." Trout knew all about the Spanish explorers. Their names had been drummed into his head every year at school: Oñate, Don Diego de Vargas, Coronado, and Cabeza de Vaca. Their portraits were painted on the school walls, and the children dressed like them for school plays.

"The Spanish said to the Indians, 'This is our land now.' Ownership of land was a new concept to the Indians. They were caught off guard. Then the Spanish started settling on the land and killing the Indians if they tried to fight. 'Show us the deed if this is your land,' said the Spanish. Of course, the Indians had never heard of a deed before. They had no proof that the land was theirs, apart from the bones of their ancestors resting in the soil."

Trout's mind began to wander as Ruth continued her monologue. He had heard all this stuff before about the Europeans taking the land from the Indians. Not at school—at school, Trout was taught that the conquistadores were liberators who had rescued the Indians from their terrible lives—but from listening to Gordon talk with his friends. He watched Heaven bat a marble around with the kittens on the rug. She looked quite a bit like Trout, but her hair was longer and blonder than his, and her skin paler. She was skinnier, too, skinnier than other kids her age. Trout heard Ruth say the word hippie, and his ears perked up.

"They were artists and activists," she said, pouring boiling water into a teapot. She placed two mugs on the table along with a jar of honey. "The hippies fought for social reform. They used phrases like peace, love, and freedom. These words can be interpreted many different ways, Trout. Well, lots of hippies had fantasies of a simpler, more natural way of life. Many of them began to move into small towns and into the mountains. Some of them landed right here in Cielo. There was lots of land for sale, and people here have more freedom than they would in a city to live as they want to.

"Trout, do you think all twelve-year-olds are like you?"

Trout thought of the kids he went to school with. "Definitely not."

"Right. Just because a bunch of people are all twelve doesn't mean they're all the same, see? That's just how it is with hippies. It's the same with Hispanics and Indians. Lucinda and Mr. Garcia are very different people, don't you think? But if you didn't know them, they might seem very alike.

"So, all these white people began moving into the small towns of New Mexico, like Cielo and Madrid, Taos and so on. Some of them considered themselves hippies; others did not. What they had in common was that they were all outsiders, and so, to many of the Hispanics, they were all the same. And every Hispanic person had his or her own feelings about what was happening. Some liked it, some did not, some felt sort of middle of the road. But to many of them, it felt like an invasion."

Trout's head was spinning as Ruth poured the tea. He had never heard her talk so much at once. He struggled to pay attention, though his eyelids were beginning to droop. She placed a mug of tea in front of him. The steam smelled sweetly of chamomile and peppermint. Ruth sat still for a few moments, her hands wrapped around her cup, her head down and eyes slightly closed. She looked up and smiled.

"What I am getting at, Trout, is that there is a very traditional way of life going on up here. In come the hippies with their free love and peace and marijuana, and most of the Hispanics don't like it one bit. They see people walking around without any clothes on, and they consider that disrespectful. They see women without shirts on and men with long hair, and to them, all of this is strange. Our food is strange, our music is strange, our clothes and language are strange. They don't like the fact that some of us use drugs. And here we land, plop! In the middle of their world. If that isn't hard enough for them to deal with, there are some hippies who steal from the locals. They steal their chickens and other animals, and eat them. They steal wood from their neighbors' wood piles to burn. They steal gasoline from the tanks of cars and put it in their own. They leave garbage around and keep their yards messy. I could go on and on, but do you see what I am getting at, Trout? It's not you who the woman at Lucinda's hates. It's what you represent. It's the invasion of the hippies."

"Why did we come here, then? If nobody wanted us here in the first place?"

"For the very same reason the Spanish came here when the land belonged to the Indians: there was no room for their dreams in the world they came from. But it's the way you come in that's important. And unfortunately, many of us have not come in very nicely."

The sun was sinking fast. Ruth's words hung in the room like smoke. Trout did indeed feel that he had just finished a grown-up conversation. His head was filled with images of bare feet, teepees, and conquistadores. He mentally caressed the new awareness Ruth had given him. The conflicts of his day melted away like snow on a mountain. Heaven had fallen asleep on the rug. A fluffy kitten was curled on her back, cleaning itself with a pink tongue.

Ruth stood and smoothed her apron. She kissed Trout on the top of his head and began to rummage about in the kitchen. "Don't you worry too much about all this, Trout. You have a few precious years left to just be a kid. I'll be outside. You two better get home so your Mama doesn't worry." She softly touched the cuts on Trout's neck as she passed.

Trout carried the bowls to the sink and washed them with water from a bucket. He placed them to dry on the counter and went to wake his sister. She looked scared for a moment until Trout reminded her where she was. She rolled over, and the kitten flopped onto the rug.

"I don't want to go home," Heaven said.

"I know, but we have to. Come on."

Heaven stood and rubbed her eyes. She looked like a real little girl to Trout, not the mute doll she usually was. Her shoulders weren't scrunched up toward her neck anymore, and her cheeks had a light pink flush to them.

Outside, Ruth was emerging from the hen house. She handed Trout a basket. "This is for your Mama. Tell her I'd like her to visit me sometime."

Trout nodded as he took the basket. He knew Lotus would never come. "Thank you, Ruth."

Ruth bent and kissed each of them on the cheek. "Don't wait too long before coming to visit me, my munchkins." Heaven impulsively wrapped her arms around Ruth's legs, then let go and smiled.

They started off down the hill. Trout looked through the basket as they walked home. There were eggs, dried apples, jarred green beans, two heads of lettuce, a bundle of dandelion greens, dried tomatoes, goat cheese, jarred strawberry jam, and two loaves of homemade bread inside. He felt like crying again.

4

Thursday

Trout awoke early the next morning. The family lay fast asleep around him in the crowded loft except Heaven, whose small bed on the floor was empty. He dressed and went down to the kitchen to pack his lunch for school. Sheets of newspaper covered the table and countertops, upon which stems of pot had been laid to dry. The air was thick with the musty, rich smell of it. His parents had helped Forest pick the pot from his greenhouse the day before. They had come this far with the project last night and then abandoned the idea of hanging it, afraid people would see it through the windows. Trout pushed some plants aside so he could make a sandwich from Ruth's basket.

Heaven came in the door, bits of sticks and leaves stuck in her hair. She was always the first one up, and she and Trout had established a morning routine. Heaven would awake at dawn and slip outside. Trout knew all the places she went on her morning walk. First, she would go to the acequia to drink some water. Along the *acequia* was a tiny path that led into the willow and rose hips, so faint one could easily miss it. There were footpaths like this all over the property and beyond, made by Heaven on her daily outings. Heaven would duck onto this path and make her way along the creek, sometimes crawling beneath branches. Several bird nests were tucked in there, and Heaven would stop to check on each of them. Once, she had brought a tiny blue egg to Trout, and he had made her put it back, telling her not to touch any more. The next day, Heaven found the egg on the ground below the nest, grown cold, cast out by the mother. After checking on the nests, Heaven would follow another path to the woodpile. She often brought crumbs for the deer mice that lived in there. They knew her by now and would scamper out for their breakfast when she came by. From the woodpile, she'd make her way to the back creek. There, she checked on the birds, skunks, snakes, mice, and rabbits that made their homes near the mountain stream. Some days she would wander up the slope behind Forest's house, stopping in to see his chickens along the way. After she had made her morning visits, she would come back to the house in time to see Trout off to the school bus. She'd watch him pack his lunch and then walk with him to Ruth's road. That was as far as Trout would let her go. In the afternoon, she would return to the spot to greet him, sometimes bearing flowers or a snack. Some days they would walk up the road to Ruth's before going home.

Trout turned as Heaven walked inside. "Top of the morning to ya."

This made her laugh.

"How are your friends?" he asked.

"Good."

"Any eggs hatched yet?"

"No. Soon, though." Heaven stepped up to the counter to spread jam on a slice of bread. "I checked for eggs at Forest's, but there weren't any. There were some smashed on the ground, though. Do you think the mama chickens did that because we touched them?"

"No. Somebody probably just dropped them." Trout felt a twinge of guilt at his lie. He didn't want to revisit yesterday's encounter with Lotus. He pushed it out of his mind along with the dropped eggs.

He wrapped his sandwich in newspaper and slid it into his backpack along with some dried apples. "Ready?"

Heaven followed him out the door, her mouth full of bread. The crisp mountain air smelled like new paper. The birds were in full morning song. Trout and Heaven walked quietly beside the creek. They savored the pale light and the rim of sun peeking over the hill in front of them. It was nice in May, when day was breaking during their walk. Much nicer than in winter, when they walked in the dark through crisp snow.

They said good-bye at their usual spot, and Trout continued on alone. Heaven watched him until he disappeared and then turned back to the house. Her day would be filled by the routine she had designed for herself. Trout felt guilty many days, leaving Heaven alone. He knew she missed him while he was gone, and he also knew that nobody kept an eye on her during the day.

Cielo Elementary was a small school of fifty or so children from Cielo and the surrounding villages and hills. Trout was one of four hippie children who attended. Most of Trout's friends went to school in San Pedro, a town about thirty miles from Cielo. There were more hippie children there, who were able to stick together, but there wasn't a school bus that went from Cielo to San Pedro.

Trout hated the school. Most of his days at Cielo Elementary were spent trying to avoid fights and stealing naps whenever he could. As he climbed off the school bus with the other kids, he made a beeline for his classroom. School didn't start for another fifteen minutes, but staying on the playground would be a mistake. With his pale hair and ripped jeans, Trout was hard to miss. And ganging up on the gringo was a popular playground game.

There were three classrooms: one for kindergarten through first grade, one for second through third grade, and the other for fourth through sixth. Trout was in sixth grade. Sometimes he considered dropping out, like Jade did after eighth grade, but Ruth had drummed it into his head plenty of times that school was the most important thing he could be doing, and he needed to finish school if he ever wanted to be an architect like James. Besides, as awful as Cielo Elementary was, it sure beat staying at home with Gordon and Lotus. Trout slipped into the empty classroom, shutting the heavy door quietly behind him. Fluorescent lights flickered overhead, and the screams of children on the playground seeped through the windows. His teacher, Mrs. Trujillo, was probably on the playground with the kids or in the teachers' lounge.

Trout placed his lunch in his cubby. Somebody had drawn a cross-eyed fish next to his name. He went to the reading area, which was formed by three bookshelves arranged into a u-shape, and laid down on the brown carpet to read the spines of books. When the bell rang, he went to a desk at the back of the room. He always took a desk before the other kids came in so he could avoid having anybody sit behind him. Too many days he had gone home with spitballs plastered to the back of his head or some kid's snot smeared on his shirt.

His classmates swarmed in like a hive of bees, yelling and shoving. Mrs. Trujillo came in behind them, plump and not much taller than her students. She yelled at the students until they took their seats. Trout laid his head on his desk and fell asleep. He awoke to the sound of the morning recess bell. The kids were swarming inside again. He hadn't even heard them leave. As they came in, two boys whacked Trout on the head, one after the other. There was a ruffle of laughter throughout the room. "I'm gonna getchoo today at lunch," the older of the boys said. Trout glared at him. His name was Manny, and he had flunked several grades. He towered over the other children. His hair was cut close to his head, and he had a cut on his chin from shaving. Trout had already had three fights with him during the year. Manny swaggered to his seat, turning to give Trout one last menacing glare.

Mrs. Trujillo instructed the kids to take out their spelling books. She began to write the week's words on the board. Bruise, celebration, grandparent … Trout soon grew bored. He pulled a book out of his backpack, slumped in his desk, and read. Schoolwork was easy for him. He usually had his homework finished before the day was over. Mrs. Trujillo had given up on trying to get Trout to pay attention back in the fourth grade. He did his own thing during the day and still managed to stay ahead of the rest of the class.

After math, the lunch bell rang. Trout made his way to the cafeteria in the swarm of children. He sat at a long table far from his classmates and was soon joined by the three other hippie kids, all of whom were in different classrooms. Tuesday, the youngest, was six. She lived a few miles up the road from Trout. Max was seven, and his sister, Sage, was eight. They lived on the other side of Cielo, near Lucinda's. Max and Sage sat down with plastic trays, each of which held a wilted burger on a thin bun, a sloppy scoop of macaroni and cheese, a carton of milk, and a square of red Jell-O. The food was lifeless and limp except for the Jell-O, which trembled excitedly.

An apple core came flying through the air and landed with a splat on Tuesday's lunch tray. Her face crumpled into a pink scowl, and she burst into tears. Sage took the core and threw it in the direction from which it had flown. There was a low booing sound from the other kids, and somebody yelled, "Slut!" Trout took the goat cheese sandwich and dried apples from his bag. He was again grateful for Ruth's gift of food that saved him, at least for today, from the slimy slop of school lunch.

"Hey," said Max with his mouth full, "are you gonna be at Winnie's party tomorrow?"

"I dunno," said Trout. Winnie was an old hippie who had a huge party every couple of months. The parties usually started fun enough. There were outdoor games of Frisbee and baseball, and people came from all over Cielo bringing food and drinks. Musical instruments would be brought out, and there would be all sorts of kids for Trout to play with. The parties dragged on into the early hours of the morning, sometimes until the next day. After dark, a bonfire was built, and people gathered around to play music, tell stories, drink beer, and pass joints. In the dark fields and in the house, the harder drugs came out, and Trout would have to be careful not to stumble upon people having sex in the corners. The last party at Winnie's, he had stepped on a large piece of broken glass. Unable to find Gordon or Lotus, he pried the shard free himself and spent the rest of the night limping around on his throbbing foot. "It's not bad," people had said to him. Nobody wanted to leave the party to take him home.

"You should come," said Max, twisting about in his seat. "My brother's making pot brownies. Have you ever had those?"

"Uh ... "

"Me, too. They get you sooo high."

Sage grunted in disgust. "What are you, Max? Like, six?"

"I'm seven!" yelled Max. He raised his lunch tray above his head and brought it slamming down on the table, splattering the other children with Jell-O and macaroni. "Gaahhhh!" he screamed. Tuesday began a fresh bawl, and Trout wiped macaroni off his shirt.

"Thanks a lot, Max," Trout said. Sage put her thin arms around Tuesday.

When the cafeteria had emptied, Trout and the others rose and deposited their trash in the large can by the door. They always waited until the other kids left before going to the playground. The goal for lunch recess was to stay unnoticed. They stepped out into the harsh sun. To their right, students ran around the playground and basketball court, screaming and playing. Sage held Tuesday's hand, and the four of them walked to the left, away from the crowd.

They sat near the steps that led into Tuesday's classroom. A metal dumpster stood between them and the playground, shielding them from view. By now, the rest of the kids would be involved in other games. As long as they could remain unseen, they were likely to avoid harassment before the bell called them back to class. Some of the Hispanic children were nice to them, but it wasn't enough to hold back the bullies.

"Let's make a city for the ants," Sage suggested. She began to collect pebbles and sticks, and before long, they were all involved. Max and Trout worked on the castle together until Max decided that they needed an enemy castle and went to work on it alone. Trout worked at digging a moat with a stick. Sage built bridges across the moat and then went to work on a school made of sticks and leaves. Meanwhile, Tuesday had found a large beetle whom she named King of the Ants. She happily chatted away with him while she wove a crown from blades of grass. Trout tried to steer the ants across his drawbridge, eager for them to move into the castle.

"Sage," he said, "do you know what a hippie is?"

Sage shrugged. "It's someone like us."

He had not forgotten his discussion with Ruth the day before. It had tainted his view of Cielo Elementary all that day. His position in school seemed even more precarious than before. His right to be there, previously unquestioned, shook beneath him like the wobbly drawbridge he had made. He busied himself with the ants, feeling the presence of the playground pressing upon him. He had not seen Manny, but he knew it was only a matter of time before the threat was carried out. They always were. The only nice thing about a fight was that afterward the kids left him alone for a few days.

The bell rang, and the children reluctantly abandoned their city. "See you later," Trout said and walked toward his classroom. He lined up with his classmates, trying in vain to blend in. Back in the room, Trout's usual seat was taken. The kids scrambled into desks, shoving Trout aside. A foot or body quickly blocked every desk he tried to sit in. Hope of finding a seat was disappearing. He knew none of the students would willingly let him sit by them. Mrs. Trujillo waddled in. She pretended not to see Trout standing in the middle of the room. He knew not to expect help from her. Sometimes he thought the hippie kids were hated more by the teachers than by the other students. She sat behind her desk and silently organized papers. Spitballs began to fly at Trout. He felt his face turning red, and he turned to retreat to the reading area. A leg flew out in front of him, blocking his way. He turned the other way. Another leg. The children snickered. A hand shoved his back. He turned to face Manny.

"Where were you, punk?" Manny demanded, his face inches from Trout's. "Are you afraid to fight me, punk?"

Trout looked into Manny's hard, brown eyes and said nothing. He glanced around for an escape route. He made a move to climb over an empty chair nearby. Manny shoved him. Trout fell over the chair, his elbow slamming into the floor. Laughter erupted around the room.

"Hey!" yelled Mrs. Trujillo. The room grew silent. "You there, güero!" The children snickered again. "No fighting in my classroom! Go see Mr. Quintana." She returned to organizing papers, not looking up again.

Trout picked himself up off the floor and made his way to the door. "Burn!" somebody yelled. "You're busted!"

The halls were empty. Trout stood in front of a portrait of Don Diego de Vargas, debating what to do. He knew what to expect if he went to see the principal. He had been to his office many times already that year. Mr. Quintana had a long paddle with holes in it that he used to spank troublemakers.

Trout wandered slowly down the dim hall until he came to the metal door that led to the playground. Max's second grade class was playing kickball for gym period on the basketball court. Peering out the window, Trout could see Max's blond head shining at second base. He walked into the bathroom. Soon he would have to decide what to do. A teacher was bound to see him eventually, and he couldn't go back to class without a note from the principal confirming he had been to his office. He stared at his face in the scratched mirror above the sink. He practiced looking mean. He was not a bad fighter, but the boys attacked him in groups, and he didn't stand a chance. His strategy had become to act crazy. He found that if he screamed randomly and waved his arms wildly, the attackers stayed back long enough to give him a chance to make a run for it. He was a fast runner. He was small and light and a good jumper. He could usually make it off the school grounds, and at that point, the kids would let him go. Then he would be stuck walking home. Sometimes, the school bus passed him on the way, kids yelling out the windows and throwing garbage at him.

Trout wandered from the bathroom to the doors that led out to the front of the school. He stepped outside and decided to walk home even though his backpack was still in the classroom. He couldn't face another paddling from Mr. Quintana, and it seemed pointless to wait an hour for the school bus.

The afternoon had grown warm. Trout walked along the side of the highway. To his right, the land dropped steeply away into a deep ravine of juniper and piñon trees. Tuesday's father had driven his motorcycle off this highway several years ago. Trout remembered the funeral. Tom had been a woodworker, and a dozen trees were planted around his property in remembrance of him. People tied messages to his axe handle, and then Tuesday's mother threw it into a fire while they stood around and sang. Mark, Ruth's husband, played Tom's favorite song on the fiddle. Tuesday was only three at the time. She wandered amongst the mourners, playing peek-a-boo and chasing Heaven.

Every time Trout went by the ravine, he peered down its steep slopes, looking for a sign of Tom's bike.

Trout was a mile away from Cielo when the school bus passed him. He was glad he was not on the bus with Manny and his friends. He rounded the curve in the road before town, wondering how much longer he could avoid one last fight before summer vacation, when he saw Manny and four other boys waiting for him. They spotted Trout and began to walk toward him. Trout sized up his situation. To his right was the drop-off; the ground plummeted away to the valley floor, hundreds of feet down. To his left rose a slippery dirt bank. Behind him, the highway snaked back toward school. Trout squared his shoulders and walked toward the boys.

"Hey, Manny," he said jovially.

Manny shoved Trout in the shoulder. His friends laughed. "Don't talk to me, hippie! I didn't say you could talk to me!"

Trout stepped away. Two of the boys circled behind him. "Yeah, don't talk to him," one boy said. Tension crackled in the air. Trout's heart raced.

Manny shoved Trout again. "I don't like it when you talk to me, hippie. Why don't you cut your fucking hair?"

"Yeah, what are you, a *joto*?" The boys laughed appreciatively at Trout being called gay.

"Are you a *joto*?" Manny shoved Trout again.

Suddenly, anger erupted inside of Trout. He screamed and shoved Manny back. All the boys laughed except Manny, who looked surprised. Manny thumped his own chest. "C'mon! Do it again! I'd like to see you fight me, punk!"

Trout stood uneasily in the circle of boys. The anger left as quickly as it had appeared. Fear slid over him like a sudden shift in the weather. He saw something glinting in one of the boy's hands.

"Let's cut this fucking *joto's* hair!" said the boy. Manny shot forward with two of the boys. They grabbed Trout around the arms and legs and flung him to the ground, face up.

"No!" Trout yelled. "No! Fine! You can cut my hair! I don't give a shit!" He was lost in a swarm of arms and fabric.

The boys laughed as they held him pinned. Manny climbed onto Trout's chest, his big knees pinning Trout's elbows. Two pairs of hands held Trout's feet.

"You cry like a girl!" Manny said. "You look like a girl." He took a knife from his friend and held it above Trout's face. It was a small hunting knife with a black, plastic handle. Trout squirmed uselessly on the ground. Manny stared intently at Trout with wide, wild eyes and then puckered his lips as though to kiss him. "Are you a fucking *joto*?" he asked, making kissing sounds at Trout. "You know what we do to *jotos* around here, don't you? We cut off their balls."

"No!" screamed Trout. "No! You fucker! Fuck you!" Trout knew he was about to cry. He turned his face away from Manny. The pain in his arms was becoming unbearable.

"He's gonna cry," somebody said.

A voice, one voice, spoke up uneasily. "Don't play around, Manny."

Trout clung to that voice. "Listen Manny!" said Trout. "Your friend's right. This is stupid! We can work this out! Just put the knife away."

"Cut him!" yelled another voice.

"Fight!" chanted the boys. "Fight! Fight! Fight!"

A sharp, piercing pain slid across Trout's cheek. He knew Manny had cut him. He began to thrust his body with all his might, trying to throw the boys off him. His breath heaved in and out, his cheek felt on fire. Manny sat, heavy and immovable. From the corner of his eye, Trout saw one pair of feet run off. Probably the lone dissenter. Then, the sound of approaching tires and the sound of a horn.

The boys froze and then jumped away from Trout. He rolled over and slowly rose to his feet. He put his hand to his cheek and pulled it away to see blood. A door slammed, and somebody was yelling. Manny and his friends yelled back, and then they were running away. Trout felt a hand on his shoulder and looked up to see his neighbor, Bob.

"Come on," Bob said. He led Trout to the truck and opened the door for him. Trout was shaking. He climbed slowly into the cab. Bob shut the door and walked to the driver's side. He started the truck and pulled onto the road. Out of the corner of his eye, Trout could see Bob looking over at him every few moments. They passed Manny and his friends walking along the road. Manny faced the truck and raised his middle finger to them. The other boys laughed and made obscene gestures with their hands and crotches.

They drove in silence. Trout felt ashamed at having been seen losing the fight so badly. He wished Bob would say something, that he would acknowledge what had just happened, but Bob was not a talker. He seemed awkward and mildly angry most of the time to Trout. Still, Trout felt comforted by his presence. He looked out the window at the passing landscape. The colorful houses and brown earth seemed foreign to him, pushing him away with hostile indifference. The truck slowed and rounded into Bob's driveway. Bob turned off the engine, and they sat in silence.

"Well," said Bob, "let's get you cleaned up." They climbed out of the truck and went into the trailer.

Bob's wife, Mary, had died the year before of cancer. Since then, the trailer had been overtaken by clutter. Trout followed Bob along the narrow path that cut through piles of books and papers, dishes and clothes, to the kitchen. Bob went to the bathroom and returned with a bottle of rubbing alcohol. He had Trout lean his head over the kitchen sink and then poured alcohol over the cut. Trout cringed at the sting. Bob screwed the cap back on, then strapped the cut closed with several band-aids. "Keep that clean, Trout."

Trout nodded and wiped his cheek on his shirt. He heard a car pull up outside. It would be John and Lucy, Bob's kids, returning home from school. They usually caught a ride with Cookie, whose son, Joaquin, was in the same grade as John at San Pedro.

"And Trout," said Bob, "next time you see those boys, run. Don't let them gang up on you like that."

Trout nodded again. He knew Bob was trying to comfort him in his awkward way. Bob went outside to greet his children, and Trout followed.

John stopped when he saw Trout. "What happened to your cheek?"

"I got in a fight."

"That's a big cut, bro."

"John! Trout!" Bob called from the truck. He had backed it up to the stable. The boys walked over, and Bob put them to work unloading hay from the truck bed. They stacked the bales inside, and then John climbed into the truck and began to sweep it out with a broom.

"Should we go for a ride?" John asked.

"Yeah," Trout answered. He was not eager to get home. Gordon was likely to give him a hard time about losing the fight, and Lotus would probably shake her head and give Trout her unhappy look. He helped John saddle up the horses. Diablo, the stallion, was Trout's favorite. He was muscular and black with a white star on his forehead. Because he was young and unpredictable, only John and Bob were allowed to ride him. Trout threw a blanket on the back of Santa Ana, Diablo's mother. He gently lifted the saddle onto her, then cinched it on and led her out to the corral. The boys lifted themselves easily onto the horses and guided them out the gate.

"John," Bob called, "an hour."

"Yup," John answered, and they set out.

Trout loved being on the horse. He relaxed into the swing and sway of Santa Ana's step as they trotted past Trout's house and followed the road, heading left at the split toward the swimming hole. There were very few houses this far from town. Many ranchers brought their cattle out here to graze. The cows looked up as the boys passed, then returned to their methodical chewing.

"So what happened?" asked John. "Was it Manny?"

"Yeah. And four of his friends." Trout told of his decision to leave school rather than face another paddling and then of meeting the boys along the road.

"You are so lucky my dad came along," John said. They climbed off the horses and left them at the stream to continue on foot. They climbed the rocky slope that led to the swimming hole.

"I know," Trout answered. He didn't know what would have happened had Bob not arrived. Trout would be attending school in Española next year, and he wasn't sure Manny would make it out of sixth grade. Manny must have known his opportunities for proving himself against Trout were slipping away as summer vacation neared. Nobody had pulled a knife on Trout before.

They reached the swimming hole and stripped off their clothes. They slid into the clear water, pure snow runoff from Truchas peak, and gasped.

"That's cold!"

"I know, man! My nuts are the size of peas."

"Mine are the size of a chipmunk's."

"Mine are the size of a worm's!"

They laughed and splashed each other. Trout thought briefly of Manny's threat to cut his balls off. The cold water had numbed his cheek. He looked at John, whose wet, brown hair hung past his shoulders.

"Maybe we should cut our hair," Trout said.

"What? No way, man! I want to look like an Indian."

"Well, I'll never look like an Indian. More like Goldilocks."

"Shut up," said John, hoisting himself onto a rock. Trout climbed out of the water, and they sat shivering until the sun warmed them. John reached into his crumpled pants and produced two crooked cigarettes. He handed one to Trout and then lit them with a paper match. They propped themselves on their elbows and watched each other self-consciously.

"You don't inhale," John said.

"Yes I do! Watch." Trout took a long drag and sucked the smoke into his lungs. He began to cough. "See? Maybe I just don't inhale as much as you do."

"Watch," John said and inserted the end of his cigarette into one nostril. He closed the other nostril with his finger and breathed in, then exhaled smoke from his mouth.

They finished the cigarettes and dressed. The horses stood by the creek, staring meditatively at the ground.

"Lemme ride Diablo back," Trout said.

"Nope."

Trout asked every time they rode together, and John always said no. John hoisted himself proudly onto the black horse and patted him on the neck. They set off toward home.

"Are you serious about cutting your hair?" asked John.

"Yeah."

"Is it because of Manny?"

"No! I'm just sick of looking like a freak."

"You're not a freak."

"Look," Trout said and pointed to a large eagle overhead. The bird circled twice above their heads and then sailed off toward Winnie's house.

"Trout, you're not a freak."

"I know I'm not a freak, but I'm sick of looking like one."

"What are you talking about, bro? You don't look like a freak at all."

"Maybe to you I don't, but I'm the only kid in my class with long hair."

"So? You're different from them."

"I don't want to be different," Trout said. "I'm sick of being different. I just want to be normal!"

"If you came to school in San Pedro, none of this would happen."

"Well, I don't. I go to a shitty school because my shitty parents don't want to drive me in their shitty car."

"So get a ride with Cookie."

Trout was silent. The idea of riding to school with Cookie had come up after his last fight a few weeks ago, but his school said it was too late in the year to transfer. They steered the horses off the road at the sound of an approaching car. An old Chevy came rattling toward them with two men in the front seat, a plastic crucifix dangling from the rearview mirror. The car slowed as it approached the boys, and John waved at the two men inside. The car sped up, and as it gunned past the boys, an empty beer bottle came flying out the window. It skimmed Santa Ana's chest and shattered on a rock at Diablo's feet. Diablo reared up and whinnied.

"Goddammit!" yelled John. He threw a finger at the disappearing truck. "*¡Chinga tu madre!*"

"*¡Pinches cabrónes!*" yelled Trout.

"I hate those guys," said John.

"Do you know them?"

"They used to sell firewood to my dad. They tried to rip him off, and you know how my dad is … "

He trailed off, but Trout knew what he meant. Bob may be quiet and reserved, but he had a nasty temper and held a grudge for life.

The cows had gone from the fields. A light breeze drifted toward the boys, carrying the smell of snow off Truchas peak. The yellow grass rolled around them, tinged orange by the setting sun.

"Hey," said Trout, "how come you haven't asked me about my house?" He hadn't seen John since the night of the fire.

John shrugged. "What do you mean?"

"You know, the fire."

"I don't know. I thought you didn't want to talk about it."

"Why wouldn't I want to talk about it?"

John didn't say anything for a while. He could be silent like his father. Usually Trout liked this about his friend, but other times, like now, it was extremely irritating.

"I guess I thought you'd be, I don't know. Like you wouldn't wanna talk about it because it was torched."

"Oh." Trout didn't understand what John meant, but he decided not to press it.

They returned the horses to the stable and fed them fistfuls of hay. Trout stroked the white star on Diablo's forehead. "Well," he said, "I'd better get home."

"See ya," said John.

"See ya."

Trout squeezed through the barbed wire fence that separated their properties and crunched across the broken glass left by Jade crashing through the window.

5

Thursday

Lotus looked up from the wood stove when Trout walked in. "What happened to your cheek?"

"I cut it at the swimming hole."

Trout picked through the stems of pot. A pair of scissors lay on the counter. He fingered them for a moment and then took them in his hand. He walked out through the new front door Gordon had hung and across the field to a large rock by the creek. He sat down and contemplated what he was about to do, then took a strand of hair and cut it close to his scalp. Slowly and carefully, he cut his golden hair. The strands fell at his feet, some of them drifting into the creek. He finished and looked up to see Heaven watching him. She didn't say anything, just stared at him fixedly.

Trout smiled. "Do you like it?"

Heaven shrugged, then nodded. She came to sit by him on the rock.

"Should we do yours?" Trout asked. She smiled and shook her head. "Are you sure? We could give you a mohawk." They both laughed at the image of Heaven with a mohawk.

"What happened to your cheek?" Heaven asked.

"I fell. At the swimming hole." Trout didn't like lying to his sister, but he was supposed to be the big brother who could take care of himself. They rose and returned to the house for dinner.

"Oh my God!" said Lotus, who was opening a can of tomatoes with a serrated knife. "What did you do to your hair?"

"I cut it."

"It looks terrible." Lotus stared at him for a moment, then, "I'll fix it for you after dinner."

Trout could not remember ever getting a haircut. He didn't think Lotus knew how to do things like that. "What's for dinner?" he asked.

"Tongue."

"Oh."

Cow tongue was a weekly affair in their house, a reprieve from rice and beans or potatoes and chicken parts. Much of what they ate depended on whose crop was ripe. Bob grew corn; Forest grew tomatoes in his greenhouse, and Winnie grew peas and greens. Bartering was common in Cielo. Just about everybody had a skill or commodity to trade. Gordon knew how to fix cars, and he often did repairs in exchange for food or help with his property. Lotus sometimes helped people weed and plant, but she didn't have many skills. Their own vegetable garden was scrawny and feeble, barely producing enough food for a meal at any one time.

"Trout, cut these up," said Lotus, and she placed two onions on the counter. Trout examined the dull edge of the knife. He thought about the bartering in Cielo. He was counting in his head, trying to place people in order by who had the most to trade. Ruth had goat's milk and cheese, vegetables from her garden, and she sewed and knitted. Mark had tools for people to use and could build all sorts of things. Bob grew corn and had manure from his horses, and his truck was good for hauling. Gordon fixed cars and spoke fluent Spanish. People were always asking him to translate things to their neighbors. They built up favors like bank accounts, nothing ever formally recorded but based on a sense of who helped each other out when they needed it. Somebody would come by with a car to fix, and Gordon would fix it, and then, it was understood that he could ask him or her for something when he needed it, or vice versa. Trout decided that Ruth and Mark had the most to barter. His family was only a little better than Cookie, who gave people rides and sometimes babysat.

"Lotus," he asked, "how come you don't know how to sew?"

"I know how to sew," she answered, stirring the tongue in the boiling water.

"Then how come you never do?"

"Well, I guess I don't really see the point."

"What do you know how to do?"

"Watch it, Trout. I know how to do a hell of a lot more than you."

This was how all their conversations seemed to end lately, with Lotus snapping and Trout wondering what he had said to make her mad. It was true he didn't know how to do much. Gordon had been teaching him to work on cars, and Bob had recently taught him how to fish. Ruth had shown him how to milk a goat, and Forest and Mark were teaching him to use their tools. He could garden a little and knew how to build a sweat lodge. He knew how to cook some things and could play a little guitar, but already that seemed to be more than Lotus could do.

Jade and Gordon came through the door. Trout could tell by their narrow, red eyes that they were stoned.

"Aw, Lotus. Look what you did," said Gordon, pointing to some marijuana stems she had walked upon.

"You shouldn't leave them all over the floor."

"Where the hell am I supposed to leave them?"

"If you'd build us a fucking table ..."

Gordon sighed and kicked the stems out of the way. It occurred to Trout that the arguments between his parents never fully played themselves out. They were left unfinished so that whenever his parents were in the same room together, an uneasy tension hung in the air. It was only when one or both of them had been drinking that the arguments got loud and sometimes led to hitting. Nevertheless, they made Trout uncomfortable.

Dinner was not a formal affair in their house. Only two or three nights a week did they all eat at the same time, and that was almost always by accident. Lotus usually got dinner started, enlisting Trout to help. Gordon and Jade could never be found until dinner was ready, when they miraculously appeared at the doorway just as Lotus would say, "Dinner." Then, whoever wanted to eat would take one of the mismatched plates from the shelf above the sink and serve him- or herself, claiming a seat somewhere around the house or outside. Because there were five of them and only four chairs, they ate in shifts, or sometimes Jade ate standing up. Some nights, Lotus didn't cook, and everybody foraged through the cupboards as they grew hungry, piecing a meal together from whatever was around.

Trout dished up two bowls of tomatoes tossed with fried onions and boiled tongue. There was no use not liking what was made because there was rarely another option. He gave one bowl to Heaven and sat in a chair beside her. The others dished themselves up and sat down. Jade squatted against the wall near the stove. They ate in silence except for Jade, who rattled on, trying, it seemed, to get some sort of a reaction from his family members. It was impossible to get any reaction out of Heaven, who ate her tongue placidly and seemed oblivious to the other people in the room. Trout occasionally responded to his brother's comments but mostly just listened. Lotus appeared infinitely annoyed at every sound Jade made, sighing and scraping her chair this way and that, but it was mainly to his father that Jade spoke, searching exhaustively for a sign of approval.

Jade stretched his long legs out on the dirt floor. "Oh man," he began, "somebody drove through Colin's fence. They knocked the whole thing over, practically, and then they just drove off! Can you believe it? They didn't even try to put it back up. That's totally not right, man. That's bad karma. I guess once, I did that. Well, not me, really, but I was in Boonray's truck with him, and he drove through some fence in Seco, and we just drove off. That sucks, man." He paused, opening the room for comment. When none came, he chose a new topic.

"Tomorrow night is Winnie's party. It's for May Day, he says, even though that was, like, two weeks ago. I don't know why he needs a reason to have a party. We should just celebrate being alive. We should just get together like the Indians and sweat and smoke and stuff. Dance. Sing. What the fuck is May Day, anyway? Some day where a bunch of bored Viking housewives got together and drank their husbands' liquor while they were away on a raid, and they got so drunk they tied their hair ribbons to trees and danced around naked, throwing eggs at each other. Ha-ha! That's what I think happened. The only days I celebrate are every day, man. Boonray says they're going to roast a pig. I don't know whose pig. Maybe one of Allen's big, fat ones. Damn, those are some big pigs! I mean, you could, like, ride one of those into town! Forget cars and horses, man. You could ride one of those hogs lying on your back, falling asleep. Ha-ha! That would be so cool. It'd probably stink, though."

Jade paused again. Trout recognized this manic monologue as Jade's typical stoned behavior. Pot turned some verbal faucet on in Jade's brain. Gordon dragged a hunk of Ruth's bread around the bottom of his bowl. Jade stirred his stew, which had probably grown cold by now. His eyes lit up as he thought of another subject.

"I went to town yesterday, and there was this beautiful Mercedes-Benz—a black convertible—parked in front of Lucinda's."

Trout's ears perked up. Was Jade going to tell the story of stealing the car? He hadn't thought about the car all day. He felt his stomach grow cold as he remembered what they had done.

"So me and Boonray stopped to have a look, and the owner comes out and starts talking to us. He says he's scoping out Cielo to film a movie! We asked if we could be in it, and he said he had parts for us. That would be awesome! He was looking for the falls to check it out for a scene. I was like, 'Dude, you do NOT want to take this car to the falls.' So we offered him a lift, and he came. He was cool. His name was Fred, and we smoked a bowl. I am totally going to be in that movie."

Lotus groaned and scooted her chair closer to the fire. She scowled at Jade but said nothing. Trout tried to catch his brother's eye. He could not, for the life of him, think what his brother was doing. Why was he mentioning the car at all? It was stupid! And Fred sounded like a totally made-up name; nobody was ever going to believe it. But Gordon and Lotus were absorbed in their own thoughts. Heaven had fallen asleep. Her half-eaten bowl of stew was trickling onto her flowered dress. Trout reached over and took the bowl, then worked at finishing it himself. Jade was quiet for a few moments. The fire popped loudly.

"So later I went to town with Boon and Espi, and we were sitting in front of Lucinda's, and one of the redheads who lives next door to her shop starts throwing rocks at this dog. We told him to cut it out, but he didn't stop, so then Boon picks up a rock and throws it at the kid and says, 'See how it feels?' And then the kid's older brother comes out of the house and says, 'Pick on someone your own size,' and Boonray goes, 'I'm ready,' and then I stand up next to him. You could tell he wanted to fight us, but there were two of us and only one of him, so he just stood there looking at us, and then he looks at me and goes, 'Your house was burned, hippie. That means it's time to go.' I was like, 'What the fuck are you talking about? I was BORN here, man.' Well, not *in* Cielo, but in New Mexico. But he says, 'It's not your home. We were here first.' I felt like punching him, man! Whose home is it, anyway? Why can't it be everybody's home? These people have no idea what sharing is all about. No wonder this world won't move forward."

Gordon grunted, and Jade sat up, aware that he had a winner. He took a moment to gather his thoughts and then forged ahead.

"What the hell did we ever do to them, right? I mean, this land belongs to us, and we have the right to be on it and to live however we want to on it. Who the hell are they to get pissed off at us because we are here? Nobody owns the fucking planet, right?"

Gordon was nodding his head in agreement as he slurped his second bowl of tongue. Trout sat quietly, watching this interaction between Jade and his father. Lotus stared into the fire, chewing thoughtfully. She actually seemed to be listening to Jade, which was a rare thing. Jade placed his empty bowl beside him on the floor and rocked on his heels as he spoke.

"That's the really beautiful thing, man, is that nobody owns the planet. We all do. But these fucking people up here think that because they were here before us they have more of a right to be here than we do. That's bullshit, man! If anybody owns it, it's the Indians, right? I mean, can you imagine living in a world where there was no owner-ship? It'd be beautiful, man, but these people up here can't see that. They can't see how much they are hurting themselves by not giving in to change. We need a revolution, man. Not all this talking about it. We need huge change that even these tiny towns couldn't resist."

"That's what I'm always saying," Gordon said. "What the world needs is a little change. We need to move backward, not forward. Back to the simpler days of living but forward into the modern ways of thinking. Different ideas of marriage and child-raising and jobs."

"Exactly!" said Jade. "Totally different ideas. Like, why is everybody supposed to go to their fucking nine-to-five job every day so they can buy their stupid crap for their own spoiled, rich kids? There isn't enough community. It's every man for himself, and that just sucks."

Gordon shifted his weight in his chair and cleared his throat. "I knew a man," he began. He gazed at the fire in the wood stove. "A long time ago. He was from a far-off country on the other side of the Atlantic. Prague, I think. He came to America looking for space to breathe, room to grow, somewhere that he could stretch his enormous feet in front of his own fire. He came to New Mexico because he had heard about it. He moved into the mountains, miles away from the nearest town. He somehow found himself a wife and moved her up there with him, and they started a family. He became a trapper and a woodcutter. He and his family lived simply and in harmony with the land. They lived in a two-room log cabin he built with his own hands. Their nearest neighbor was seven miles down the road. This man was so good. Sven was his name. He had a heart of gold. He was a real man. Honest. He had a little trouble with the locals, but mostly, they left him alone, and he left them alone."

Trout rolled his eyes to himself and tried not to snicker. Gordon liked to make up stories on the spot that sounded like well-worn fables.

"One day, he was out in front of his house, stripping aspens, when a truck full of hunters drove up. They said they were lost. Sven thought this was strange because the road led from town and came to a dead end just past Sven's. The only way to go was back to town, so you couldn't really get lost, you know? I mean, it wasn't like you could take any wrong turns. But Sven was a good man, so he put down his knife and asked them where they were trying to get to. His wife came out onto the porch, and the hunters climbed out and pulled their guns on Sven and his wife."

Lotus stood up suddenly and moved to add more logs to the fire.

"Well, to make a long story short, they raped his wife, torched his house, shot his goats, chickens, and dog. All of this while Sven and his children watched at gunpoint. After that, his wife moved to California with the kids, but Sven was destroyed. He took to wandering in the mountains and became a mountain man, living out of caves and streams. He's still out there … Wandering around …"

"Man," said Jade, shaking his head, "that is totally fucked up."

Lotus stood by her chair. She had rolled a joint and held it between her lips while she spoke, trying to light it. "Yeah, well, maybe he shouldn't have moved up there with his family in the first place."

"But that's exactly what we're saying," Jade said. "People should be able to live wherever they want without getting hassled."

"Jesus Christ, Lotus," said Gordon, reaching for the joint, "listen to yourself. Do you think that what happened to this guy's family was his fault or something?"

"I don't want to talk about this anymore," she said and took another hit before handing the joint to Gordon. She stood shaking her head and holding the smoke in her lungs. After a few moments, she exhaled and noticed the stew spilled on Heaven's lap. "Jesus, this child is a wreck."

"Oh, man," said Jade, grinning and watching his father labor at the joint, "that is totally why things like that happen. Nobody wants to talk about it!"

Gordon nodded in agreement and handed the joint and lighter to Jade. "Yep. Yep." His voice was thin and strained as he held his breath.

Jade and Gordon passed the joint back and forth and continued to complain about the state of the world while Lotus woke Heaven and helped her up the ladder to bed. Trout soon grew bored of the conversation. He carried his bowl to the sink and then took the bucket by the wood stove and went outside to fill it from the acequia.

Thousands of stars littered the black sky. Coyotes yipped in the distance, and crickets chorused in the crisp, spring air. Trout crouched by the creek to fill the bucket. The water was ice cold. He walked back toward the house, lugging the water beside him. He filled a large pot with water and set it on the stove to heat, then went back outside to pee. He stood in the field, his head thrown back, marveling at the vast sky above him, all those stars, when an engine approached. He turned to see a car pull in front of the house. It sat for a moment, headlights off, engine idling, and then reversed out of the driveway with a loud roar and a great deal of smoke. It turned onto the road, and the driver gunned the engine, roaring away with a few backfires as Gordon, Lotus, and Jade came running out of the house.

"Goddammit!" yelled Gordon. "what the hell was that?"

Trout stood watching the taillights of the car as they disappeared around the bend. He recognized the sound of the engine. It was the same people who had torched their house two nights earlier. Trout zipped his pants and walked toward his family. His heart shot about in his throat like a scared rabbit.

Jade paced anxiously near the porch. "What the fuck?"

Gordon wordlessly disappeared into the house. They heard the creak of the ladder as he climbed into the loft. Lotus followed. Trout and Jade stood tensely beside one another, shifting their weight from one foot to the other, glancing at the road and listening to their parents arguing inside. Gordon emerged from the house, his boots on his feet and a bottle of tequila in the back pocket of his jeans. "Let's go," he said, and the boys obediently followed.

They walked quickly across the field to Forest's, where they found Forest sitting in his living room with Colin, Boonray's stepfather.

"What's up?" asked Forest as they came through the door.

"Hey, Colin," Jade said.

"Hey."

Gordon took the bottle from his back pocket and unscrewed the cap. "The guys who lit the house were back."

Forest rose unsteadily from his chair. He had obviously been working on his own bottle for a while. "When?" he asked.

"Just now," Gordon answered. "They pulled into the driveway and sat there for a minute, then drove off. I think they came by to see if we were home. They're gonna do it again."

There was silence for a long moment. Colin leaned back in his chair, fingertips on his pursed lips as though he were praying. Forest weaved in front of Gordon, his long hair falling into his eyes, apparently still working toward comprehending what Gordon had just said. Trout watched his father grow exasperated. This was obviously not the angry mob he was hoping to gather. Jade shifted nervously from foot to foot.

Forest suddenly peered at Gordon as if he were seeing him for the first time. "Fuck 'em," he drawled and then walked slowly to the door. He pulled on a fringed, suede jacket and reached behind the door for his shotgun and rifle. He handed the shotgun to Gordon and then shuffled out the door. After a few pensive moments, Colin rose to his feet and followed Forest out the door, the others on his heels.

Forest drove a 1952 orange Chevy pick-up truck that he called Red Eagle and left parked on the other side of the creek from his house. The truck was a mess. Its tires were old and showed thin cracks; the tailgate was missing; the turn signals didn't work; the side view mirrors were gone; the interior was cracked and torn, and the windshield looked like a rolled egg shell. Gordon took the wheel, and Forest and Colin sat beside him on the bench seat. Trout and Jade climbed in back with the guns. The night had grown cold, and Trout wished he had brought a jacket. Jade pulled a pack of Lucky Strikes from his pocket and lit one.

"Can I have one?" Trout asked. He normally smoked only with his friends, in secret, but that night he felt daring. It felt like a special occasion. Jade scowled and then handed him a crooked cigarette. Trout lit it from the end of his brother's and puffed away as Gordon backed the truck slowly up the steep bank. Gordon tapped the window and shook his finger at Trout in a mock reprimand, then grinned and swung the truck onto the road. Trout sighed and leaned back against the window.

The night sky rolled above them, brilliant and clear. Here he was, in charge of a shotgun on a school night, smoking in full view of his father. Surely, he was nearly a man now. He savored the moment until Jade stood up, his hair streaming back in the wind, and whistled loudly. They were passing Esperanza's house, and Jade brandished Forest's rifle proudly, a cigarette dangling from the corner of his mouth. The truck rattled on; Esperanza didn't come out. Jade let out a loud whoop and fired Forest's rifle at the sinking barn to their right. The truck swerved sharply and nearly ran into the creek. Gordon banged the outside of his door and yelled angrily at Jade. Jade whooped again and laughed, his mouth wide open as if to drink in the stars. Trout stared up at his brother. He looked enormous, towering above him, framed in the huge sky. Trout stood up. There was a thin lip of metal that framed the rear window. They clung to this, leaning against the cab for balance.

"Jade!" yelled Trout, his mouth filling with wind. "Why did you tell Gordon and Lotus about the car?"

Jade glanced at Trout. "What?"

"Why did you … " His words were lost in the wind. Jade's eyes shone ahead. He had his wild expression on, which told Trout that Jade would comprehend nothing that was said to him and was, in that mood, capable of doing anything. Sometimes, when this side of Jade came out, Trout yearned to be a part of it. He would go along with the craziness, laughing and pretending to enjoy himself, all the while terror growing inside of him. He would go along, wanting to be a part of Jade's experience, until he realized that his brother wasn't aware of him at all, that Jade was lost inside some vast, internal wilderness Trout couldn't get into, no matter how badly he wanted to follow. Inevitably, Trout would back out of every situation he followed Jade into, his stomach knotted in fear, and Jade would go on without him. Jade wouldn't be angry at Trout, or disappointed. He wouldn't even realize Trout was no longer with him. He would be completely swept away. Trout yearned to feel, to abandon himself, but for some reason, he couldn't.

Soon the truck rounded a bend, and the dirt road gave way to asphalt. Gordon slowed to a stop and shut off Red Eagle's headlights. He leaned his head out the window and called to Trout in a loud whisper.

Trout leaned forward. "Yeah?"

"You saw the car, right?"

Trout hesitated. He had seen the lights of the car and heard the engine, but he sensed something coming in Gordon's tone. "Not really."

Gordon was annoyed. "Yeah, well, can you try to look for the car that you didn't really see?"

"Yes."

The truck rolled forward, and Trout peered into the dark night. Red Eagle crept past the trailers and low, adobe homes of Cielo, waking a few angry dogs. Some of the houses had lights on, and Trout searched the driveways, but he had only a vague idea of what he was looking for. He knew the car had a long front end and a loud engine, so it was probably a V8, maybe an El Camino or an Impala. Cielo was full of cars like that. Trout knew there was no way he could be sure of the car. He also wasn't sure how he felt leading a truck full of angry, drunk men with guns out to do God-knows-what. He knew they weren't going to kill anyone; it was just how things were done up there: late night confrontations required guns. Trout clutched the shotgun to his chest uneasily, glad that it was he who had it and not Gordon or Forest.

Red Eagle rolled past Lucinda's, and Trout still had not seen the car. They rolled out of town and Gordon flicked on the headlights.

"Oh, shit," said Jade. Trout turned to see they were being followed. A lowrider with its lights off was cruising quietly on their tail. Trout and Jade thumped loudly on the cab's window.

"They're behind us!" Trout yelled.

Gordon craned his head around. Cursing, he elbowed Forest awake. Trout gripped the side of the truck, his heart pounding. He stared at the lowrider. It was impossible to tell how many people were inside.

Gordon found a wide place on the shoulder and pulled over. The lowrider pulled over behind them. Immediately, Gordon and Colin were out of the truck and walking toward the car. Forest stumbled out of the cab, shaking his hair out of his face. Jade leapt out after him, skidding a bit on the dirt, and strutted behind his father, the rifle slung casually over his shoulder.

"Put that away," hissed Gordon.

Trout stayed in the truck, scooting up to the edge of the bed, unwilling to part with the shotgun in his lap. Jade stepped back to the truck and leaned against the rear bumper.

Three men emerged from the lowrider. Trout saw that it was an El Camino.

"Lucio," called Gordon. Trout recognized the driver as Lucio Garcia, the son of Mr. Garcia and the husband of the woman with the spider eyes at Lucinda's. Lucio said nothing but took two steps forward. His friends stood behind him, one tall and lean, the other short and stocky. Lucio was somewhere in between the two in size except for his arms, which were huge and menacing. Gordon held his ground and looked at the three men. "Lucio, what's going on here?" He tried to sound casual, but fear swam in his voice.

Lucio glared at Gordon, his eyes revealing his distrust. "You know, hippie. You know what's going on here."

"No," said Gordon, "why don't you tell me?"

Lucio smiled at his friends, and they chuckled. "What are you doing, driving around with no lights on and guns in the back, *ese*?" Lucio stood with his chest puffed out at Gordon, fight pose.

"I could ask you the same thing," Gordon replied.

"Yeah!" yelled Forest. He was so drunk Trout was amazed he was standing on his own two feet. He stood wobbling in the headlights of the El Camino, occasionally flailing his arms about uselessly.

"You could," said Lucio. Lucio's friends chuckled nervously with every word Lucio said. Lucio was growing cockier, slowly edging closer to Gordon, his head extended off his neck like a snake tasting out its prey.

"Well," said Gordon, taking a step back, "I was hoping we could talk this over like men."

"The problem is," Lucio stepped closer to Gordon, "you aren't a man."

The viciousness behind this statement surprised Trout. He wondered what Gordon could have done to incite such hatred from Lucio. A thousand possibilities came to mind. Lucio's friends laughed appreciatively, and Gordon threw his shoulders back at the insult. Colin edged discreetly toward the truck. Terrified, Trout saw that Gordon was the only one worth anything if a fight were to break out. He clutched the gun and glanced at Jade, who was watching the scene with fascination.

"All right, all right," Forest said, one hand up by his head as though surrendering. "We don't want any trouble."

Lucio's tall friend stepped forward. "You don't want any trouble, *ese*? Well it's too late for that 'cause you're in a whole lotta trouble now."

"Yeah," said Lucio, "you should have thought of that before you came up here with all your dirty hippie people."

A car slowed as it neared them and came to a stop. The driver, an old Hispanic man, reached across the seat to unroll the passenger window.

"*¿Qué esta pasando aquí?*" he spat in quick Spanish. Lucio's short friend slipped into the shadow of the El Camino. "Manuel? Manuel?" the driver called. Sheepishly, the short man came out of the shadows and approached the car, his head hung low. The driver shouted a string of angry words at the man, who climbed into the car and slid down in his seat. The car drove off, and Lucio and his friend looked at each other incredulously. While Lucio's head was turned, Gordon shot forward and laid a fast punch square on Lucio's jaw.

"Oh shit!" Forest yelled and skipped backward to the truck. Trout scooted back into the bed, breathing rapidly. Lucio turned and smacked Gordon hard in the face. Lucio's friend had scurried to the El Camino and returned with a baseball bat. Gordon staggered back, and Jade strode forward, peering down the barrel of the rifle he had aimed at Lucio. Forest was climbing into the truck, Colin right behind him.

"Put down the gun, *niño*," said Lucio to Jade. "Fight me like a man." He was fingering his jaw where Gordon had hit him. His chest heaved heavily like a bull's. Gordon recovered from the hit and charged Lucio, screaming, overcome with rage.

Trout screamed, "NO!" as Lucio's friend brought the bat down on Gordon's shoulder. Forest had started the truck and was backing it up.

Jade held the rifle on Lucio. "Come on, Gordon!" he yelled. "Let's get out of here!" Lucio glared uneasily at Jade, who said, "I'm one hell of a shot," and cocked the gun.

Lucio spit on the ground at Gordon's feet. "You better get out of here while you still have a chance."

Gordon was breathing hard, bent over from the blow to his shoulder. His eyes did not move from Lucio's face. "I can leave anytime I want." He raised his chin and shook his hair back from his face, confidently. Neither man moved. Forest had backed the truck up to them, and it sat there, idling stupidly. Trout stood. He held the shotgun forward from his chest a few inches, wanting to make sure Lucio knew there was a second gun, terrified he might be asked to use it.

"Come on, Gordon," Jade said again.

Lucio's friend touched his arm. "Come on. Tonight's not the night."

Lucio backed toward the car, keeping his eyes glued on Gordon's. "That's right. Tonight's not the night. But soon, *pendejo*. Soon." He climbed into the car with his friend, and the El Camino shot backward.

Gordon walked to the truck, Jade's hand on his back. Gordon nudged Forest over and climbed behind the wheel. Jade climbed in back with Trout, and they waited for Lucio to pull out before them. When the El Camino didn't move for several moments, Gordon peeled onto the road. Jade threw the finger to Lucio and then dropped his pants and shook his bare bottom at the disappearing car. The men up front laughed and banged on the window in approval. Trout clung to the side of the bed and watched the El Camino swing out after them and follow at a respectful distance. Jade screamed insults and shook the rifle at the car.

Gordon swung the truck left onto the road that led into the town of Cordova. They bounced and bumped down the steep hill. Red Eagle roared through the sleeping town, and Trout watched several porch lights go on in their wake. They passed through Cordova and then began to climb an old logging road up the side of a mountain. Trout and Jade held on as the truck banged over the holes and ruts. The El Camino fell farther and farther behind. Gordon plowed ahead for a mile or so and then shut off the engine and climbed out, confident he had lost Lucio and his friend. He whooped loudly, a deeper version of the whoop Jade made right afterward. Forest and Colin stepped out from the passenger door. Gordon opened the bottle of tequila from his back pocket and took a slug. He held it out to Jade, who took a long drink and passed it back. Gordon looked at the bottle thoughtfully and then offered it to Trout. Trout took it and had a tiny sip. The liquor burned down his throat like a lit match. Gordon laughed and reclaimed the bottle. "Good job, boys." He squeezed the nape of Trout's neck affectionately. His left eye was swelling shut where Lucio had hit him. "Did you cut your hair?" he asked, looking at Trout.

The pine forest loomed about them, dark and watchful. Trout shivered in the cold.

Forest took the bottle from Gordon. "What do we do now?" he asked.

Gordon grinned. "Did you hear Jade when he said, 'I'm one hell of a shot'?" They all laughed, Jade hardest of all.

They recounted the events of the fight to each other and took turns pissing on the side of the road. Trout opened the cab of the truck and lay down on the bench seat, suddenly exhausted. He curled into a ball for warmth and fell asleep listening to the drone of the men outside, and smelling the smoke from their cigarettes as it came drifting through the open door.

6

Friday

The blue van sped down the long hill out of Cielo. Trout looked out the window at his school, at the playground swarming with children. There was no way he was going to school today to face Manny and his friends. Nor was he interested in hanging around the house while Gordon cursed at the adobe bricks they'd made, which were now crumbling and sifting away on their plywood boards, taking out his aggression on whoever was nearby. Lotus had a doctor's appointment in Española, and after much shouting and pleading, Trout had convinced her to take him and Heaven along. The radio blared a song Trout recognized.

"This is the blues," he told Lotus. She didn't answer. She was grumpy for having the kids with her. Trout couldn't think of the last time he had taken a trip out of Cielo. He bobbed his head in time with the music.

Lotus reached over and shut off the stereo with a loud sigh. Trout stared at her profile as she drove. He knew his mom was pretty because people often told her that, and he could see what they meant. Her delicate features were neatly ordered on her face. Her sandy blonde hair looked as shiny and soft as soap bubbles. Her eyes were bright blue and her lips a strong plum color. But to Trout, all of this was undone by the chronic foul mood that caused her eyebrows to stitch angrily together and the corners of her mouth to scowl down. Her eyes darted about constantly, hunting for something to criticize. Her shoulders rolled sharply inward as if she was always ready to throw a hard punch. He could remember times when they used to sing together. Lotus used to be a lot happier, he thought. He turned to look at Heaven. She sat limply on the bed in the back, staring out the window.

"Heaven," he called. She looked at him, and he made a face. She smiled faintly and turned back to the window. Trout stared out his.

Trout climbed onto the bed with Heaven and spent most of the trip drawing on his jeans with a ballpoint pen and trying to get Heaven to play tic-tac-toe with him, but she continued to stare out the window and eventually lay down and curled away from him.

Española was a short strip of fast food restaurants, gas stations, and car dealer-ships, with long arms of lush green valley spanning away on either side. Lotus pulled onto a side street and then parked in front of a low, beige building.

"Stay here," she instructed Trout and Heaven.

"But Lotus, I have to pee," said Trout, purposely whining to annoy her.

"So take a leak outside, what else is new?" She slammed the door shut and walked through a door that read County Health Clinic. Trout climbed out the passenger door and peed onto a patch of grass. He climbed back into the van and tried to wake Heaven so they could play a game. She opened her eyes and looked at him blearily.

"Hev? Come on, wake up! Let's play Indians!" She blinked her eyes slowly at him and made a small movement with her head that he took to mean no and then closed her eyes again. Trout looked closer. She didn't look quite right. Her face was flushed and shiny. He put his hand on her forehead. It felt warm.

"Hev?" He shook her gently. She moaned and flopped her arm around. "Hev, are you okay? Heaven?" He shook her more forcefully. It seemed as though she was deeply asleep except that she kept opening her eyes and looking at him curiously. "Come on," Trout said and slid an arm under her neck. He propped her up and half dragged her off the bed. She stumbled onto her feet. Trout helped her out of the van and into the clinic. The waiting room was cool and carpeted. A family of Mexicans occupied one corner, toys and magazines splayed about them. Lotus sat by a scraggly plant, flipping through a magazine. She looked up as the children approached her.

"What are you doing in here?" she hissed. "I told you to stay in the van!"

"Heaven's sick," said Trout. He guided Heaven toward Lotus.

Lotus set down the magazine and felt Heaven's forehead. "She's fine." She picked the magazine up and resumed flipping the pages.

Trout led Heaven to a chair and sat her down. She curled into the armrest and closed her eyes. "She's really sick," said Trout.

Lotus looked over at Heaven for a moment and then glared at Trout. "*I'm* sick, Trout. Okay? I have fucking chlamydia. She's fine. She just has a little bug or something. She sleeps all the time, so what else is new?" The magazine went up. Trout stared at the cover; a tall woman in a red dress with very large breasts puckered her lips at him. He went to sit near Heaven. The Mexicans were unwrapping something crispy from tinfoil. It smelled delicious. Trout folded his hands over his stomach and waited.

A nurse in a blue dress stepped into the room and called, "Lotus … Ajna?"

"Finally," Lotus grumbled and got to her feet. She followed the nurse through a swinging door, her fringed purse smacking her hip as she walked.

Trout watched the Mexicans. The two men sat facing each other in cowboy hats and button-down Western shirts. They spoke in Spanish and periodically reached out to playfully stroke or lift one of the five children playing on the floor. The woman sat holding a sixth child, obviously the sick one, cradled in her arms. Trout looked at Heaven. Maybe she had what this little boy had. The woman caught Trout staring at them and smiled. He smiled back, wishing he could talk to them. The woman said something to a little boy, and the boy walked over and offered Trout one of the crispy things wrapped in tinfoil. Trout took it and thanked him. He looked at the woman and said, "*Muchas gracias.*"

"*De nada,*" she answered and smiled.

Trout hungrily unwrapped the foil. The fried doughy thing inside tasted as delicious as it smelled. It was stuffed with meat and spices. Trout took some to Heaven, but she shooed him away without opening her eyes. He wrapped the rest of the pastry in foil to save for her.

A nurse walked by them on her way to the Mexican family, but she stopped when she saw Heaven. She looked at Trout and then put her hand on Heaven's cheek. "Where's her mother?" she asked.

Trout pointed to the swinging door.

"What's wrong with her?" asked the nurse.

"Chlamydia."

The nurse mumbled something and made the sign of the cross over herself.

"No, my mom has chlamydia. Lotus. Lotus Ajna. This is Heaven. I don't know what's wrong with her, but I think she's sick."

"Yes" said the nurse. "She has a fever. She needs to see the doctor. Wait here." She headed back through the swinging door. Her sneakers made a dry, squishing sound as she walked. After a few moments she returned with a thermometer. "Okay, '*jita,*" she said as she opened Heaven's mouth. "We're going to take your temperature." She slid the thermometer underneath Heaven's tongue and kept one hand on her jaw so it wouldn't fall out. She turned to Trout. "How long has she been like this?"

"Just since this morning." Trout stroked Heaven's foot as he spoke, suddenly very protective of her. "Is she gonna be okay?"

The nurse smiled. Trout liked her smile. "She's gonna be fine," she said. But when she pulled the thermometer out a few minutes later and read it, her eyebrows went up. "Come on, '*jita,*" she said and prodded Heaven into a standing position. "We're going to go lay down, okay?" She turned to Trout. "You can come keep her company. Help her walk, okay?"

Trout wrapped his arm around Heaven's shoulders and followed the nurse through the doors, down a hallway, and into a small room with a bed and two chairs. The nurse helped Heaven climb onto the bed and arranged the pillows under her head.

"Wait right here," she said to Trout. "The doctor will be here in a little while. I'm going to get your mother as soon as she's done with her appointment. Just call if you need anything. My name is Mrs. Sena."

Trout thanked her as she left. He put his hand on Heaven's small wrist. "It's okay, Heaven, it's okay."

Heaven seemed oblivious to him, and Trout knew he was trying to reassure himself more than his sister. Many long minutes passed before he heard quick, clipping footsteps in the hallway. Lotus strode into the room, her eyes sharp.

"What's going on?" she asked.

"Heaven's sick," Trout said. He looked at Lotus as if to say, 'I told you so.'

"Come on," Lotus said and pulled on Heaven's arm.

"No!" said Trout and placed himself between Lotus and Heaven. "She's sick! The nurse said so! The doctor is coming right now!"

"Yeah, Trout. Of course she's sick. Everybody's sick in the doctor's eyes. Believe me, I know sick, and she's not sick. She just needs sleep. I have to be somewhere right now, so let's GO!" She had succeeded in getting Heaven out of bed. Heaven wrapped her arms around Lotus's leg. Lotus peered down at her and patted her awkwardly on the head. "Trout, get your sister, and go back to the van."

Trout shook his head and refused to budge. Heaven looked from Trout to Lotus and back but continued to cling to Lotus's leg. Trout felt Lotus's glare like cockroaches crawling down his shirt. Lotus turned, brushed Heaven off her leg, and then left the room holding Heaven's hand. Trout followed behind. In the hallway, they bumped into Nurse Sena.

"Are you leaving?" she asked.

Lotus said nothing, just continued to walk determinedly toward the swinging door.

"Miss, miss!" called Nurse Sena "Your daughter is very sick. I think she should wait to see the doctor."

Lotus turned at the door. "That's a fucking joke. I've been waiting all morning to hear your fucking bullshit. You think we're such dirty freaks, don't you? Fuck off." She walked through the door, leaving the nurse in a stunned silence. Trout scurried after Lotus, too embarrassed to look at Nurse Sena. He ran to the van, afraid Lotus would drive off without him if he let her.

They drove along a river and down a winding dirt road. Lotus drove fast, shifting the gears forcefully and braking and accelerating suddenly. Heaven flopped onto the floor several times but just kept climbing onto the bed with her mute doll face on. Trout clung to the handle above his door. He didn't dare say anything.

"Goddammit, Trout!" Lotus yelled and smacked her hand on the dashboard. "Why the fuck do you come with me if you're gonna pull shit like that? I'm sorry I brought you. You can't fucking leave anything alone, can you? The little hero. Savior. Goody two-shoes boy. Always trying to get attention for yourself, aren't you?"

Trout stared dumbly out the window. He rubbed his lips together and shook his head. It's not true, he thought to himself. She's just mad, that's all. She has chlamydia. Maybe she's dying. What is chlamydia, anyway? It sounded dangerous. The van swung into a long driveway that dipped down into a valley. Heaven plunked onto the floor. A brown cat darted off the road in front of them and into the bushes.

"You think I don't know how to be a mother? You think you know better than me, Trout? Huh?"

Trout stared firmly at the passing landscape.

"You don't know the first thing about raising snotty-nosed brats like you. You think you're so much better than me, don't you? I see you. I see the way you look at me. You hate my guts, and that's fine, because I hate your guts even more."

Trout began to hum softly to himself. He wouldn't give her the satisfaction of knowing she was getting to him. In his mind, he sang, "I can't hear you, I can't hear you."

Lotus stopped the van in front of a brown house. She turned to Trout. "Look at me." Trout looked. He flared his nostrils and glared. "Stay. Here." She climbed out of the van and slammed the door behind her.

"Bitch," muttered Trout as she walked away, too quietly for her to hear. As soon as he said it, he felt afraid and ashamed. In the back, Heaven had curled into a tight ball on the floor. Trout went to her and helped her back on the bed, then sat next to her. "God, Lotus can be such a bitch!" Heaven said nothing. "We'll be okay, Heaven. We'll be okay."

They waited. Heaven fell asleep. Trout walked around outside the van, threw rocks in the creek, and went looking for the cat they'd almost run over. He returned to the van, lay beside Heaven, and fell asleep.

When he awoke, Lotus still wasn't back. He thought longingly of the fried treat the Mexicans had given him, the remains of which he had forgotten at the health clinic. He looked in the glove compartment and under the seats for something to eat. Nothing. He found a half-smoked cigarette in the ashtray, lit it, and smoked it in the driver's seat, hoping Lotus would come out and catch him. He wanted to make her much angrier than she had been, to make her as angry as he could. He wanted to make her so angry she would hit him, and then he'd be justified in hitting her back, and then she would realize what a terrible mess she had gotten them into.

The cigarette made him feel dizzy and nauseous. He put it out and closed his eyes. Lotus had taken the keys with her, so he wasn't able to listen to the radio.

"Are you hungry, Hevy?" he asked. She didn't answer. The light outside had turned the rich and golden color of a late summer afternoon. Trout made up his mind and climbed out of the van. "I'll be right back," he said to Heaven.

He walked through a blue gate and up a cement walkway to the brown house. He could hear music and voices coming from inside. He self-consciously straightened his shirt and knocked on the front door. The noise inside stopped for a moment, and then a large man with curly, black hair opened the door. He looked at Trout curiously and jerked his chin upward, as if to say, 'What?'

"Er … is my Mom here?"

The man looked confused and then started laughing. He wore a necklace of tiny seashells that tinkled when he laughed. He turned away from Trout. "Lotus, you got a kid?"

"Oh shit," Lotus said. Trout peered behind the man into a dark living room. Lotus sat on a green couch in front of a messy coffee table. Two other men sat near her, one of them asleep in his chair. Lotus stabbed out a cigarette then got up and walked toward the door.

"What the fuck are you doing here, Trout?"

"I came to look for you. You've been gone a really long time."

"What time is it?" Lotus asked the man.

He started to laugh again. "You've had kids in your car all this time?"

"Shut up, Carlos," she said and then started to laugh herself. Trout shifted his weight to his other foot. He smiled so he would be included in the joke. He glanced around the house for signs of food.

"I'm hungry," he said. At this, Carlos laughed even harder. Lotus joined in, clinging to his arm.

"He's ha-hungry?" said Carlos.

The man in the chair woke up and looked groggily around the room. "Who's hungry?" he asked. Lotus and Carlos, in a fit of laughter, clung to each other to avoid falling over. Trout continued to smile even though he was feeling confused about what was so funny.

"Shit, Lotus. What kind of mother are you?" asked Carlos.

Lotus stopped laughing and straightened up. "What the fuck is that supposed to mean?"

Carlos stepped back. "Nothing, babe. I'm just teasing you." He reached out and grabbed Lotus by the waist. "You're an awesome mama, I'm sure. You sure know how to make 'em." He started rubbing his hips against Lotus, who giggled and threw her head back. Trout blushed and looked at the floor. Lotus allowed her neck to be kissed for a few moments and then shoved Carlos, who stumbled backward, laughing. He roared and charged at Lotus. Trout tensed, ready to stop him, but Lotus was laughing. The two of them pushed and shoved each other, which led to wrestling on the floor. Trout walked around them into the kitchen and began to quietly open the cupboards. He felt a little afraid that he would get into trouble for taking food without asking, but on the other hand, he had already asked, and probably nobody would care. He saw cans of Spam, chiles, some alcohol, and a bag of rice. Trout opened a can of Spam, pulling the ring top off with a wet shhhloock, and ate the pink meat with his fingers, standing over the sink. He took another can for Heaven.

In the living room, Lotus was sitting on top of Carlos with her shirt off. His shirt was off, too, and her mouth was on his chest. The other two men sat on the couch watching. Trout slipped by them and out the front door. In the van, Heaven tossed fitfully in her sleep. Her face was bright pink, her hair matted about her head. Trout set the Spam down and untwisted Heaven from the covers she'd become tangled in. He began to feel very lonely. He desperately wanted to leave this little valley and return to Cielo's bright, open fields. He heard a mewing outside the van and stepped out to see the cat he had gone looking for earlier. It was a scrawny tabby with green eyes. It flopped onto its side when it saw Trout. Trout knelt beside the cat and stroked its ears and back. "Wait here," he said and went back into the van to get the Spam, but when he returned, the tabby startled and ran off.

Trout smoked the rest of the cigarette he had put out earlier and crawled onto the bed beside Heaven. He curled up on his side and put his head on her shoulder. Her clothes were wet with sweat. Trout remembered what the nurse had said, that Heaven was really sick. He studied her small face. She wasn't throwing up, so she probably couldn't be *that* sick, he reasoned. Nevertheless, he decided to try to get Lotus again. He knew she was probably doing it with Carlos, so he waited a few more minutes and then quietly returned up the cement walkway. The music was louder than before, and the front door was open. Trout stood in the doorway, peering into the dim house. When his eyes adjusted to the dark, he stood very still, taking in the scene before him. He wasn't sure what he was looking at, exactly. It was naked people, but what they were doing was unclear to him. There was a tangle of arms, legs, and hair. Lotus had something in her mouth; Carlos was holding something long and black, and another man had a hold of Lotus's arms. Did he have a gun?

"NO!" Trout screamed and ran toward his mother.

Trout held the bump on the side of his head. He marveled at the van window, which hadn't so much as cracked when Lotus had slammed his head into it. He didn't think the glass was that strong. The van sped along the winding road back to Cielo. Lotus sat slumped behind the wheel, her eyes staring dully ahead. Trout closed his eyes. He had to pee, but he had sworn to himself, a half hour ago, never to speak to Lotus again, so he was unable to ask her to pull over. He felt tired and numb. His stomach hurt from all the Spam. His eyes were tender and swollen from crying. He hated her. He hated her for hitting him and saying the horrible things she had. He hated her for hating him. He hated her for having such power over his emotions.

They climbed the last hill into Cielo and drove through the town, tinged pink in the sunset. Trout knew he had to make a plan, to be ready in case things got really bad with Lotus and Gordon. Jade was hardly ever around. Trout knew he had to take care of himself and Heaven. He had to protect Heaven. He turned in his seat and peered back at the lump of her in the bed. They would have to run away. Where would they go? Maybe to Mark and Ruth's. Trout began to devise a plan in his head. He would pack their bags that night when Lotus wasn't looking. Winnie's party. She would probably go. Trout could pack a bag for them and take Heaven to Mark and Ruth's. He would tell them all about what had been going on: the drinking, fighting, hitting, and name-calling. He would ask them for money and promise to pay it back someday. Then he could take Heaven to Santa Fe. He would get a job and rent them an apartment. Heaven could go to a real school. So could he. Trout began to get excited as the plan unfolded in his mind. But Heaven was sick. There was that. She would have to go see a doctor right away. Maybe Ruth could take them to the hospital tonight.

Lotus pulled into the dirt driveway. She shut off the van's engine and, without looking at Trout, said, "Get your sister." Then she climbed out, shut the door, and disappeared into the house. Trout sat still. Should they leave right then? Why bother going in at all? He watched the sun sinking to his left. His heart sped. He crept back to Heaven.

"Come on, Hevy. We're home." He pulled her up into a sitting position. Her head flopped forward. Trout put his hand near her mouth and felt for breath. It was there, shallow and faint. "Come on, Hevy. We have to go." He couldn't wake her up. He heard a door slam and looked out the windshield to see Lotus walking quickly across the field toward Forest's. The house was dark. "Come on, Hevy." He shook her gently, then harder when she still didn't wake up. She opened her blue eyes briefly and looked at Trout. There was no recognition. Her eyes closed, and Trout's chest tightened into a cold knot. He jumped out of the van and took off running to Forest's. He hadn't even reached the outhouse when he saw Red Eagle speeding off toward Winnie's. "Lotus!" he screamed, running after it. "Forest! LOTUS! MOM!!!" The truck disappeared. Trout turned and ran in the other direction, to Ruth and Mark's. His legs pumped furiously against the dry, packed dirt road.

Ruth saw him coming. She ran toward him from the garden, her face tense and concerned.

"Ruth! Ruth, Heaven's sick! I don't know what's wrong! I can't wake her up! Please come!"

Ruth had a hold of his shoulders. "Where are your parents?"

"Winnie's."

Ruth ran into the house. "Mark!" she called. "Mark? Get the truck; Heaven's sick!"

A moment later, Mark came running out, buttoning his shirt. Tall and lean, with silver hair and weathered skin, he was as spry as a man half his age and had the truck started and pulled around in seconds. Ruth followed. She motioned Trout toward the truck, and he climbed in between them. The three of them sped off toward Trout's house.

"How long has she been sick?" Ruth asked.

"Just for today. But she got real bad all of a sudden."

Ruth didn't say anything but squeezed Trout's hand.

Mark parked behind the van. Ruth was opening her door before he'd stopped the truck. She ran to the van, slid open the side door, and climbed inside. Mark climbed in after her. Trout hung back, afraid to get in the way, until he heard Heaven call his name. He sprang into the van and took hold of her hand.

"I'm right here, Hevy. It's okay."

Ruth placed a thermometer under her tongue.

"A nurse took her temperature in Española today. She said it was high."

Ruth nodded. "Lotus took her to the doctor already?"

"No. Lotus went 'cause she has chlamydia. Lotus does. While we were there, a nurse took Heaven's temperature."

Ruth touched Heaven's bright pink face. "Trout, go get a washcloth, and wet it in the creek. We need to cool her down."

Trout returned a minute later with the cool cloth. Ruth placed it on Heaven's forehead and then withdrew the thermometer. Her face tensed but her voice remained calm.

"It's 106." She looked Trout gravely in the eye. "Trout, Mark and I are going to take Heaven to the hospital. She is very, very sick. I need for you to get Bob next door. If he's not home, go for somebody else because you need to get to Winnie's quickly and tell your parents."

Trout nodded. Mark gathered Heaven in his arms, and Trout stepped back to let him pass. He watched Heaven's limp form drift away from him. Ruth gathered up her skirt and followed Mark, Trout on her heels.

"Is she gonna be okay?" Trout asked. His voice broke.

Ruth turned to him and wrapped him in her arms. "I hope so, Trout. It's good you came to get us. Come as quickly as you can. Heaven will want you with her." She released Trout and helped Mark settle Heaven on the truck's bench seat, her head in Ruth's lap. Ruth waved as they sped off. Trout's throat closed up.

"Please God," he whispered, "please don't let this be the last time I see Heaven." He turned and sprinted toward Bob's, jumping over the barbed wire fence, calling Bob's name as he ran.

7

Friday

Trout climbed out of Bob's truck, Lucy and John behind him. The three of them fell behind Bob and walked up the dirt road toward Winnie's. Cars lined the road for what seemed like miles. Dark was setting in.

Winnie's house sat nestled in the rolling, yellow pastures that lay to the Northeast of Cielo. He was one of the Old Timers. He'd been living in Northern New Mexico for twenty-three years, Cielo for ten of those. Winnie threw parties often. His house, though far away from the center of Cielo, had become a center for the hippies. People came and went from Winnie's. Out-of-town guests could always find a bed there, no matter who they had come to visit. Backpackers and wanderers eventually ended up at Winnie's, smoking pot and pitching in on the upkeep of the property, building sweat lodges, clearing fields, picking up trash after parties, mending fences. There was never a shortage of work at Winnie's nor was there a shortage of play.

The party had been going on for some time by now, and Trout could already tell it was going to be big by the number of people they passed, scattered in and amongst the cars, talking and smoking, making out, flowing out of the party in search of privacy. Trout recognized a few people, but most of them were strangers. This didn't surprise him. The hippie population in Cielo was fairly small compared to other nearby towns. Winnie had lived in so many of these towns, it seemed that everybody knew him.

They walked quickly up the hill. John and Lucy were excited at the idea of a party, but when they reached the posts of Winnie's driveway, Bob turned to them and said, "Stay here," then strode toward Winnie's and disappeared into the front door. The kids settled themselves on the wooden fence and took in the scene around them. Winnie's house was lit up by candles and lanterns, which made the windows glow with a warm, orange light. A steady stream of people flowed in and out of the front door, talking and laughing. Trout could smell the pig roasting. It would be in a pit behind the house. A group of people gathered around a keg to the left of the house. Behind them another group played horseshoes. Trout saw Jade filling two glass jars from the keg and called out to him. Jade sauntered over in brown corduroy pants and a button-down, white shirt embroidered with yellow flowers.

"Hey, little bro!" he said. "Do you like my new threads?" He puffed out his chest and turned a full circle. "Espi gave it to me."

"Yeah," said Trout, "it's cool. Where's Gordon and Lotus?"

"They're around. Somewhere. What's up? You guys look like the serious group over here."

"Heaven's sick," said Trout. "Ruth and Mark took her to the hospital. Bob's looking for our parents."

"No shit? What's wrong with her?"

Trout shrugged. "She's been sick all day." He filled Jade in on what had happened.

"Huh. Well, I'll go look for them. You guys should come join the party. The pig's coming out soon, and Winnie's setting up volleyball."

"Yeah, okay."

Jade nodded and walked away to join the horseshoe game.

"I'll be right back," Trout said and jumped off the fence.

"Where are you going?" asked John.

"To find Lotus and Gordon."

"Wait for me!" John jumped down and caught up with Trout.

"Me, too!" said Lucy, running to catch up with them. They passed the horseshoe game and walked behind the house.

The field behind Winnie's was packed with people. Smoke drifted up from a large pit a few hundred feet from the house. Several men and a few children stood around it, peering in and poking at the pig with sticks. A large bonfire illuminated the field. Some people roasted marshmallows in the flames while others played instruments and sang. A long pole had been erected in the ground, and colored ribbons were wrapped around it, their ends floating in the breeze. People were dancing, laughing, kissing, and eating from a long table covered with food. Far off in the field, Trout could make out several dark figures hanging lanterns on two posts between which hung a net. His eyes scanned the party in search of his parents. He saw Forest by the food table, dishing food onto a plate and talking to a woman in a yellow dress. Trout made his way toward him.

"Forest!"

John and Lucy each took a paper plate and began piling it with food.

"Trout! Hey! This is Sierra." Forest pointed to the woman next to him.

She smiled and bowed her head. "Greetings, Trout."

"Er … greetings. Forest, have you seen Lotus or Gordon?"

"Yeah. Lotus is inside talking to George Fair. He's here! Sierra brought him. I don't know where your dad is. I think he's helping Winnie with the volleyball net. Hey, you should have some food. I made spaghetti, and Sierra here brought samosas."

"Thanks. Nice to meet you." Trout headed toward the volleyball net, leaving John and Lucy to the food even though his stomach growled in protest.

He found Gordon squatted down, wedging a rock against one of the posts. His matted, brown hair was tied back into a ponytail. He looked up when Trout called his name. "Hey, Trout."

"Heaven's sick. Ruth and Mark took her to the hospital."

Gordon stood up. "What?"

"Heaven's sick. I came to tell you guys."

"Oh, Jesus." Gordon snorted, then spit a large wad of phlegm on the ground. "I'll be back, Winnie. Come on." He and Trout headed toward the house. "What do you mean she's sick? What's she sick with?"

"I don't know. She just got sick." Trout was beginning to feel anxious. Didn't anybody take him seriously? He glanced longingly at the food table as they passed. A man lay on his stomach by the pit, his arms disappearing inside.

They squeezed through the throng of people gathered around Winnie's back door. The house seemed to be made out of people. Trout pressed against Gordon's back and followed him through the crowd. The noise of so many people talking and laughing filled his ears. Gordon stopped periodically to say hello to friends. A hand ruffled Trout's hair. He looked up to see Cookie, Espi's mom, a wilted pink rose sticking out from behind her ear.

"What'd you do to your hair?" she asked. Several people turned to look.

Trout scowled. His hunger was making him irritable. "Somebody stole it," he said. Laughter rang out around him.

"What's so funny?" somebody asked.

"This kid just said somebody stole his hair."

Trout heaved a sigh and followed Gordon into a second room that was quiet except for the sound of a guitar, on which somebody was picking a beautiful, lonely melody. Gordon stopped, and Trout looked up. The crowd of people in the room stood perfectly still, concentrating on the music. This must be where George Fair is, thought Trout.

George Fair was a famous folk musician who had played with Bob Dylan and James Taylor. Trout knew all about him. Everybody knew all about him. He was a hippie icon, and anybody who played guitar or sang knew at least one George Fair song. "True Love Blue," "90 Miles from Fairfax," and "Camp Freedom" were the three songs of his Trout knew. Trout tilted his head and listened. George Fair was playing a song off his new album. Trout recognized it, but he couldn't think of the name. His parents owned a small radio that ran off batteries, and it was the only source of music in his house. Bob had electricity, though, and Trout sometimes listened to music with John on Bob's old record player. George Fair began to sing, and the room grew even quieter. His voice, soft and lilting, filled the room. It rose and fell like soft wings caressing Trout's ears.

"I just came to say,
I'll be back again someday,
But right now I got to be movin' on.
Once I was a child,
But it's been a long while,
The magic I believed in is gone."

Goose bumps popped up on Trout's arms. He looked at Gordon, whose mouth was open slightly, his head swaying to the music. Everybody in the room seemed entranced, listening intently, their eyes either closed or fixed on George Fair, whom Trout could not see through the crowd. Trout took a deep breath. This is an important moment, he thought. Gordon's rough hand reached back and squeezed Trout's shoulders. Trout closed his eyes and leaned into his father, enjoying the musky smell of him. I'm sorry I wished you would die, he thought. He reached his arms around Gordon's waist and squeezed hard. He felt like there was a cavernous hole in his heart where his father should be, and he wanted to press Gordon right into it. Trout thought of Heaven in the hospital. He thought of the distance that had grown between him and Jade. He thought of his fight with Lotus earlier in the day, when he had stumbled upon her in Carlos's house. He had thought they were hurting her; he was trying to save her; he hadn't understood. He had never seen her so mad. Trout was sure that if Carlos hadn't stopped her, Lotus would have beaten him up pretty bad. He felt enormously alone as he thought of these things. He squeezed his eyes shut against the tears welling up in them. Gordon's hand pulled him closer, hugging Trout to his side. Trout pressed his face into his father's shirt. He felt a shudder pass through Gordon and looked up to see his father crying, as well. Tears ran openly down Gordon's face, leaving pale tracks in the ruddy dust on his cheeks. Trout and Gordon swayed together to the music. People joined in on the second chorus:

"And oh, I like the idea of being free.
And oh, I like the idea of you loving me.
But my sweet little honey, if the truth be told,
My heart's gettin' tired and my body's gettin' old.
I just can't pretend anymore,
And I got to be movin' on."

The song ended, and the room erupted in applause. Trout dried his eyes on Gordon's shirt. Suddenly, everything seemed okay. His worry for Heaven had vanished. His distress over his family had been smoothed over and softened into a feeling of calm acceptance. Trout looked around the room. These were his people. He found himself wishing that he hadn't cut his hair.

The crowd was breaking up a bit, and Trout edged his way forward until he could see George Fair. He sat on a rug on the floor, pillows piled around him. In photos and on album covers, Trout had always thought George Fair looked a lot like Gordon. Now, seeing him in person, the resemblance was striking. George had long, stringy, brown hair like Gordon's and a shaggy, brown mustache like Gordon's, long at the sides, over a short beard. George Fair wore glasses, and Gordon didn't, but the two could easily be brothers. Apparently Lotus thought so, too, because she was sitting at George's side, one hand resting on his knee, saying, "Oh my God, you look *exactly* like my husband. I'm totally not coming on to you. Well, I *am*, but that isn't why I'm saying this. Not that that's a big turn-on or anything, to look like somebody's husband. For you, I mean. Oh my God, I should just shut up right now. There he is! Gordon! Get over here; I found your twin!"

Gordon made his way over, wiping his cheeks, and settled on the floor next to George, extending his hand. "That was beautiful, brother. My name's Gordon."

George Fair took Gordon's hand and wrapped the other around Gordon's shoulders, as much of a hug as he could give with the guitar still in his lap. "Holy shit, brother! You and me really are twins!" He held Gordon at arm's length, still clasping his hand. The two men laughed. George took off his glasses, and they laughed at that, and then Gordon put on George's glasses, and they laughed harder at that. Gordon took George's guitar and began to clumsily pick out the melody to "Camp Freedom." Lotus wrapped her arms around George and smooched his cheek.

"If anybody walked in right now, they would think you guys were each other." No sooner had Lotus said this than Forest walked into the room, nodded at Gordon strumming the guitar with George Fair's glasses on, and clapped the real George Fair on the back.

"How's that net coming?" he asked. At this, everybody in the room fell into hysterics, and when the joke was explained to Forest, he was incredulous. Gordon and George got such a kick out of it that they decided to be each other for a while. Gordon got the glasses and the guitar; George got Lotus, who immediately led him out of the room and down an adjacent hallway that led to bedrooms in the back. Trout felt a confusing mix of emotions rising in him. On one hand, he was embarrassed by his mother's behavior, but on the other hand, he felt proud that it was Lotus whom George Fair chose. Suddenly, he remembered Heaven.

"Gordon! We forgot to tell Lotus about Heaven!"

Gordon stopped strumming the guitar and looked at the floor for a moment. "Oh, well. There really is nothing we can do tonight, Trout. I'm sure Ruth and Mark are taking good care of her. We'll head down there in the morning."

Trout pondered this rationale for a few moments until the pangs of hunger in his stomach became the most important thing of all, and he made his way to the food table, where he ate until he was stuffed. The pig was just coming out of the pit. Trout marveled at its charred, crisp body. Winnie cut into it and, after much examining and conferring with nearby people, decided it wasn't quite done and stuck it back in the ground.

Trout's thoughts continued to shift to Heaven in the hospital. He knew she'd be afraid and want him with her. He had given up on trying to find Bob; he assumed they had left long ago. The party was exploding around him. People were dancing, singing, wandering around, getting crazy. Faces were painted; juggling balls rolled about; musical instruments circulated; people tried crazy tricks with the bonfire; somebody was arranging the coals from the pig pit for fire walking. It was as if a traveling circus had stumbled upon a country fair. Trout stumbled upon Max, who urged him to try one of the pot brownies his brother had baked. Trout, with one last thought of Heaven, chewed the chocolate brownie, much to Max's delight.

Boonray drove up in the stolen Mercedes with Espi in the passenger seat. Trout went to say hello and stumbled upon a heated argument between Jade and Boonray, something about Boonray not showing up to help with the pig earlier and taking Espi to Taos with him. It was right about then that the pot brownie began to take effect. Trout found himself laughing uncontrollably at the sight of Jade arguing in the ridiculous, flowered shirt. Espi shifted uncomfortably from foot to foot until Trout exclaimed that with the ribbon in her hair, she looked just like a giant bee, and she sighed and walked away, leaving Jade and Boonray to continue arguing until Winnie rallied them to help haul the pig from the pit again. Trout followed.

Black boils and blisters covered the pig's body. Its snout was split open and stiff; its eyeballs had exploded, a pole rammed through it from mouth to anus. Trout watched Jade and Boonray help several men prop the pole upon two forked posts in the ground, leaving the pig dangling heavily between, its feet bound with thick wire. Once again, it was cut into. Winnie examined a strip of flesh pulled from the side and tentatively bit it.

"Dig in!" he yelled. "SoooIE!"

People cheered and lined up with paper plates. Trout found himself staring into the pig's eye socket, gaping and black with crisped strands of eyeball poking out. The deep hole seemed infinite to him. He stuck his finger into it.

"Is this done?" he heard somebody ask.

"I don't know," another person answered.

"How do you tell if a pig is cooked enough?"

Trout turned, his finger still in the pit of the eye, and said, "You check the eye holes. Feels good to me."

The diners shrugged. "Okay," they said and tucked in. Trout shuddered at the sight of the stringy, pink flesh jiggling into their open mouths. He let his hands wander down the pig's side, over the bloated cheek, the hardened jowls. His hands took in every sensation, every crevice and wrinkle, every thick hair poking out of every blister. At the rump was a large hole from which people were digging clumps of pale meat. Trout watched the knife sawing through the carcass. Ribbons of juice and blood squirted from the blade. The pig was enormous. It hung from the poles like a blimp in the sky over Hell.

"Whose pig is this?" he asked the line of people waiting for a piece.

"Everybody's," came the answer.

"He's his own pig!" said another.

"He's God's pig."

"Don't start that God shit with me."

Trout wandered away. An arm encircled his shoulders, and he looked over to see John grinning from ear to ear.

"What are you doing here?" asked Trout. "I thought you left."

"We did, but I came back. I rode Diablo."

"No way! Your dad's gonna be pissed."

"He won't know. He and Lucy went to spend the night at Kirsten's in Dixon. I said I wanted to stay home."

"Where is Diablo?" Trout suddenly felt it imperative that he see the horse right away. John pointed to the volleyball net. Diablo was tied to one of the posts, happily grazing away. He looked huge and majestic. Trout yearned to ride him. "I have to ride him." His feet turned toward the horse.

John steered him the other way. "Forget it. Did Max give you a pot brownie?"

"Yeah."

John laughed, and then Max was there, too, laughing, and that made Trout laugh, and then it was just the three of them, stoned and together, and they laughed and spun around and around until they fell onto the parched earth, still laughing. They each ate another brownie and spent the next several hours wandering through the party, a tight trio of troublemakers, rowdy and giggling. John stole a bottle of whiskey and somebody's cigarettes, and they made their way to the dark of the far field where they smoked and drank and pondered ideas.

"I'm getting naked!" Max declared and began to strip. Trout and John followed suit, and the three of them streaked back to the party, naked butts shining in the moonlight. Whooping loudly, they tore through Winnie's yard and across the fire-walking pit. Everywhere they ran, people cheered, and some began to take off their own clothes, as well. Before long, they had a line of naked people trailing behind them, children and adults, whooping and screaming. "This was my idea!" Max yelled, his voice bursting with pride and excitement, his hair a pillow of straw flying in front of Trout's face. Suddenly, Trout had to pee, and he broke from the group. Panting heavily, he looked up to find that he was near the side door to Winnie's house. He peed and listened to the group tearing down the other side of the hill. Thirsty, he went inside for water.

Inside the house, it was warm and quiet. A radio played soft music, and voices murmured around him. Trout filled a cup three times from the kitchen sink and drank Winnie's cool well water. He wiped his mouth and listened. He could hear George Fair's guitar from somewhere in the house. He had forgotten all about George Fair. What was he doing running around outside, naked, when he could be talking to George Fair? Cupping his hands self-consciously around his penis, he walked through the house toward the sound of the music. His head was spinning from the whiskey. The house tilted around him, and Trout laughed.

He followed the music to a half-open door. He quietly opened the door enough to peer into the room. George Fair was lying on a bed, naked except for his glasses. The guitar lay across his chest, and he was lazily plucking at the strings. Beside him, a woman, also naked, had her leg draped across his middle. She was twisted, so she faced away from George and Trout, her breasts bared and shiny. Trout knew it wasn't Lotus. He felt embarrassed and wanted to turn away, but another part of him wanted to look. He stood there, torn, curious, and then the woman turned to look at George Fair, and Trout saw her face. He shrank back, surprised, and then George Fair sat up and put his mouth on Esperanza's nipple. Trout stared at the tattoo of a large, green, six-armed goddess.

He heard a familiar voice call his name, and he sprang into the hallway to intercept Jade, who was walking toward him. Jade must not see this. Trout stepped toward Jade and did his best to appear nonchalant.

"Where are your clothes?" asked Jade.

Trout shrugged. "Around."

Jade laughed and pushed past him. He put his hand on the door.

"Don't go in there!" yelled Trout.

Jade looked at him curiously and then shoved the door open. For a moment, Trout stared at his brother's stiff, solid back inside the embroidered shirt, and then there was just the empty doorway and screaming. Trout froze. From inside the room came Jade's voice yelling at Gordon and Esperanza, and Esperanza screaming back at him and then a crash and something breaking. There was silence for a moment and then the unmistakable thud of flesh hitting flesh, and Esperanza screamed, "You idiot! You fucking idiot!" She came running out of the room clutching her turquoise dress to herself, her face balled up and flushed. She ran past Trout, and this jolted him out of his petrified state. He stepped toward the door, toward the sounds of fighting. He looked into the room, afraid of what he might see but needing to see it all the same.

Jade was shoving Gordon, who kept stumbling backward stupidly. "What the fuck is the matter with you? What the fuck is the matter with you?" Jade asked this over and over until Trout began to wonder the same thing. What *was* the matter with Gordon? What kind of father had sex with his son's girlfriend?

"All you think about is yourself!" Jade yelled, his face purple with rage. His hands looked enormous and full of energy as he shoved his father around the room.

People had begun to gather in the hallway behind Trout, asking each other what was going on. Trout grew embarrassed. He stepped into the room. "Cut it out!" he yelled, but neither Jade nor Gordon seemed to hear. "You guys, quit it!"

Jade had backed Gordon into the corner by the door, and he was punching his shoulders. Gordon cowered, his hands over his face, yelling Jade's name. Forest pushed into the room, seized Jade, and pulled him away from Gordon. Gordon stumbled over to the bed and began to pull his pants on. "I'm sorry," he said. "I'm sorry."

Trout turned to the crowd of people standing behind him, shaking their heads and talking quietly. "What are you looking at?" he yelled. "Get away from here!" His face burned with anger and shame. He turned to face his brother, who was still held by Forest. Tears covered Jade's face as he stared at his father. Nobody spoke. Trout was stunned. The last of his family's alliances, besides his and Heaven's, had just been broken. Gordon, Jade's lifelong hero, sat uselessly on the edge of the bed, his hands dangling between his knees, his head shaking back and forth. George Fair's glasses lay broken on the floor.

"Did she know?" asked Jade, his voice thick and cracked with tears.

Gordon looked up with a bewildered expression. He said nothing but stared at the space between Jade and Trout.

"Did she know who you were?" Jade asked.

After a long moment, Gordon shook his head. "No."

Jade sobbed, Forest's arms around him. Forest stared up at the ceiling. They stayed like this for a while, and then Trout went to find his clothes. People stared at him as he walked through the house. They were hushed and wide-eyed. From snatches of conversation around him, Trout gathered that they all knew what happened. The real George Fair was in the kitchen with his arms crossed, several people standing around him. They glanced at Trout as he passed. He was still naked, but he didn't care. He felt completely detached from everybody as though he were floating through somebody else's dream.

He found his clothes in the field. John and Max came walking toward him, already dressed.

"What happened?" asked John. Empty of people, Winnie's property looked smaller, the house closer. He realized that everybody must have heard the yelling. How long had he been in that room? The party seemed over. Where was everybody?

He pulled his shirt over his head and turned toward them. "I don't know."

They walked through the field to check on Diablo, but when they got there, the horse was gone. The post he'd been tied to lay on the ground.

John looked all over the ground as though maybe Diablo had not run away but just shrank. They peered out into the darkness. There was no sign of the horse.

"He probably went home," said Trout.

"Dammit!" yelled John, kicking at the post. "I gotta find him."

Trout felt exhausted. His head was heavy and aching. He wanted to eat, drink, sleep, and go home all at once. John began to call Diablo's name, and Trout let out his best whistle, knowing it was useless. Diablo wouldn't come to anybody except Bob, and even that depended on the horse's mood.

"Trout, we gotta find him!" John repeated. Trout didn't answer, but he followed behind Max and John as they walked the perimeter of Winnie's property, calling off into the darkness. Trout's head hurt; his feet were tired; his eyes stung. He thought of Heaven in the hospital, and he said another silent prayer to the night sky, this time that she would be waiting for him at home when he returned.

They circled the wide field, tracing the border of Winnie's wooden fence, and then found themselves in Winnie's driveway. Trout looked over at the stolen Mercedes, blocked in by a half dozen cars, looking gaudy and pretentious amidst the beat-up station wagons and buses. Jade sat behind the wheel, staring ahead. "I'll see you guys later," Trout said.

John began to protest, his voice near desperation, but he watched Trout go and then resumed his search, Max trailing behind with his matted, blond hair.

Trout walked around the car and stood beside the passenger door. "Are you all right?"

Jade nodded.

"Can I get in?"

Jade nodded again. He sniffed, and Trout saw that he was still crying. Trout climbed in and settled beside his brother. The leather seat felt cool and made a nice rustling sound. Trout sat still for a few moments, unsure of what to say. He wanted to say something to Jade, something to let him know that he was on his side, that Gordon was an asshole, but he couldn't think of the right words. He traced the outline of the glove compartment.

"Where's Esperanza?" As soon as he said it, he regretted it. He wanted to talk about what just happened, but he wanted to talk about it for his sake. He wanted Jade to verify that Gordon was self-centered and selfish because Trout had been feeling those things in secret for so long. He wanted the alliance with Jade that had been Gordon's. He wanted Jade to turn against Gordon with him so everybody would know that Trout had been right all along, and his parents had been wrong, mean, and selfish. But none of this could be put into words, so he waited for Jade to talk about Esperanza, who, at this point, Trout did not care about one bit.

"Boonray took her home," said Jade.

"Do you think she really didn't know?"

Jade turned his head to look at Trout, his face twisted in pain. He raised his eyebrows and looked at the sky. "This is so fucked up."

Trout looked up at the sky, too. A million, trillion, tiny, white stars spun overhead. "Tell me about it."

8

Saturday

Trout awoke at dawn, shivering. He lay across the front seat of the Mercedes, Jade's green jacket pulled atop him. A wild chorus of birds filled the air. He sat up and looked around. Paper napkins and plates littered Winnie's property. The pig dangled from its pole, half eaten. Trout vaguely remembered hearing coyotes in the night. He was surprised they hadn't eaten the rest of the pig. He felt like he could sleep for much longer, but he was worried and cold. He made his way to the fence, where he peed and thought about Heaven, Jade, Gordon, and Diablo. Then he walked into the house in search of his family.

A sea of bodies covered the living room floor. Trout picked his way across the sleeping figures. He found Gordon and Lotus asleep in the same bed that Gordon had been in the night before, with Espi. Trout shook them awake.

"Heaven is in the hospital," he said. "We have to get to her right away."

His parents looked at him curiously.

"Jade's missing."

Gordon sat up, hung his legs over the edge of the bed, and coughed.

"I'm cold and hungry."

Lotus rolled over and put a pillow over her head.

"We have to get home right now. We're not doing so well."

Gordon smacked Lotus on the hip. She glared at him but got out of bed anyway. As they dressed, Trout walked back through the house. It felt good to take control. He found Forest by the fireplace, Sierra wrapped in his arms, the two of them curled inside a crocheted, pink blanket. Trout shook Forest's shoulder. Forest rolled over and peered at him. "We need to use your truck, Forest. Heaven's in the hospital, and we've got to get home."

Forest rummaged around in the pile of clothes beside him and then handed Trout the keys. "I'll catch a ride home from someone else," he said and snuggled back beneath the blanket.

Trout walked outside and spotted Forest's truck parked crookedly by the fence. Gordon's van was wedged in the tangle of cars with the Mercedes. Trout felt urgent but calm. He had watched his family come apart at the seams last night, and this morning he was going to calmly and smoothly patch things together again. He pulled the choke out and started Red Eagle up on the first try. He sat gunning the engine, feeling powerful and determined. He honked the horn, and Gordon and Lotus came out of the house. Gordon peed and then tore off a chunk of the pig to chew on. He offered some to Lotus. She shook her head, her arms crossed. They came trudging toward Trout, messy and squinty-eyed. Trout scanned the fields for Jade. He wasn't sure Jade had left the party, but he had a hunch Jade was gone. Gordon nudged Trout over to the middle of the seat, so Trout's legs straddled the gearshift, and Lotus climbed in on the passenger side. Gordon backed the truck up and pulled onto the road.

"Where's Jade?" asked Lotus, yawning.

"He's gone," Trout answered, trying to sound dramatic. He looked at Lotus. "Heaven's in the hospital."

"I *know*, Trout. You don't have to keep telling me that. God. I don't want to think about that right now."

"Well, you're gonna have to think about it because she could be dead."

Gordon and Lotus yelled at him at the same time.

"Don't say that shit!" Gordon shouted.

"Jesus, Trout!" yelled Lotus. "What the fuck is the matter with you? She's not dead. She wasn't even that sick. I don't know why Ruth had to poke her nose in and take Heaven to the fucking hospital. I can't pay a bill. Why does everybody have to jump in and try to take over my life all the time?" She looked accusingly at Trout, who slowly wiped his nose on his sleeve and turned away. He didn't think he wanted to talk to Lotus just then.

The truck rumbled down the road, and Trout stared fixedly ahead. He would not let Lotus get to him. He would take charge of getting Heaven home. He would let Jade know that he understood what it felt like to be on the slanted side of Gordon's selfishness. He would show his family that he wasn't willing to be pushed around anymore. They were going to get their act together and pull through. Trout planned to retrieve Heaven from Ruth and Mark's as soon as they got home. While she recuperated, he would finish the addition Gordon had started with the adobe bricks, and he would clean up their property. Get the grass cut. Maybe build a new sweat lodge by the river. But when they pulled around the bend, all of Trout's thoughts fell away.

"Oh God," said Gordon, stopping the truck in the middle of the road.

The most bizarre feeling Trout had ever known came over him just then. As he stared disbelievingly at the column of smoke drifting upward, at the scorched grass and blackened ground, at the fire trucks lined up along the road, and at Jade, standing alone by the creek and rubbing his arms, a feeling of enormous desolation washed through him. A primal, vicious terror gripped him at the base of his spine. This was all wrong, terribly wrong. This shouldn't be happening.

Lotus climbed out of the truck, and Trout followed. He ran toward the coals feeling that somehow he could reverse this; there must be a way. If he could just talk to the right person. This had to be a mistake! Were they absolutely positive this was their property? Maybe somehow they were confused, and this was somebody else's house. Trout ran to Jade, who was shaking his head mechanically, like a broken toy, his eyes wide and vacant. Trout stared desperately at his brother, searching his face for answers but finding only questions. He stood beside Jade and stared into the mound of smoking rubble.

Gordon and Lotus stood in the driveway, talking to a few of the firemen. Two of the fire trucks had backed out of the driveway and were pulling away. The sky grew brighter as the sun climbed over the hill. Trout saw that the woodpile had burned, and he thought of the family of mice who lived inside it. Gordon walked over to the ashes and began kicking through them while Lotus leaned against the remaining fire truck and rolled a cigarette. Trout walked over to join Gordon. A bitter, nostril-burning smell hung in the air. Gordon kicked at the ashes. His pants had turned black up to the thighs. Trout kicked a little, too, but there was really nothing to find. The woodstove stood in the middle of the rectangular pile. Trout saw nothing else he recognized. Whoever had done this had done it very well.

"Those fuckers," said Gordon. "THOSE FUCKERS!"

Just then, they heard the rumble of a motor. Trout looked up to see Mark's truck pulling into the driveway. The truck stopped, and Mark climbed out, open mouthed, staring at the spot where the house had been. Trout sprinted across the yard, his mind full of Heaven.

"I heard the fire engines," Mark was saying to Lotus. "I thought they were going to Winnie's, that a bonfire had got out of control or something."

Lotus sucked violently on her cigarette, not looking at Mark.

"Where's Heaven?" Trout asked.

Mark blinked. He put his hand over his mouth and squinted at Gordon squatting in the ashes. "Lotus, I need to talk to you and Gordon for a minute."

Lotus closed her eyes, irritated, and then walked with Mark toward Gordon. Trout followed silently, determined to find out where his sister was. He didn't trust anyone else to take immediate action. But Mark turned and shook his head at him. Trout veered away and went back to join Jade, who sat on the ground, his head in his hands.

Trout watched the three adults carefully, trying to discern their words by their body language. Mark stood a few steps back from Gordon and Lotus, his arms crossed. He looked at the ground as he spoke, swinging his head up every few moments to look at one of them and then quickly back at the ground again. His shoulders were hunched forward, and he kept touching his mouth. Whatever he was saying was difficult. Gordon craned his head toward Mark, following his words closely, though by the tilt of his head and his furrowed brow, Trout could tell that Gordon was having a hard time comprehending Mark's words. Lotus looked defensive, her chin thrust out and her arms folded tightly around herself. Suddenly, she cried out, "What?" loud enough for Trout to hear and then threw her arms open and stepped back. Mark continued to touch his face and talk, though it looked to Trout like he didn't want to say what he was about to say. He spoke a few more words, and Gordon fell to his knees in the ashes, a great, animal-like cry bellowing out of him, and then Trout knew. Heaven was dead. He ran to his parents, ran as fast as he could, a resounding "NO!" trailing after him in the ash-sifted breeze. Just before he reached them in the pile of ashes, a flash of movement caught his eye from the hills, and he turned his head to see Diablo running furiously through the cedar and piñon.

PART II

9

October 13, 1984

Saturday

Trout sat up on the couch and swung his long legs over the edge. He picked up the beer that sat on the floor and took a long swig. A girl sat next to him, and he watched her out of the corner of his eye. She had a bright green mohawk about six inches high. Her nose was pierced between her nostrils with a silver ring, and thick lines of black make-up framed her eyes. She talked animatedly to a group of people about San Francisco. Probably a friend of somebody in Jade's band.

Trout's eyes scanned the crowded room. He had fallen asleep without meaning to, and the party had grown until it pushed against the adobe walls of the house. A motley crew of people crowded into the living room and kitchen and spilled out the front and back doors. The stereo blared The Specials while Jade's band tuned up in the back yard, the electric guitar and bass vibrating loudly through the floor. It was Trout's birthday, and Jade had insisted on throwing him a party, saying, "You don't turn twenty-one every day, man!" Trout was doing his best to enjoy himself, but he felt exhausted. He had just finished his midterms and had been working overtime for Ruth's son, James, trying to finish up construction projects before the cold weather set in. On top of all that, he had spent the last few months applying to graduate schools. He took another swig of his beer and looked around for people to talk to.

Trout knew most of the guests: friends of Jade's, friends of the band members, Trout's and Jade's coworkers, friends from school. His eyes settled on a pretty redhead standing in the kitchen, leaning against the counter. She was talking to Courtney, one of the carpenters who worked for James. Trout ran his fingers through his shaggy, blond hair and stood up. He was tall and strikingly handsome. His hair had kept the bright blond tones of his childhood, and his blue eyes possessed at once a fragile innocence and world-weariness. His features were masculine yet not rough, his jaw solid and tilted up a bit, almost defensively. It was apparent he was strong and muscular even through his flannel shirt and jeans. He made his way through the crowd and into the kitchen. He stood next to the redhead and drained his beer into the sink. "It got warm," he said to her.

She smiled. "Mmmmmm."

Trout's stomach lurched.

"There you are!" Courtney said and kicked Trout squarely in the butt. Trout whacked into the counter and turned to splash Courtney with water. Courtney shrieked and punched Trout in the arm, hard. "Where have you been?"

He motioned toward the couch. "Asleep."

"At your own party? Trout!" Courtney admonished.

Trout smiled and extended his hand to the redhead. "I'm Trout."

She took his hand. Her skin was cool and soft. "Laura. Happy Birthday."

"Thanks." Trout took three beers from the fridge. He opened one each for Courtney and Laura, and they toasted one another.

They made small talk. Trout tried not to stare at Laura too much, but his eyes kept drifting over to her face. She had strong, almost masculine features with full lips and wavy, red hair that kept falling into her blue eyes. She'd shake it away, and then it would fall right back. Trout's fingers itched to tuck it behind her ears. She and Courtney were cousins, it turned out, and she had just moved to Santa Fe from Minneapolis. She was taking classes at the acupuncture school and worked at one of the downtown clothing stores. She caught Trout looking at her a few times and smiled slightly, though when she smiled, the corners of her mouth turned down, and it looked almost like a frown. Trout nervously sipped his beer. Courtney was trying to embarrass him, he could tell. She liked to give him a hard time, especially in front of women. Trout usually didn't mind it, but now he found himself blushing as she spoke, trying to think of a way to shut her up.

"Laura, you should have seen it. There he was, balancing on the beam, trying to show us what good balance he had and—wait, did you bet somebody? Yes! Yes! You bet José that you could do a handstand on the roof beam! How much did you bet him?"

"Twenty dollars."

"Ha-ha! So Trout does this handstand on the beam. It did look pretty cool, I must say, while it lasted, anyway. But just then, this mouse, this fucking gray, tiny mouse as big as my pinkie comes running down the beam toward him, and it runs right onto his hand, and so he screams and falls, right? He falls off the beam and lands on top of his circular saw. Show her your scar." Courtney reached over to pull up his shirt, but he shyly pushed her hand away. "Come on, Trout! Let us see!"

Embarrassed, he pulled his t-shirt up to reveal the three-inch scar on his side.

"Ooohhh!" Laura said and reached out to touch it. "Did it hurt?"

"Not really," he lied. He pulled his shirt down and tried hard to control the blush that was creeping over his face.

"Where did you get the name Trout?" Laura asked.

"My parents named me after Truchas Peak, which is a mountain near the town I used to live in. Truchas means Trout." He shifted his weight. He didn't talk about his parents much.

"It's a really cool name."

"Thanks." Beer ran into his windpipe, and he choked. He turned away from her, coughing. What an idiot I am, he thought.

Laura slapped him on the back. "Are you all right?"

He nodded, very red by now.

"Trout's parents were hippies," said Courtney. "As if you couldn't tell by his name."

"Wow. What an awesome way to grow up."

Trout shrugged. "Not really. It was kind of chaotic."

Laura's blue eyes stared at him in a way he really liked.

"Are your parents still hippies?" she asked

"I don't know."

"Do you mean you don't know if they'd still be considered hippies?" she asked.

"Well … I don't know where they are, actually. I haven't seen them in seven years."

"Oh."

Courtney fiddled with her pigtails and glanced back and forth between Laura and Trout. "You guys would make a really cute couple."

Trout set his beer down and picked Courtney up. "That's it. I think it's time for you to go outside now."

Courtney shrieked and whacked him on the back. He pushed through the crowd, gripping her legs tightly, and into the backyard toward a kid-sized, plastic pool that Jade kept filled with water for his dog, Conrad. "No!" Courtney shrieked. "Don't you even think about it, Trout! I will get you so bad!"

He grinned and stepped one foot into the pool. People yelled encouragement as Courtney wriggled wildly in his arms. His foot caught on the pool's rim, and he slipped. The two of them fell into the water with a huge splash, and then Courtney had her hands on his shoulders and was dunking his head. Trout laughed, feeling much better. Courtney's boyfriend, José, dove into the pool with them and pulled Courtney away. The two of them screamed and wrestled. Trout sat back, laughing and watching, and then a deafening screech came from a nearby speaker. Jade's voice, muffled in the microphone, said, "This one goes out to my little brother. Happy birthday, Trout! One-two-three-four!"

The band lunged into a loud, foot-pounding tune, and Trout climbed out of the pool. It was October, and the water was freezing cold. He shivered and walked back to Laura, who stood on the back porch.

Trout couldn't stop smiling at her. "I'm gonna go change," he said. "Don't go anywhere."

"Okay."

He returned inside and edged his way through the crowd and to the bathroom. He grabbed a towel, went into his bedroom, and closed the door. He felt nervous. He couldn't stop smiling, thinking about Laura. He stripped down and dried off, rubbing his skin vigorously to warm up. He had just soaked his last clean pair of jeans, and he opened the closet, wondering what to wear. He hadn't given much thought to his outfit before the party, but now it seemed infinitely important. He changed into a pair of casual slacks and a sweater and wrestled his unruly hair dry with the towel. There was a knock on his bedroom door.

"Just a minute!" Trout called.

He opened the door, and there stood Heaven in a dark blue dress, her long, blonde hair tied back with a blue ribbon.

"Hi," she said and held out a box wrapped in blue velvet.

"Hey! I was wondering when you'd get here. Did you bring Michael?" he asked, referring to Heaven's boyfriend.

Heaven shot him a quizzical look. "I didn't realize he was invited."

"Well, sure. Why not? Here." Trout sat on the edge of the bed and began to unwrap Heaven's gift.

It was a painting. His fingers ran over the rumpled texture of the oil paint for a moment. Three solid rectangles—yellow, blue, and red—coated the canvas. Peering out from the center of the painting was a beautiful, perfect bluebird surrounded by delicate, gold leaves. He turned the painting over and saw an inscription on the back: *Happy Birthday, Trout. No matter what happens in this crazy life, we will always be together. I love you, Precious Heaven.*

Trout stood and held his arms out to her. She stepped forward from the doorway, and they hugged. "Thank you," he said. "It's beautiful."

She was sixteen but like a child in his arms, frail, still such his little sister. Trout held her tight, savoring this moment with her, this closeness that had been increasingly absent between them. After a long moment, Heaven pulled away and smiled shyly at him.

"Do you really like it?" she asked.

"Hey, it's beautiful!" Trout held the painting before them. "Beautiful's not the right word. It's perfect. I will treasure it. And you know, I've been having those nightmares again, and so I think that if I just hang this right here …" Trout climbed onto the bed and held the painting on the wall above it. "Yes. I think this little bird will be my guardian angel."

Heaven smiled.

Jade's band was reaching deafening tones.

"Probably won't be too long before the cops show up," Heaven said.

"No," Trout said, stepping down off the bed. "We'd better go dance."

They looped through the house and into the backyard. Trout looked around for Laura. Jade jumped up and down on the stage, the microphone half buried in his mouth, screaming something incomprehensible. He saw Trout standing on the back stoop and motioned into the crowd to where Laura was dancing with an older man in a jean jacket. Trout started toward Laura but then stopped, wanting to watch instead. It felt like ages since he'd had a girlfriend. Between school and work and helping Heaven get through high school, he was too busy. That's what he told himself, anyway.

Laura looked up to catch him watching. She smiled and waved shyly. Her dance partner was doing what Trout called the Freaky Hippie Dance. With arms stretched above his head, his stance wide, he swayed back and forth, sweeping his arms to the sky, occasionally bending at the waist to touch the ground. Laura didn't seem to know what to make of it. She looked at Trout, and they laughed. He walked down the stairs and pushed through the crowd until he was by her side, and her hand was in his, and he stole her from the Freaky Hippie Dancer.

"Thanks!" she yelled over the music. "You guys throw a wild party."

"My brother does," Trout yelled back. "I'm pretty boring, actually."

"Yeah, I doubt that."

"No, really. Can I take you out stamp collecting sometime? Or turtle watching?"

She laughed. "What's turtle watching?"

"It's like bird watching but, you know, more boring."

"I'd like that."

"Good."

"Good."

"Good."

"Good."

Trout laughed. "We're off to a great start."

They danced.

10

Sunday

Trout woke with a start. Blankets laced about his legs, and his entire body was damp with sweat. He looked around the room for a few moments before he got his bearings and then took a deep breath. It had been a nightmare; that was all. He reached out to touch Heaven's painting leaning against the nightstand. The barest hint of dawn tainted the light coming through his window, and the painting seemed to glow from within. The perfect, little bluebird stared at him intently with one wide eye. Trout closed his eyes and lay back on his pillow. He had been having nightmares on and off for years, but lately they had been visiting him more frequently. Vague, dark dreams in which something was chasing him. He could never see who or what, just that he was in extreme danger and had to get away.

After a while, he gave up on sleep and climbed out of bed. His head felt heavy and his mouth dry. The party had lasted until around three in the morning, when the cops showed up for the second time and issued Jade a citation for noise. Trout had felt so good about asking Laura out that after she left, he proceeded to get drunk. He was glad it was Sunday, and he didn't have to work, although he had plenty of homework to catch up on.

He took a hot shower and then went into the kitchen to make breakfast. Empty beer bottles had taken over the house like ants. He let them be for now and mixed up some pancake batter. He heated up a frying pan and thought about when he should call Laura. His fingers itched to pick up the phone and invite her out that day, but he waited. Play it cool, man, play it cool, he told himself. He poured batter into the pan and watched it bubble. He turned on the oven and began to stack the pancakes on a plate. Lotus did this sometimes, he remembered. She would make big batches of pancakes and keep them warm on the woodstove until everybody was ready to eat. One of the rare times they ate together as a family. Trout whistled as he started up the coffeemaker. Conrad stirred from his corner and came creaking over to Trout on stiff legs. Trout patted the dog's black head and poured some food into his bowl.

He made about thirty pancakes and left them in the oven to warm. That should be enough for him, Jade, Jade's girlfriend, Holly, who lived with them, Heaven, and whoever the two people asleep on the couch were. Strange, thought Trout, to remember Lotus's pancakes all of a sudden. He hadn't thought of that in years. Certain memories visited him frequently, but others, especially the good ones, came less and less often. One day, he would remember Lotus's pancakes for the very last time.

He got out a garbage bag and began to collect beer bottles from the backyard. He heard the shower go on inside the house and returned inside to clean up the rest of the bottles. He filled three garbage bags altogether, then set the kitchen table for breakfast. Trout had tried hard to make their house homelike ever since they left Lotus and Gordon in Abiquiu and moved to Santa Fe. Jade had taken on the financial load of the household so Trout and Heaven could go to school. Trout had always felt good about doing the cleaning and cooking, and now he was so used to it, he hardly thought about it anymore. "The Little Hairy Maid" Jade called him. Where's the clean laundry? Heaven would wonder. Go ask The Little Hairy Maid was always Jade's reply.

Jade came wandering into the kitchen, his hair wet from the shower. "What's all the racket?"

"Breakfast."

"Oh." Jade pulled a beer from the fridge and opened it.

"There's coffee, too."

"Naw. This is the only thing that cures a hangover. Besides, it's Sunday. Why sober up now, when there's still some weekend left?"

Holly came into the kitchen wrapped in an orange robe. Holly and Jade had been dating for several years. She was short and energetic. Her brassy red hair had strands of purple dyed into it. She shook her head, smiling at Jade, and poured herself some coffee. Holly was usually in a good mood, which Trout appreciated. It helped ease some of the tension between the siblings. Trout motioned toward the mound on the couch. Jade walked over and peered beneath the blankets. "Boonray got lucky."

The blankets stirred, and Boonray's disheveled hair poked out. "Shut up." The blankets stirred again, and Trout caught a glimpse of a flattened, green mohawk.

"Let's wake up Heaven," said Trout, starting back toward her room.

"No jive, my man," said Jade. "She stayed at Michael's."

"What?" Trout opened the door to Heaven's room and stared at her empty bed. "No." He walked back to the kitchen. "No, Jade. That is not okay."

Holly sat at the kitchen table and pursed her lips. This conversation had been happening a lot in the household lately. Jade sighed and rolled his eyes.

"Trout, man, they've been together for almost a year. When are you going to get over this?"

"I'm not going to 'get over it,' Jade. There's a rule. We have to stick to it. No sleepovers."

"Sleepovers? Man, she's not a kid anymore. She doesn't have 'sleepovers.'"
"Whatever, Jade. But we made an agreement, and you're not backing me up. Besides, we don't really know anything about this guy. He could be a total psychopath."

"We've met him plenty of times," said Jade. "He seems all right."

"I met him," said Boonray as he sat down at the table with a cup of coffee. "He seemed cool to me."

Trout pulled the pancakes from the oven. "When did you meet him?"

"Last night. When he picked Heaven up from the party."

"Where was I?"

There was silence as Jade, Boonray, and Holly glanced at each other. Then they raised their eyebrows at Trout and burst into laughter.

"I don't know," said Jade, "Private Dancer." Boonray and Holly laughed even harder. The mohawk stirred again.

Trout crossed his arms. "What?"

Nobody could look at him, they were laughing so hard. The girl with the mohawk sat up. "Dude, you did a striptease for everybody while lip-syncing to Tina Turner."

Trout felt his face turning red.

"You have a nice ass, Trout," said Boonray. "For a guy, I mean."

"Shut up!" Trout's good mood was rapidly turning sour. He hadn't been *that* drunk. Anyway, he never did things like that, get out of control. Even when he did get drunk, he didn't do anything stupid, and he always remembered what happened.

"It's okay, Trout," Jade said and clapped his brother on the back. "Your new girlfriend didn't see."

Trout shook his head and busied himself setting out the syrup and butter. He went into the living room and picked up the telephone. "You got any chai?" asked the mohawk girl. Trout ignored her and shuffled through the mess of papers by the phone, looking for Michael's number. He found it and dialed. He could hear the others in the kitchen, still chuckling over their Tina Turner joke.

A sleepy-sounding man's voice answered. "Hello?"

"Yeah, put Heaven on the phone." The kitchen fell silent. Trout could practically hear Jade shaking his head. He was feeling angrier by the moment. Why was he the only one trying to enforce the rules?

There was some muttering on the line and then Heaven's voice, small and croaky, "Yes?"

"You need to get home right now."

Silence.

"Did you hear me, Heaven? You're not allowed to stay at Michael's. We made an agreement."

"I know, Trout, but I thought we made an exception."

"What? We didn't make any exception!"

"Yes we did! I asked you last night if I could stay here because I couldn't sleep! The party was too loud! And you said yes!" She was yelling again. He hated it when they started yelling.

"When did you ask me that?"

"Right after you did your Tina Turner dance!"

"I did NOT do a Tina Turner dance!"

Uproarious guffaws from the kitchen. Heaven was giggling. This was not working out the way he wanted it to. He wanted her home, safe, following the rules. Not laughing at him.

"Look, Heaven. I don't care what I said last night. I got carried away and maybe said and did things I shouldn't have. But now you need to come home, okay? And we can talk about this."

There was a long silence, and then Heaven said, "Okay," and hung up. Trout suddenly wished he'd said, 'I love you.' He returned to the kitchen and did his best to ignore the smothered giggles as he spread butter on his pancakes.

"Trout, lighten up," said Boonray. "Man, she's okay. You're, like, freaking out about nothing."

Trout glared across the table at Boonray. "Not 'nothing,' Boonray. You should know that better than anyone else."

Boonray held Trout's stare for a moment and then shook his head and piled a few cakes on his own plate.

Jade had finally poured himself a cup of coffee like a normal person and settled into the chair beside Holly. "Okay!" he exclaimed. "Let's talk about something else now. Please. It's Sunday, and I'm in a good mood, and we're all here together to eat this beautiful breakfast that my brother, our very own Private Dancer, has made for us all." He bowed toward Trout and began to eat.

"Amen," said Holly. "Thank you, Trout. This is awesome."

They were silent for a while. The pancakes had turned out perfect, and the weight of them settled pleasantly in Trout's stomach.

Boonray got up to make another pot of coffee. "Hey, I gotta talk to you guys about something later."

"Why not now?" asked Jade.

"Well, it's kind of, you know, personal." He glanced at the girl from San Francisco, whose green hair was sticking out sideways like the wing of a parakeet.

"I'm cool," she said. "You can talk about that kind of stuff in front of me."

Boonray filled the coffeemaker with water. "Well ... it's about Lotus and Gordon."

The room fell quiet for several long moments.

"What's up?" asked Jade.

Trout felt his stomach tighten. "Maybe we should talk about this when Heaven's here."

"Okay," Boonray said and shrugged. "So Jade, I'm serious about wanting to join in on the band. You guys sounded awesome last night."

Trout tuned the conversation out while he ate. He knew this day would come eventually, when he would have to face the reality of his parents again. Were they dead? No, Boonray wouldn't have brought it up so casually if they were dead. Trout did his best to never think of Gordon and Lotus. If he did, he was overwhelmed with feelings of guilt and anger. He hardly ever spoke of them with his siblings. Occasionally, one of them would voice a memory that they all might chuckle over and then fall silent, the weight of what wasn't being said hanging over them like something passing before the sun. Sometimes somebody, usually Heaven, would wonder aloud at where they were, and did they ever think of their children, but that was the extent of it. None of them had made an effort to contact them. It was as if their parents had just ceased to be. Boonray keyed into that long ago and followed suit, so it was odd to Trout that Boonray should bring them up. Something must have happened.

They cleaned up after breakfast, and Holly showered and went to work. She worked as a waitress at one of the ritzy, downtown hotels that catered to the tourists and movie stars who were constantly passing through Santa Fe. Boonray left to give the mohawk girl a ride home, promising he'd return afterward to deliver his news.

Heaven got back before Boonray. She walked in standing tall and trying to look composed. She looked more like Lotus the older she got. Sometimes, Trout found himself staring at her when she wasn't looking, a universe of emotions spiraling through him, questions he wanted answers to piling up inside his head like leaves beneath a tree. And then he would remind himself that it was Heaven, not Lotus, he was looking at, and he would get busy doing something else before the vast desert of sadness inside of him had a chance to sweep up and bury him forever.

Trout was sitting on the couch when Heaven walked in. He had recently remembered Laura's phone number and was enjoying the happy glow that came along with that, a wonderful respite from the anxiety he had been feeling since Boonray brought up his parents. He also had time to cool down his anger a little. Heaven *had* asked him, after all, and he had said yes, supposedly, so she'd really done nothing wrong. He smiled at her when she walked in.

Heaven set her purse down on a chair and smoothed the front of her dress. "I'm pregnant."

Trout sat perfectly still. His mind turned into a great, gaping chasm. He cradled his forehead in one hand. "Oh my God, Heaven."

She stood and looked at him for a few moments. "I'm not really."

"WHAT?" Trout smacked the pillow beside him. "That's not funny, Heaven!"

"Yes it is, Trout. It is funny. It's funny because I could get pregnant if I wanted to, and it would be my decision. I could marry Michael and run off to join a cult. I could become an astronaut. I could move into a trailer and get fat and eat Ho Hos and watch the Home Shopping Network all day, and it would still be my decision! See? 'Cause it's MY life, Trout!"

"Heaven, Heaven," Trout leaned forward and put his hands up. God, don't let this turn into yelling!

"It's MY life. Not YOUR life. I know you and Jade have taken care of me, but I'm sixteen, and I can take care of myself! And I have a wonderful boyfriend who is so sweet and would never do *anything* to hurt me, and you can't keep me from being with him, Trout!"

Trout stood up and walked to his sister. He wrapped his arms around her. "Shhhh," he said. "Shhhh."

She pushed against him, but he didn't budge. "I'm sorry, Heaven. I'm sorry." She relaxed and let him hug her. Just then, Jade walked in. Don't say anything stupid, Trout willed him. It was just like Jade to make a joke in moments like these, and then Heaven would laugh and step away from him, and the spell would be broken. Trout looked over Heaven's shoulder at Jade and shook his head. Then, he surprised himself and held an arm out to his brother. Jade came over a bit awkwardly and got in on the hug.

Heaven squeezed them both tight. "I love you guys. But you're not my parents."

It was Jade's turn to eye Trout.

The door opened, and Boonray walked in.

"Aw," said Boonray, "you're bringin' a tear to my eye."

Jade stepped away and went over to punch Boonray on the arm. Trout gave Heaven one last hug and then held her at arm's length. "We'll talk later, okay? I'm not mad."

She smiled and nodded.

Trout went into the kitchen to put a pot of water on the stove. "Boonray has something to tell us. It's about Lotus and Gordon." He couldn't look at Heaven when he said this. He didn't want her to go back to them. He wanted to hide her from them forever. "I'm making tea, and then we can talk." He looked for things to do. He wiped the table. He finished the breakfast dishes. He poured boiling water into the pretty, red teapot Ruth had given them. He cleaned the stove. He walked into the living room to see Boonray, Heaven, and Jade sitting on the couch staring at him. He returned to the kitchen and got mugs out of the cupboard. He carried everything into the living room on a tray and set it down on the coffee table. Boonray cleared his throat. Trout carried a chair over to the table, sat down, and shifted uncomfortably.

"Well," said Boonray, "I went up to see my folks." He paused. Nobody liked it when he mentioned his stepfather, Colin. "And I ran into Winnie. Gordon and Lotus are staying with him. See, Gordon has cancer."

Nobody said anything. Boonray's words rippled in the air.

Finally, Heaven spoke. "What do you mean?"

"I guess he's real sick. It just happened all of a sudden."

"Is he gonna die?" asked Trout.

"Yeah," said Boonray. "Yeah. I'm real sorry, you guys."

Jade ran his hand through his hair. "Fuck."

"Well," said Heaven, "what do we do?"

They all looked at each other. Trout felt as if he'd just run into a door. Hard. "I don't know," he said.

"More drama," said Jade.

"Jade!" said Heaven. "It's not like he did this on purpose or anything!"

"No? Well, what do you expect after living like they do for so many years?"

"God, listen to you! Cancer just happens! It's nobody's fault."

Trout leaned forward to pour tea into the mugs. "Do you know how long he has?"

Boonray stirred honey into his cup. "No, man. It could be three months; it could be tomorrow. I don't think he has long, though."

Jade folded his arms. "Well, I'm not gonna go see them."

Trout nodded. This was the big question. Heaven had seen them only twice since the state took her away eight years ago. Both of those times were when Lotus and Gordon came to visit her while she was in the foster home. Trout had stayed with them for another year before he and Jade left together and got Heaven back with Ruth and Mark's help. That had been it. One night, he and Jade had driven off in Boonray's truck, and that was the last time they had seen Gordon or Lotus. There had been sporadic communication over the next year, mostly with Gordon, who kept saying, "You guys will come back when you're ready." But they never went back. The last conversation was six years ago and had ended with Gordon saying just that, "You guys will come back when you're ready." Was Trout ready now? He couldn't imagine seeing them. There was too much hurt and anger, too much confusion in his feelings about them.

"I can't believe they're still together," said Trout.

Jade nodded. "I know, man. They hated each other."

"Remember when Gordon took another wife?"

"Yeah," said Jade. "Whatever happened to her?" He turned to Boonray, who shrugged.

"Fuck if I know. What was her name?"

"Ivy," said Trout.

"No," said Jade, "it wasn't Ivy. It was, like, Daisy or something."

"I forgot all about that," said Heaven.

Trout swallowed his tea. "Well, this is probably our last chance to see Gordon."

"I don't care," said Jade. "I was already planning to never see him again."

"I want to see him," Heaven said softly.

A pang went through Trout. "Why?"

"Because, Trout. He's my dad. Even after everything that happened, he's still my dad."

"Well," said Jade, "you guys can go. I'm not gonna go."

Boonray turned to face Jade. "Jade, man, he *is* your dad. This is death. You're not gonna get another chance."

"He had his chance. And he blew it. He stopped being my dad a long time ago." Jade stirred his tea so hard it splashed onto the table. "Besides, they could have called us or something. What, was he just gonna die without telling us?"

Trout had been wondering the same thing. "They may not want to see us."

"Well, I'm gonna go," said Heaven. "You guys can come or not. It's up to you."

Trout sat back. Why did this have to be happening? He wasn't ready for this. "I'll go with you Heaven," he said before he knew he was going to say it.

"Fuck!" Jade yelled. "Fuck! Fuck! FUCK! This is BULLSHIT!" He slammed his cup down so hard it broke, and tea spilled all over the table. Heaven put her head in her hands. "Goddammit!" Jade yelled and got up and stepped over the coffee table. He returned with a dishtowel and began wiping up the tea.

"I'm sorry, you guys," said Boonray.

"When did you find out?" asked Jade.

"Just yesterday. Before I came to the party. I went up to help Colin fix his truck."

"Don't say that asshole's name!" Jade yelled. He lunged at Boonray, who dove over the side of the couch. Jade fell on top of him and wrestled him to the floor.

Heaven stood up. "STOP IT! JADE, STOP IT!"

Trout pulled Jade off Boonray, who stood up and smoothed his hair. "What the fuck, Jade!" Boonray yelled. "I thought we were over this!"

"Over this? OVER THIS? After what that fucker did to my sister?"

Heaven burst into tears and ran into her room, slamming the door behind her.

"Jade!" yelled Trout. "Cut it out, man! This isn't what this is about. Just cut it out."

Jade's face crumpled into tears. He held his head and sobbed. "I'm sorry, Boonray. It's not your fault. I'm sorry, man. FUCK! This is so fucked up."

Trout put his arm around Jade's shoulders.

Boonray shook his head and looked at the floor. "It's all right, man. No hard feelings. This is tough."

Trout went back to Heaven's room and knocked on the door. When she didn't answer, he opened it a crack and said, "Heaven? Hevy?" He opened the door farther and saw her sitting on the bed, her back against the wall, her knees to her chest. He went over and sat beside her. "Are you okay?"

She shook her head and reached her arms out to him. He held her. "I don't want him to die," she sobbed.

Trout sat and held his sister. In his heart, the cold stone where he kept his parents turned over indifferently.

11

Sunday

Trout looked at the people gathered around the table. Ruth sat across from him, her eyes closed, her head bowed. Every meal at Ruth's house began with a few moments of silence. Trout tried to close his eyes and say a few words of thanks to himself, but he loved looking at everybody else, their faces peaceful and lit by the candles on the table. Mark sat next to Ruth, looking sharp in a red, button-down shirt, his silver hair and beard sparkling brilliantly. James and his wife, Anna, sat with their two-year old son, Oliver, between them. Jade sat next to Trout, his eyes closed, his knee bouncing a restless rhythm. They all opened their eyes and smiled at each other.

"This is so awesome, Ruth," said Trout. "Thank you."

"Yes, thank you," the others murmured.

"Thank *you*," Ruth said to him. "You've given us a reason to celebrate."

Trout smiled and dished a piece of the steaming lasagna onto her plate. Ruth had been holding birthday dinners for him, Jade, and Heaven since she moved to town four years before. She had become the closest thing the children had to a mother. Actually, she was the closest thing to a mother Trout had ever known. Lotus had sometimes forgotten her children's birthdays altogether when they were growing up.

"So," said Mark, "how was the party last night?"

"Good," said Jade. "It was really big. I'm sorry you guys couldn't make it."

"Oh, pshaw," Ruth said and waved her hand at Jade. "I'm sure you didn't want us old fogies there."

"Actually, we did," said Trout. "You would have really liked the slam dancing. How have you guys been?" Trout and Jade both worked for James. Anna managed the office, so Trout saw the two of them every day, as well as Oliver, who was often riding on the hip of one of his parents. But lately, Trout was so busy with school and work that he hadn't been able to see much of Ruth or Mark.

"We've been well," said Ruth. "No big news. Just being grandparents, you know?"

Ruth and Mark had moved to Santa Fe from Cielo when Anna was pregnant with Oliver. Ruth spent her days watching Oliver, gardening, and cooking. Pretty much the same way she had spent her time in Cielo, minus the goats, plus electricity and running water. Mark had a woodshop set up in his garage where he made furniture, and many days, he would drive out to a jobsite and work with James. Trout loved to be with them. Their family was palpably tight-knit. He felt envious but at the same time knew he was included, at least somewhat.

"How's the application process coming?" Mark asked.

"Good," said Trout. "It's expensive, though."

"You know, I've never understood why you have to pay to apply to college. It's expensive enough just to go."

"The whole concept of paying for university is ridiculous," said Anna with her crisp British accent.

"Yeah," said Trout. "I've really racked up the school loans. That's okay, though. It's worth it."

"It certainly is," Ruth agreed.

"Yup," said Jade. "Trout here is gonna make the big bucks so he can take care of his older brother."

"Big bucks!" shouted Oliver.

"Yeah!" said Jade. "Moolah, *dinero*, wool, lana, the good stuff."

"That's assuming you don't become a famous singer," said James, addressing Jade.

"Yeah, well, you know. That, too." Jade grinned and poured himself another glass of wine.

They chatted about work. James had just picked up a lucrative contract to build another gated community outside of Santa Fe. They would begin construction in the spring.

Oliver picked up his glass of milk and dumped it onto his plate.

"Oliver!" said Anna.

Oliver sucked his cheeks in and looked wide-eyed around the table. Trout tensed, waiting for the reprimand, the smack to Oliver's head, but Anna smiled and shook her head. Right, thought Trout. Not all parents are like Gordon and Lotus.

"So, do you plan on going to see your parents?" Ruth asked, looking at Trout and Jade. Trout had given her the news about Gordon over the telephone.

"I don't know," said Trout. He wiped his mouth with his napkin. "It's weird, you know? Heaven says she's going to go. I suppose I should go with her—I told her I would—but it'll be intense."

"What about you, Jade?" Ruth asked.

Jade set down his fork and cradled his glass of wine in both hands. "Nope."

Everybody was silent for a moment, and then Ruth said, "Well, that's certainly understandable after everything that's happened. You boys will let us know if you need anything?"

"Yes," said Trout.

The subject of Gordon's cancer had been at the table all night like an invisible guest. Trout didn't want to think or talk about it, but talking about anything else felt superficial and strange. Nobody seemed to know quite what to say.

James cleared his throat. "You can take as much time off as you need, guys."

"Thanks," said Trout.

"No problem. This is heavy-duty. When Anna's mom got cancer, it took over our lives for a while."

Anna nodded. "Yes, it did. It's a lot to handle."

Jade poured himself more wine. "Yeah, but this is different, you know? I mean, not to discount what you're saying, Anna, but it's like, we don't even know Gordon and Lotus anymore. It's not like we're close or anything like that. To me, they're just two people I don't like very much. And I happened to live in one of their stomachs for a while. A long, long time ago."

Trout looked at his brother. Jade sure had a strange perspective sometimes. "It is weird," Trout said. "I don't know. I guess we should make our decision, though, 'cause he may not have much time left."

"I've made mine," said Jade, sounding a bit defensive.

Anna stood and began clearing the dishes. Trout stood to help, but she shooed him back down. "You're the birthday boy. You get to just sit there and be pampered. Jade, hop to it." Jade got up and helped clear the table.

Trout leaned back in his chair and rubbed his stomach. "Triple yum, Ruth. Thank you so much."

Ruth came to sit in Jade's empty chair beside Trout. She patted his knee and leaned across him to smile at Oliver. "Somebody looks like a sleepy boy." Oliver held his arms out to her, and Trout swung him out of his highchair and onto Ruth's lap. Oliver rested his head on her chest and played absentmindedly with the buttons on her dress. "I remember when you used to do this," she said to Trout. He smiled, suddenly feeling sad and nostalgic.

Mark left the room and returned with his pipe and tobacco pouch. "Trout," he said, "whatever decision you make about Gordon will be the right one. But as a parent and an old man, I can tell you that life is brief. It's gone before you know it." He eyed Trout while he packed his pipe. "If you've got anything you need to say to Gordon, now's your chance."

Trout nodded. He knew Mark was right, but what did he have to say to his father? Thanks for nothing? Hey, Dad, it's been real not talking to you for seven years and taking all your shit for the fourteen before that? He didn't feel ready to face all of this yet, but ready or not, here it was. Gordon was going to die. Maybe he already had.

"I never really knew your parents," said James. "You guys moved to Cielo after I'd left. It seemed like they loved you, though."

Trout snorted. "I don't know where you got that from."

Ruth reached out to caress Trout's hair. "They did love you, Trout, in their own way. How could anybody not love you?"

"You were more of a mother to me than Lotus ever was."

"Well, I don't know about that. I certainly felt, and feel, like a mother to you. Lotus was very young when you were born. She wasn't equipped to be a parent."

"She was older than you were when James was born."

Ruth smiled. "It's hard for you, isn't it?"

"I don't know. I'm over it. I feel fine, felt fine, until this news today. I just don't know what to do with it, you know?"

The lights went out just then, and Anna and Jade walked into the room singing "Happy Birthday." Anna carried Trout's favorite, German chocolate cake, ablaze with twenty-one candles. The others joined in, and Anna set the cake in front of Trout. When they were done singing, he stared at the flames, pondering his wish. He'd always been a wisher. As a boy, he would wish upon all sorts of things: stars, falling leaves, airplanes flying overhead, untied shoelaces, eyelashes. Crazy wishes: make Gordon stop drinking, Heaven start talking, Lotus notice him, Jade like him. He still made crazy wishes, but he hadn't included his parents in a wish in a very long time. He wondered if he should wish for Gordon to live. This was his twenty-first-birthday wish; it seemed powerful. He closed his eyes and had a thought. He smiled. *I wish Laura would go out with me.* He blew out the candles, and the others cheered.   They sat around the table and ate cake and ice cream. The air seemed to have been cleared of Gordon for now. Mark got out the whiskey and poured them each a glass. "Now that you're twenty-one, Trout," he said, which made Trout laugh because he had been drinking whiskey with Mark for a few years.

When they'd finished with dessert, Anna gathered Oliver, who was fast asleep, in her arms. She leaned down and planted a kiss on Trout's cheek. "I've got to get this lad to bed. Happy birthday." Trout smiled and squeezed her hand.

Ruth picked up her glass of whiskey and turned to Trout. "Let's you and me go talk." Trout got up and followed her out to the back porch. She took a couple of shawls from a hook by the back door and handed one to Trout. They wrapped themselves up and sat side by side on the porch swing. Ruth took her own pipe from beside the swing and began to fill it with tobacco. Trout grinned. He had always liked that Ruth smoked a pipe. It seemed contrary to her wholesome grandmotherliness. She lit the pipe and sucked on it until the tobacco burned bright. "So. It's too bad Heaven couldn't be here."

"Yeah, she wanted to be with her boyfriend."

Ruth looked at him sideways. "I haven't yet met this new boyfriend."

"It's hardly new. They've been going out for a year."

"You don't like him."

"How can you tell?"

"Ha! That's funny. Why don't you like him?"

"I do. He's a nice guy. Just not for Heaven."

"And why not for Heaven?"

"He's just like, you know, he's old, for one."

"How old is he?"

"Twenty-one. My age."

"Well, Heaven has always been very mature for her age."

"Yes, but she's still only sixteen. I just wonder why he can't get a girlfriend his own age."

"Huh. What else?"

Trout pushed the swing with his legs. "He seems kind of, I don't know. Like he's hiding something."

"Maybe he is."

"Yeah, that's what freaks me out. It's like he's not presenting himself as he is."

Ruth sucked on her pipe. "Maybe what he's hiding is how much he cares about Heaven."

Trout snorted. "Naw. That's not it. It's so hard, you know? I just want her to be safe. I feel so protective of her. I *know* she's growing up, but I just don't think she's like other girls her age. She needs more time."

"For sex you mean?"

Trout was silent. "Maybe. I don't know what I mean. It's just after everything that happened. And I feel like it's all up to me to take care of her. Jade is like, 'Whatever!' He provides no parental guidance. And she's so pretty, you know? Guys look at her. It would be easy for somebody to take advantage of her."

"That will never change."

"I guess not. But she *is* still a kid. And she's my responsibility. I probably wouldn't have a problem with her boyfriend except that it's so *serious*. She's staying at his house and everything. I just don't think it's smart."

Ruth squeezed Trout's hand. "Oh, Trout. So much responsibility at such a young age. You were always like that. You'd come up to my house holding Heaven's hand, looking so worried all the time. It just broke my heart every time I'd see you."

"I've taken care of Heaven as long as I can remember."

"And then, when she was raped, I remember you said you felt guilty."

"I did. I felt like it was my fault, like I hadn't been watching out for her enough."

"We all felt that way. But it was nobody's fault."

"No. Just Colin's."

"Yes. His."

"Oh, I love that smell," said Trout, referring to Ruth's pipe. "Anyway, I'm more concerned right now with what to do about this whole Gordon thing."

"Oh, yes. I'd forgotten about that for a moment."

"I wish I could. I wish this wasn't happening." He stared at the brilliant New Mexico night sky. He felt suddenly very tired. He had to work in the morning, and there was a stack of homework waiting at home for him. He reached for Ruth's pipe and took a few puffs.

"I feel very protective of you, Trout. I wish this wasn't happening, either. You've seen so much pain in your short life and now this. It's quite a blow, isn't it?"

Trout nodded and handed the pipe back.

"It's very unexpected," said Ruth, "but maybe it's a blessing in disguise. Who knows why this is happening, but there's probably a reason behind it. There always is, it seems."

Trout wrapped his arm around Ruth's shoulders and rocked the swing with his feet. He liked that sentiment, that hard things were blessings in disguise. He wished he could believe it. The back door opened, and Jade came out holding a glass of whiskey, an unlit cigarette dangling from the corner of his mouth. "Mind if I cut in?" He squeezed between them on the swing and lit his cigarette. "Aaahhh." He turned to Ruth. "That was an excellent dinner, Ruth. As always."

"Good, I'm glad you liked it. I always love to feed you, Jade."

"Oh, stop it," he teased.

Ruth chuckled. "I was just telling Trout that it's too bad Heaven couldn't be here."

"Oh, yes. I'm sure he filled you in on the Michael saga."

"A bit. What do you think of him?"

"He's a nice kid. Very upstanding and responsible. He's a painter, too, you know."

"No, I didn't know that," said Ruth.

"Yep. He actually sells stuff. He's in a gallery downtown."

"Oh? Which one?"

"I'm not sure."

"Gerhardt's," said Trout.

"That's a nice gallery," said Ruth. "I know that one."

"Yeah," said Jade. "He and Heaven paint together and stuff. I think he really loves her."

"And what do you think about that?"

Jade glanced at Trout. "Well, I feel differently about it than Trout does. I figure, the guy treats her well, makes her happy, seems like he has his shit together. Excuse me. And she loves him. So that's all that matters."

"Very true," said Ruth. "How's your girlfriend, Jade? Holly?"

"Aw, she's great. She's the best. She keeps us from fighting with each other."

"It's true," Trout said. "She's our voice of reason."

Ruth tapped her pipe on the arm of the swing. "When are you going to get yourself a girlfriend, Trout? Or are you too busy with school?"

Trout blushed. He didn't say anything.

"He asked a girl out last night," said Jade.

"Oh, really? And who is this girl?"

"Her name's Laura," said Trout. A happy glow came over him. He loved this. He would forget all about her, and then, when he remembered, it was like asking her out all over again.

"Well?" said Ruth. "What's the scoop?"

"She's a friend of Courtney's. You know, the girl who works for James."

"Oh, yes. The peppy one. Is she pretty?"

Jade chuckled to himself. Trout nudged him.

"She's beautiful. And very smart. Nice. No, not nice. *Sweet.* Great laugh. She's going to the acupuncture college."

"Well, are you going to call her?"

"I don't know yet. Now that this whole Gordon thing has come up, I feel a little strange going on a date."

"Oh, I wouldn't worry about that. Your whole life can't come to a screeching halt."

"Yeah," said Jade. "That's bullshit, man. Call her!"

Ugh, thought Trout. He sounds just like Gordon when he drinks. "I will call her. I will. I just don't want to be like, 'Hey Laura, do you want to have dinner with me? I just have to go spend some time with my dad, who's dying of cancer and who I haven't seen in seven years.'"

"What's wrong with that?" Ruth asked.

"I don't really want her to know about my parents. I feel like … a bum prospect for a boyfriend. I'm poor, and my parents are losers."

"You can say that again," said Jade.

"Most people care about money a lot less than you think," said Ruth.

"Really?" asked Trout.

"Really! I mean, look at us. We lived for years off practically nothing in Cielo. And we were happy! Content!"

"But that's just it," said Trout. "Being a hippie is different now. It's not a good thing. I got called 'dirty' and 'freak' most of my life. I don't want to be a hippie! When I tell people that my parents were hippies, they're like, 'Wow! What a cool way to grow up!' But it wasn't! It was chaotic and scary. My parents and their friends were so absorbed in their 'free love' that nobody looked after the kids."

"Not all of us were like that," Ruth said softly.

"No," Trout said, bitterly, "but enough."

"You guys are bummin' me out!" Jade said.

Ruth chuckled and patted Trout on the back. "She's going to adore you, Trout. You're not the monster you're afraid you are."

Trout smiled and stopped the swing with his legs. "Well, thanks for everything, Ruth. Really. That was a wonderful dinner, and the cake was the best ever."

Ruth set her pipe down and stood up. "You're welcome. Don't you two be strangers. I expect a full report on the Laura story."

Trout stood and prodded Jade's foot. "Come on, Jade. Let's get home."

Jade drained the last of the whiskey from his glass and stood up. "Laura, Laura. Isn't there a song about a Laura? There should be. Maybe I'll write one."

Trout held the door open for them, hung the shawl on its hook, stopped in the kitchen to say good night to Mark and James, and then turned to face Ruth by the front door. "Good night, Ruthie." He hugged her.

She wrapped her arms around him. Her gray head didn't even reach his shoulder. "Good night, Trout. Drive safe."

"I will." He kissed the top of her head and watched as she hugged Jade, then walked with his brother to the Toyota they shared. "Keys," he said and held his hand out.

Jade grumbled good-naturedly, then put the keys in Trout's hand. "Good thing you're driving, Trout, 'cause I'm on my period!" Jade laughed hard at his joke and climbed into the car.

Trout grinned and pulled onto the road. He sang with his brother on the way home. Goofy, made-up songs about a girl named Laura and some idea of perfect love.

12

Monday

The next morning was cool and clear. Trout heaved a piece of flagstone into his arms from the back of James's truck and carried it to where Jade worked on laying out the patio. He carefully set the stone down where he thought Jade would want it. It was sort of an odd shape, and there was really only one place where it would fit. Jade glanced at the stone after Trout set it down. Trout returned to the truck, took another stone, and walked back to find Jade sitting on his heels, scowling at the stone Trout had just set down.

"Trout, just let me decide where the flagstone is going to go. Your job is to carry it."

Trout set down the slab of rose-colored rock. Under normal circumstances, he would have shrugged off Jade's comment and done what he said, but Jade had been short and grumpy with him all morning. "Okay," Trout said, "but there's no other place for that rock to go."

"Yeah, there is. I haven't decided where it should go yet."

"Jade. Look at this rock. It's shaped like a … nothing else around it. It has to go right here."

Jade reached down and heaved the stone into his gloved hands. "It doesn't *have* to go anywhere, Trout. You have to think creatively. That's why this is my job and not yours, because I think more creatively than you."

Trout clenched his jaw. Jade was trying to wedge the stone into a space that it was clearly too small for. He walked to the truck and returned carrying several small stones. He set them down beside Jade. Jade looked up and began to shove the rocks aside. "Trout! Why can't you just set the stones down over there where I asked you to in the first place? Huh? You're, like, making this ten times more difficult than it has to be!"

Trout wished he had asked James to split them up for the day. He should have seen this coming. That morning, he and Heaven had been sitting at the kitchen table having coffee and discussing what to do about Gordon. They had just decided to take the next day off school and drive to Cielo together when Jade came in slightly hungover. Trout was doing his best to make it a fun event. "We could stop for lunch in Española. Remember that taco place we used to go to?"

"I do!" said Heaven. "That would be fun. I was also thinking we could stop in Chimayo for some of that holy dirt."

"Well, then we should get lunch at Leona's."

"Yeah! I remember going there with Forest, that time Red Eagle broke down, and we had to hitchhike home."

Trout laughed. He was becoming excited about the trip. There were some good memories mixed in there, after all, and he was enjoying reminiscing with Heaven.

Jade had yawned loudly. "Yeah. Sounds real fun, guys." He opened the refrigerator and stuck his head inside. Heaven and Trout looked at each other, furrowing their brows at Jade's sarcastic tone.

"Want us to bring you some holy dirt?" Heaven asked.

Jade snorted and emerged from the fridge with a loaf of bread and a jar of peanut butter. "Sure, Hevy. I'll sprinkle it on my asshole, and maybe you guys will like me better."

"Jade!" said Trout. "What crawled up your ass and died this morning?"

"You did."

Trout immediately regretted reacting the way he did. He thought about why Jade might be irritable, and it dawned on him that Jade felt left out. Here Trout and Heaven were preparing to reunite with their parents without Jade, and Jade could not very well change his mind about going, not after the big deal he had made of refusing to see Gordon. Trout looked at Heaven, who rolled her eyes and diverted her attention to the bowl of oatmeal before her.

"All right, Jade," Trout said. "I'm sorry. I didn't mean anything."

Jade put two pieces of bread in the toaster and rolled his head in a circle. "'S okay, bro." But by the way he said it, Trout knew he was still irritated.

On the way to work, Jade drove faster than usual and slouched in his seat.

"So, I'll drop you at work tomorrow morning, and then you can catch a ride home with James or José," said Trout. He was trying to coordinate use of the car for the trip to Cielo. Jade didn't say anything, just sat and looked pouty. Trout felt more frustrated by the minute. Jade braked suddenly at a stop sign, and Trout's coffee spilled onto his lap. "Watch it, Jade!"

"Excuuu-uuse me! I'm just trying to get us to work on time since you spent so much time planning your trip this morning. It's not like you don't have all night tonight, and it's not like there's really that much to talk about. You just get in the car and drive up there. You know the way. It's not like you didn't live there half your life, and then what? This isn't a huge production, Trout!"

Trout dabbed at his pants with a t-shirt that had been lying on the floor of the car.

Jade reached over and grabbed the shirt from his hands. "What are you doing? That's a band shirt!" He shook it out and glared at Trout.

Trout stared out the window. He could tell it was going to be a long day.

Trout moved the pile of rocks to the far end of the patio, where Jade wanted them, and thought back over the morning's events. Why hadn't he asked James to split them up? Jade could be working with Jorge right now, who wouldn't take any of his shit, and Trout could be with José and the others, finishing up the hay bale house. It'd be warmer. Trout shook his hands in the cold. He had forgotten his gloves; how stupid was that?

He had unloaded the rest of the rocks before it dawned on him that he was doing the much harder job. Jade sat carefully pondering the layout of the stones. Trout felt his irritation mounting. This was not as difficult a job as Jade was making it out to be. Trout could see how the stones should go, and he knew Jade was stalling on purpose, just to irritate him. If Jade had laid them out by now, they could finish this job before the end of the day.

Trout walked over and stood beside his brother. "I see it."

"You see what?"

"I see how the stones should go."

"Would you just let me do my job?" Jade glared up at him.

"Well, I'm hungry, and I want to go to lunch soon, and I know you see the layout, but why you're not just putting the stones down beats the crap out of me."

"Maybe I'm not as perfect or as smart as you."

"Jade, cut it out."

"Cut what out? Acknowledging that there are problems between us?" Jade stood up and faced his brother.

Trout's mouth fell open. "What are you talking about?"

"I'm talking about you and me, Trout. About you and me and Heaven and all this bullshit that's been going on that you never want to talk about!"

"Jade, what are you talking about?" Trout felt his mouth go dry.

Jade's face was turning red. His tight frame went taut with tension. Trout had sensed Jade was bothered, but he had not anticipated this. He reached out to touch Jade's arm, but Jade pulled back. "Jade, come on, man. What are you so pissed about?"

Jade glared at Trout and then shook his head and walked back to the truck. He slammed the tailgate shut and pulled off his dusty gloves. "What I'm talking about,

Trout, is that you're so busy trying to organize and run our lives all the time that you can't see *shit* anymore."

Trout leaned against the truck. He was trying to understand what Jade was talking about. It wasn't like Jade to get this angry. Trout was sure that somebody must have done something really bad, most likely him, and he was trying hard to think of what it might be. The thing he kept coming back to was the trip to see Gordon. He took a deep breath, determined to stay calm. "Jade, I feel like this is all about me going to see Gordon."

"Yes! Yes!" Jade opened the truck door and took out his cigarettes. He lit one and threw his gloves onto the seat. "It *is* about you going to see Gordon. Because the only reason for you to see him is so that you can prove you're the better son. Because you're going to see him, and I'm not."

"Really?"

"Let me ask you something, then. Why *are* you going to see them?"

Trout was having a hard time looking at Jade's face. His expression of anger was so potent and personal. Truthfully, Trout still wasn't sure why he was going to see Lotus and Gordon. He knew he'd better come up with a good reason, though, so Jade would stop inventing his own. "I'm going … because I have some things to say to Gordon, and this is my only chance."

"Like what?"

"Like …" He still wasn't sure what he wanted to say, but by this time tomorrow, he'd be with Gordon, and now was as good a time as any to think of this stuff. "Like … okay. I want to know why they never really tried to get Heaven back. I want to know why they thought only of themselves. I want to know if they ever loved us. I don't know, Jade. I just want to hear some things, I guess. Maybe I just want to hear Gordon say, 'I love you' to me. To tell me he loves me."

Jade puffed on his cigarette. "He'll say it, but he won't mean it."

He glared at Trout, and Trout almost couldn't stand the confusion and pain he saw in Jade's eyes. He sensed that he didn't know the half of Jade's feelings toward their parents. Jade had looked up to Gordon. The two of them had something special. They had been friends, unlike Trout and Heaven, who had each other but had never been close to Lotus or Gordon. What that must have been like, to find Gordon and Esperanza together. Jade had truly loved Espi. They had talked about getting married and having kids. They'd been planning to go to Mexico together. After the whole Gordon thing, Espi didn't want anything to do with Jade or anybody in their family. Trout still wasn't sure if Espi had known she was having sex with Gordon or if she thought he was George Fair. Jade had gone to live with friends in Taos, breaking all communication with the family until after they moved to Abiquiu, and Jade had shown up one day, ready to forgive Gordon. But things were never the same again. By the time the two brothers left, nearly a year later, Trout knew that Jade's image of Gordon was shattered, and all respect for their father had been lost.

Suddenly, Jade's shoulders slumped, and he put his hand to his forehead.

"I'm sorry, Jade," said Trout.

Jade was silent for a long moment and then said, "I'm sorry, too, Trout. I don't mean to act like such an asshole." They stared at each other for a moment, and then Jade opened the truck door. "Come on, let's go get some lunch."

By two o'clock, Trout's hands felt ready to fall off from the cold. The day had gone from cold to nasty. The wind had picked up, and a light rain had begun to fall, bringing the sharp smell of snow with it. Trout stood up from the patio and stuck his hands in his armpits. "I'm done."

Jade nodded in agreement, and they began to clean up. It was unusual for either of them to stop working before five, but Trout couldn't stand the cold anymore, and he had decided to pick Heaven up from school. They dropped the truck at James's office, and Trout swung Jade home, then drove to Heaven's school.

Heaven went to a tiny, private high school near their house, close enough for her to walk. Trout pulled the orange car up in front of the school and shut off the engine. After a few minutes, the door to the small, brown building opened, and a handful of students came out, then Heaven, wrapped in her black winter coat, a drawing pad tucked beneath one arm and her green book bag slung around her shoulder. She saw Trout and waved.

"Hi!" she said, climbing into the passenger seat. "What are you doing here?"

"I came to pick you up."

"I'm glad you did. It's freezing!" Heaven turned the heat up as Trout started the car.

"Are you hungry?" he asked, pulling onto the road.

"Starved. I just had a math test, and I used all my nutrients doing the problems."

Trout laughed. "I always liked math."

"Well, that's good if you're going to be an architect. Where are we going?"

"I am taking you out to eat."

"You are?"

"Yes. I thought we could use a little time together."

He drove them to their favorite lunch spot, a small restaurant hidden in a neighborhood near Heaven's school. They took a table in the corner and ordered their usual: two combination plates, each with a chile relleno, beef taco, and cheese enchilada, all smothered in red and green chile and sour cream with warm tortillas on the side. They talked about school and work until their food arrived. Heaven drizzled honey on her meal.

"I want to talk to you about something," she said.

"What?"

"You're not going to like it."

Trout spread butter on a tortilla and filled it with beans, rice, and chile. "What is it?"

"Michael and I are talking about moving in together."

The food in Trout's mouth suddenly lost all flavor. He pushed his plate aside and wrapped both hands around his coffee mug.

"I knew you'd be mad," she said softly.

"No. You're too young. And you guys haven't known each other long enough."

"We've been going out for almost a year. And I'm sixteen."

"Look, I know you feel really grown-up, but you're still just a kid. You have plenty of time for living with boyfriends and stuff. Why don't you at least finish high school?"

"Well, actually, I've been thinking about getting a GED."

"WHAT?"

"Trout! Calm down!" She looked self-consciously around the near-empty restaurant. "I've been talking to my teachers about it, and they think it's a good idea. I could start taking classes at the Community College right away."

"Heaven! You need to finish high school!"

"Why, Trout? I'd be getting more of an education in college. And Jade never finished school."

"Yeah, well, let's not use Jade's life as an example of excellence."

"Why not? He's happy; he's in his band; he has a good job. What's wrong with all that?"

"You're better than that, Heaven. Jade dropped out of school so he could take care of us. You have the luxury of attending a really good school, and I think it would be a mistake to let this opportunity go."

"Jade dropped out of school way before he had to take care of us."

"Why do you want to grow up so fast? If you move in with Michael, you'll have to pay rent and get a job. It sucks having to work while you're in school, believe me."

"I'd have to work through college anyway. At least if I lived with Michael, I'd have help."

A feeling of desperation was rising in Trout's chest. This was all wrong, and he knew it. "I would help you."

"I know you would, Trout. But I don't want to live with you forever."

A pang of hurt shot through him. Unreasonable. She shouldn't live at home forever. But at least for a little while longer. Just another two or three years.

Heaven poked at her food with her fork. She looked at Trout until she caught his eye, and she smiled, then took a tortilla from the basket and began to make her own burrito. "This chile is hot today."

Trout nodded.

"Look, Trout, it's just an idea. We haven't decided on anything yet. But living with you guys is hard. There's Jade's band practice and a lot of partying on school nights. It's not you; it's Jade. And just the fact that I'm not even allowed to spend the night at Michael's makes it really hard to be with him."

"Why? You guys can hang out all you want during the day."

"I know, Trout, but it's not the same."

Trout hadn't seen the waitress in ages, so he stood up and refilled his own coffee cup from the pot by the ice machine. He sat back down and pulled his food in front of him. He felt like being done with this conversation.

"Michael and I are having sex, you know," said Heaven.

"Yes, I figured." This was a conversation he had been meaning to have with Heaven. Birth control and all that. But it was something he needed to plan, to be prepared for. Not like Jade, who had looked at Heaven over dinner the week before and asked, "Does Michael wear a raincoat?"

"Can we talk about something else now? I just, I need to think about this." He rubbed his head, feeling a headache coming on.

"Sure."

They returned to small talk. Trout asked her about painting and told her about Ruth's party, but something had changed. Their conversation trickled on like the lost water of a hose somebody forgot to turn off. Trout got up to use the restroom. On the way, he passed the dishwasher, a fat, Mexican man who was shredding chicken at a counter in the back of the restaurant. Trout raised his chin to him, and the man raised his in return, then peered at Heaven through the small window where the dishes came in.

"Your girlfriend?" He grinned.

"My sister," said Trout.

"Oh. She's pretty."

"Yeah. She's too young for you, too."

The dishwasher raised his arms and went back to the chicken. "I was just saying… "

When he returned to the table, Heaven had stacked their dishes into a neat pile.

"Where's the waitress?" he asked, looking around the empty restaurant. The other customer had left, his cake half eaten, a pile of money on the table.

"I don't know," Heaven said. "Maybe she forgot about us."

They calculated how much they owed and left money on the table. As they were leaving, the dishwasher called after them, "See you later!"

"Bye, Arturo!" Heaven called back.

Trout turned and waved and purposely walked between Heaven and the restaurant window on the way back to the car. "How do you know his name?" he asked, unlocking her door.

"Just from coming in here. I come here after school sometimes, with friends. He's nice. He talks to us out of his little window."

Trout started the car. "You shouldn't talk to men you don't know."

"Trout! He's, like, three hundred pounds. Besides, how would I ever meet people if I didn't talk to them?"

"What do you need to meet men for?"

"It's not about men, Trout. It's about people. What's your problem? You act like everyone's an ax murderer."

Trout pulled onto the road. "They could be; you never know. You don't know what these men are thinking."

Heaven reached over and turned on the radio. "Well, I'm not willing to live my life being afraid all the time just because I was raped."

Trout winced.

Heaven fell silent and stared out the window. "I'm not ashamed, Trout. Karen says we need to talk about this, to keep it in the open."

Karen was the therapist Heaven had started seeing the previous year.

"Okay, okay, but can we talk about it later? I just want to have a nice afternoon."

"Okay," she said softly. "Did you ever call that girl Laura?"

Trout's heart shot up into his throat. "Not yet."

"Trout! You have to call her. She's going to think you don't like her."

"I will; I will. I just don't know what to say. This whole Gordon thing is screwing everything up."

"What does Gordon have to do with Laura?"

"I feel like I should wrap this Gordon thing up before I go asking any girls out. I just don't want to be a drag. You know, the lame guy with the dying dad and the alcoholic mother."

"Oh, please. She is not going to think that way, trust me. Girls aren't like that."

"Yeah?"

"Yeah! You should just call her."

"Okay, then. I'll call her when we get home."

"Actually, can you drop me off at Michael's?"

"Sure. Should I pick you up after my class?"

"I don't think so. Michael has a show opening this weekend, and I'm gonna help him finish framing."

"Oh."

"Maybe he could come over to dinner sometime."

"Yeah, sure. Hey, be home kind of early tonight, so we can get an early start to Cielo tomorrow."

"Right."

Trout considered asking for directions to Michael's as though he couldn't remember how to get there, but he decided against it and pulled the car onto Galisteo Street. He parked the car a few apartments down from Michael's and put it in neutral.

"Do you want to come in?" Heaven asked.

"Nah. I should go."

Trout watched her walk down the sidewalk and into the door of Michael's apartment. She looked so grown-up, swinging her book bag, her long, blonde hair pulled back into a braid. He pulled the car onto the road. It was getting dark quickly. What was he doing leaving Heaven at Michael's so late? What time was it? 5:15. It was early. Still, it would be dark before long. What were they doing? Were they really working on framing paintings? Should he go back and check? He drove himself crazy with questions like this all the way home.

He had a hard time concentrating in his design class. His thoughts swung among Laura and Gordon and Heaven. When he got home, the house was empty. Trout patted Conrad on the head and set his books on the couch. The phone rang, and he jumped. He picked up the receiver. "Hello?"

"Could I please speak to Heaven?" a woman's voice said.

"She's not here. Could I take a message?"

"Can you just tell her Louise called, and the apartment is still available if she wants to come see it?"

"What apartment?"

"She had called regarding a guesthouse I have for rent."

"She did?"

"Um ... "

"I think there's been a mistake. My sister is not looking to rent an apartment."

"But—"

"I'm sorry to inconvenience you, Louise. Heaven has been a little confused lately. Just forget the whole thing. Have a good night."

He hung up and stood in the living room, staring blankly at the phone. He considered calling Heaven at Michael's. Bad idea, he thought, just back off. You'll drive her away. You can talk about this later. He paced in the living room until his anger toward Heaven subsided, and he could return his attention to Laura. He lingered by the phone. He felt like he had to prepare himself to call her, like he had to be in the perfect mood. Not too hungry, not too tired, not too grumpy or worried or busy. He knew he would never call her if he waited until everything was perfect. He went into his bedroom and retrieved her number from the drawer of his night stand, where he kept all important information he didn't want Jade spilling beer on. He tried to discern what he could of her personality from her handwriting. Not too frilly or loopy, that was good. It kind of looked like his handwriting but neater. He stood by the phone, one hand on the receiver, the other holding the piece of paper. Conrad yawned loudly from his place on the floor, as though mocking Trout's hesitation. He took a deep breath and dialed her number.

As soon as the phone started ringing, his heart began to beat wildly. Three rings and then, "Hello?"

"Hello, Laura?" he croaked.

"Yes?"

"Um, hi. It's Trout."

"Hi!"

She sounded pleased. Trout stood up a little taller.

"Hi. Um, how are you?"

"I'm good; how are you?"

"I'm good. I'm good."

"So, how does it feel being twenty-one so far?"

He laughed. "The same. Except I'm getting these weird brown spots on my hands. And my hair suddenly turned gray."

"That's what happens. You're an old man now. The days of your youth are gone."

"Yeah, I know. Hey, you never told me how old you are."

"I'm twenty-three."

"Twenty-three! Wow, you're practically ancient."

"Yes, I hope you like older women."

Trout laughed and settled on the couch. They fell into easy conversation. This wasn't so hard, after all. They had been talking for a while—Trout had swung his feet up onto the couch and was intensely enjoying the warm tones of her voice—when the front door opened, and Jade barged in, a paper sack under his arm, singing "DECK the halls with boughs of HOLLY! TRA-LA-LA-LA-LA!" Trout motioned strongly for him to shut up. The look on Trout's face was so stern that Jade froze, his face losing all color. Holly came in behind him and looked from Jade to Trout and back again.

"What was that?" Laura asked.

"Nothing. Just my brother coming home."

"God-DAMMIT!!" Jade yelled and stomped into the kitchen, slamming the sack down on the counter.

"What's he so upset about?"

"Nothing. Hey, listen. I was wondering if I could take you out to dinner?"

"Yes." She didn't hesitate one bit.

"Great. Um, should I pick you up on Thursday night?"

"Okay."

She gave him directions, and then they said good-bye. Trout hung up the phone and went into the kitchen. Jade was finishing a beer and putting away groceries while Holly chopped onions.

"What's up?" Trout asked.

Jade glanced at him, his face twitching with irritation. Trout looked at Holly, who shrugged and wiped onion tears from her eyes.

"Are you pissed that I was on the phone?"

"No, Trout. I'm not pissed. You just freaked me out is all. I didn't know if something had happened. You looked all freaky when I came in."

Trout was touched by his brother's concern. He wasn't sure who it was for, but it was sweet nonetheless. "I'm sorry, Jade. You're right. I was on the phone with Laura, and you came in singing. I was just about to ask her out."

"Yeah?" Holly asked.

Trout blushed, feeling suddenly proud of himself.

"So, did you?"

He paused for dramatic effect. "Yup."

"All right!" said Holly.

"Way to go, little brother!" Jade slugged him in the arm and handed him a beer. Trout looked at it, thinking of his studying. What the hell, he should celebrate a little. He opened the beer and toasted Jade and Holly.

"To the brave Trout," Holly said.

"To getting laid!" Jade proclaimed and threw back his beer.

13

Tuesday

The next morning, Jade huffed through the house getting ready for work. Trout sat nervously on the couch, not sure what to do with himself. He could hear Heaven in her room clacking hangers around, groaning loudly every once in a while as she fretted about what to wear to Cielo.

He had slept poorly, waking in the middle of the night from a nightmare. It was like the others except this time, there had been a flood. He was trying to get to his house, which had been buried in the flood. He knew Heaven was inside the house, and he had to get her out. There was something in the water with them, and it was going to get Heaven. He swam desperately about, trying to find a clue as to where the house was under all that water. Whatever was in the water was getting closer. Trout could sense it, could feel the water growing colder and darker. He gave up on sleep just before dawn. The bluebird in Heaven's painting peered down at him, its head alert and tilted to one side. Today was the day he would see them. No more pretending they didn't exist. Today, he would have to face Gordon and Lotus. Now he sat on the couch, waiting for Jade and Heaven.

"Where's all the bread?" Jade called from the kitchen.

"There isn't any," Trout called back.

"Shit!"

Trout heard the refrigerator door slam shut. Conrad whimpered and came over to sit by Trout's feet. He patted the dog absentmindedly. Holly came out from the bathroom in her orange robe, a towel wrapped around her head.

"You want me to go get some bread, babe?" she asked Jade.

"No, I just want some fucking breakfast."

"You want me to make you some pancakes?"

"No! I want some bread with peanut butter!"

"I'll go get you some."

"We don't have time," Trout called.

"Aaaahh!" cried Heaven from her bedroom, followed by a loud thump.

"What's going on in there?" Holly asked.

"Heaven's trying to decide what to wear," Trout said.

"I'll go help her," Holly said and walked down the hall.

Trout got up and went into the kitchen. Jade slammed a pot onto the stove and began filling a mug with water.

"There's cereal, too," Trout said and pulled a box of Cheerios from the cupboard.

"I'm making oatmeal," Jade grumbled.

Trout fixed himself a bowl of cereal and sat at the kitchen table. He watched Jade, whose black work boots were leaving chunks of dried mud on the floor. "Is José gonna give you a ride home?"

"Yeah, I guess." Jade scowled and put a lid on the pot.

Trout tried to eat slowly. He felt anxious. He wished there was more for him to do.

Jade heaved a heavy sigh and lifted the lid to peer at the water. "What time is it?"

"Twenty to eight."

"Shit." He turned off the stove and took a bowl from the cupboard. He filled it with cereal, poured milk over the top, and leaned against the counter to eat.

"Are you okay?" Trout asked.

Jade nodded.

"'Cause you just seem kind of on edge."

"I'm fine."

Heaven came in wearing a yellow summer dress.

"You're gonna be cold in that," Trout said.

"That's what I told her," said Holly, coming into the kitchen and kissing Jade gently on the cheek. Jade pulled away.

"I don't care," Heaven said. "It's what I want to wear." She lifted the lid off the pot on the stove. "Is somebody making something?" When nobody answered, she turned the burner on. "I guess I am."

"We don't have time," Trout said.

Heaven turned off the stove, fixed herself a bowl of cereal, and sat at the table with Trout. They all ate in silence.

"Jeez, you guys," said Holly. "It feels like … " she stopped and looked at the three siblings who were warning her with their eyes not to say anything. She sighed and left the room.

Jade finished his cereal and set his bowl in the sink. He followed Holly down the hall.

"How're you doing?" Trout asked Heaven.

"Fine." She sighed and chewed her cereal. "I was thinking we should bring them something. Like a gift."

"I was thinking the same thing. What do you think?"

"I don't know."

Jade came into the living room and began putting on his coat. "Let's go!"

Trout and Heaven stood and put their bowls in the sink. They put on their coats and stood by the door.

"Bye, Holly!" Heaven called.

Holly came out in her standard black-and-white waitressing outfit. "Bye, you guys. Good luck." She hugged Jade, and they exchanged a tender kiss while Trout and Heaven looked at the floor, then the three of them walked to the car.

Trout drove. Nobody said much of anything. Jade stared out the window and chewed the tips of his fingers. Heaven sat in the back, writing in her journal. They pulled in front of James's office.

Jade stared out the window but didn't make a move to get out. "What are you gonna say to them?" he asked.

Trout looked back at Heaven, who stopped writing and looked up.

"I don't know," said Trout.

"Me neither," Heaven said softly.

"Are you gonna tell them why I didn't come?" Jade asked.

Trout examined his brother's worried face. "What should we say?"

"The truth."

"What is the truth?"

Jade didn't say anything for a long time. He looked from Trout to Heaven and back. "Tell them that … tell them that … " He leaned his head back and sighed. "Tell them whatever you want to." Then he got out and slammed the door and walked into the office.

Heaven climbed into the passenger seat. "What was that about?" she asked as Trout pulled onto the road.

"I don't know. He seems more nervous than us."

"Do you think he's mad that we're going?"

Trout shrugged. "I don't know. It's so hard to tell what Jade's thinking sometimes. I think he's afraid."

"Of what?"

"Of Gordon and Lotus. He's afraid of them coming back into our lives. I am, too."

"I can barely remember what they look like."

"You've looked at pictures." They didn't own any pictures of Gordon and Lotus, but Ruth did, and she had shown them on a few occasions.

"I know, but I don't have any memories of them. They're all faded."

Trout drove to the drugstore. He was struck by everybody going about his or her business as though nothing special was happening. He felt like the end of the world was coming, and he was the only one who knew about it. He and Heaven went inside and stood underneath the florescent lights.

He shoved his hands into his pockets. "What should we get?"

Heaven stared around the store. "I don't know. What do they like?"

"Um … whiskey and cigarettes."

"Not if he has cancer. Something healthy."

"How about flowers?"

"Those are too, like, 'get well' or 'sorry you're dying.'"

"Yeah, you're right."

They began aimlessly wandering the aisles, picking things up and setting them down.

"Chocolate?"

"Squirt gun?"

"Candles?"

"Yahtzee?"

Everything they chose seemed to represent either life or death, celebration or consolation. Heaven held up a t-shirt that read # 1 DAD across the front. Trout raised his eyebrows.

"Too sarcastic. Hey, look at this." He held up a white shirt that had an image of the Virgin of Guadalupe printed on it.

Heaven examined it. "You know, I think that's perfect. Now, what to get for Lotus."

They split up, and Trout walked over to the calendars. Lotus, Lotus, he found himself thinking. Who the hell was Lotus? What kinds of things did she like to do? He couldn't remember a single thing. He remembered her sweeping, cooking, smoking pot and cigarettes, always scowling. What had he ever seen make her happy? Attention. From men. He picked up a calendar featuring photographs of shirtless cowboys. Heaven came up from behind. "Noooo," she said, pointing at the calendar, then held up a hand mirror decorated with glittering beads. On the back was a painting of a woman in a sari.

"Perfect," said Trout.

They bought the mirror and Heaven had the woman gift wrap it. Trout bought a bag of jelly beans for the ride up. They walked back to the car, stopped for gas, and then they were on the road.

They drove in silence, the landscape rolling by, brown and dry.

They reached the church in Chimayo about a half hour later. Trout got out and stretched his arms overhead. "Let's get some dirt."

They walked into the old, adobe church. There was a pit in the middle of the floor filled with finely sifted dirt. Heaven pulled a paper sack from her pocket and ceremoniously poured a scoop of dirt into it. It was supposed to be healing, blessed by a priest or something. Lotus always kept a jar of it in their kitchen, one of the few motherly things she had done. She would mix a pinch of it into a glass of water and make them drink it. If they had a cut, she would rub some of the dirt into it.

They walked outside and toward the small restaurant next to the church. They ordered food at the counter and sat at a small table. Trout looked around them, memories pouring down on him.

Heaven pulled her coat around herself. "It's cold."

Their lunch arrived, and they ate.

"So, what are we going to say?" Heaven asked.

"I don't even know. I wish I *felt* more, you know? I wish I felt sad or happy. I just feel nervous."

"Me, too. I don't feel happy. I feel kind of pissed, actually."

"Yeah, I feel pissed, too," Trout said, taking a sip of root beer.

"We probably shouldn't tell them we feel pissed," said Heaven.

"Why not?"

"Ech, why did I get orange soda? I hate orange soda."

"I think it's fine if we tell them we're pissed."

"Trout, he's *dying*."

"So? What better time to be honest?"

"I just don't want this to turn into a big scene."

"Heaven, Gordon and Lotus *are* a big scene."

"I know, but I just feel like it should be more sacred or something."

"Do you want to do a ceremony?"

"Don't be an ass, Trout."

"What? I just don't know what you mean by sacred."

"I don't know, either! It's just that I've never been around somebody who's dying before."

"I think we should just be normal," Trout said. "We should just act like everything's normal."

"What does that mean? Nothing is normal about this. We haven't seen them in seven years. Last time I saw them was in that foster home. And this social worker was there, taking notes."

"They wouldn't let me come."

"I remember that. I kept asking for you. Lotus was drunk. She called the social worker an asshole."

Trout laughed in spite of himself. "What a trip Lotus is. Does Michael know about that?" He was surprised he was bringing up Michael.

Heaven nodded. "I've told him everything."

"What does he say?"

"He's supportive. He feels sad that it happened to me. He says if he ever sees Colin, he'll kill him."

"Too late. I'll kill him first."

They finished their lunch and lingered in the restaurant, neither of them ready to make the last leg of the journey. Finally, Trout stood and pulled on his jacket. Outside, fat flakes of snow had begun to drift down. Trout started the car and put the heat on full blast. Heaven shivered in her summer dress. "I shouldn't have worn this stupid thing," she said.

The narrow road from Chimayo to Cielo wound through small clusters of squat houses. Trout racked his brain for what to say to his parents. He didn't want to miss this opportunity to say everything he wanted. The car began to climb the last hill before Cielo.

"He might be really sick," Trout said suddenly. He hadn't thought of that before, what Gordon might look like.

"Oh God," said Heaven. She folded her arms tightly across her chest.

They crested the hill, and suddenly there was Cielo. To their right, the road dropped off steeply, and Trout thought of Tom's motorcycle somewhere down there. He slowed down as the road narrowed and cut through town. A lowrider cruised slowly by, the driver slumped down behind the wheel. Trout peered into the window of Garcia's. All he could see was the reflection of himself and Heaven in the car, their faces wide and white.

"Look," said Heaven, pointing at what used to be Lucinda's but was now an empty house with the windows boarded up and a single, useless gas tank in front. Lucinda and Ben must have died.

The town looked the same but smaller and quieter. Many of the houses were dark and lifeless.

"There's the church," said Heaven.

Trout was amazed by how much he remembered. It was all there as though he'd walked this road in his bare feet just yesterday.

"I hardly remember this," Heaven said.

"You weren't that little when you left."

"I know, but I didn't used to come into town. I mostly stayed at the house."

Gradually, the spaces between the houses grew farther and farther apart, and then the road gave way to dirt, and the acequia was there on the left. Patches of snow dotted the landscape. The sedan bounced along on the rough road. Trout drove slowly to prevent the bottom of the car from scraping. Heaven stared silently out the window. Trout glanced periodically at her, not sure how being back here would affect her. She hadn't been back since the day Mark and Ruth took her to the hospital.

"There's Esperanza's house," Trout said. An old Dodge sat parked in the driveway. Trout wondered if Cookie still lived there.

"And the road to Ruth's," said Heaven. "I remember that. Should we go look?"

"Nah," Trout said, looking up at the dark sky. "It's definitely gonna snow. We should get a move on."

They lurched and bounced down the road until Trout saw Bob's house on the left and, just beyond, their old land. He slowed the car, peering at Bob's funny trailer, added onto bit by bit until it resembled some sort of shoebox construction. He wondered what had ever become of Bob, John, and Lucy. He and John had said good-bye in a very unceremonious way, neither of them wanting to admit that this might be the last time they would see each other. "See ya," they had muttered, and then John had hugged Trout and given him his guitar pick.

Before he knew what he was doing, Trout pulled into the driveway of their old house. The land sat empty and barren. Weeds had grown up where the house had been.

"Oh my God," said Heaven, who had been in the hospital when the house burned down. She got out and began to walk toward where the house had stood. Trout followed her. She went and stood in the middle of the patch of weeds. "This was the living room."

"The only room."

"Besides the loft."

They looked around them.

"It's so weird," said Heaven.

Trout stared out at Truchas Peak looming down on them, its crown obscured by dark, ominous clouds.

Heaven walked to the *acequia*. She peered into the dry, brown willow. "This was my secret place. One of them." Trout bent down to look. Wild willow had taken over the space where the narrow tunnel had been. They stood up and looked around.

"Should we go see if Forest still lives back there?"

Heaven paused. "Okay."

They walked across the field until they came to the faint echo of the path that led down to the back creek. Trout slid down the snowy slope, his tennis shoes soaking through. Heaven stepped down carefully behind him, holding her dress up. They came to the footbridge, and Trout walked across. It had grown rickety, and a few boards were missing. He came to the flagstone path that led to Forest's. He rounded the bend, and there was the house.

"It looks like somebody lives here," Trout said. He turned to see that Heaven was no longer behind him. "Hev?" When she didn't answer, he walked back the way he came.

He found her standing just before the bridge, her hands clasped in fists below her chin. She stared up the creek and shook violently.

"Heaven!" Trout ran and put his hands on her shoulders. Her face had turned white, and her eyes cut across the willow like knives. Trout turned to see what she was looking at, and it dawned on him. "Oh my God, Heaven!" He wrapped his arms tightly around her. "I didn't think! I'm sorry! I didn't think!" The way she shook against him made him feel like his heart was tearing in two. "Come on," he said and turned her gently away from the bridge. She covered her face with her hands and began to sob. Huge, animal-like bellows tore out of her. Trout wanted to get her back to the car, but Heaven couldn't move. She seemed frozen to her spot, bent over, wailing fiercely.

"Oh my God, Heaven!" Trout cried. He didn't know what to do. He felt himself beginning to cry. How could he have been so stupid? That was the place; that was where Colin had brought her, down by the creek to one of her hiding places. Heaven seemed to have lost all awareness of where she was. She fell on the ground crookedly and clutched at the snow with her hands. Trout got down beside her and tried to pull her toward him. She leaned into him, and then the thrashing of her sobs jerked her in the other direction. Her mouth opened wide, and her eyes rolled back. Trout racked his brain for what to do but found nothing. He was suddenly and keenly aware of how isolated they were. Heaven was screaming at the top of her lungs. He felt he had to get her out of there, but the snow was so slippery and the hill so steep. He didn't know how to get her up the slope short of dragging her. His heart pounded. He was sure she was having some sort of nervous breakdown.

"Okay, okay," he said. It seemed good to talk. He wrapped his arms tightly around her. "It's okay, Heaven. It's okay. Shhhh. Shhhh. You're okay. You're safe. There's nobody here but me, Trout. It's just me, your brother. Shhhh. I'm not gonna let anybody hurt you. It's okay. Shhhh."

Heaven began to calm down in his arms. She stopped thrashing and buried her face in his coat, continuing to sob. Trout kept talking to her and began to rock gently back and forth. He squeezed her as hard as he could without hurting her, murmuring into her ear. It was working. The sobs began to subside and gradually gave way to weeping. Trout stroked the top of Heaven's head. "It's okay. It's okay."

His fingers had grown numb with cold long before Heaven finally stopped crying. She looked up at him. "Can we go?" She was shivering, and the bottom half of her summer dress, where her coat stopped, had soaked through.

They made their way up the hill, holding onto each other's hands. Trout kept his arms around her as they walked across the field to the car. Heaven looked at the ground the whole time, not talking. They got into the car and pulled away, blasting the heat.

"I am so sorry, Heaven. I just didn't think!"

"It's not your fault." She put her hand in his. He squeezed it and looked at her face. She looked like she was going to start crying again any second.

"Are you all right?"

She nodded, paused, then shook her head.

"Do you still want to go see Gordon and Lotus?"

"Yeah. I do."

"Do you want to talk?"

"No. I just ... I'm sorry."

"Don't be sorry! What are you sorry for? I'm the one who should be sorry. I can't believe I asked you to walk down there with me."

"No, I thought I could handle it. I didn't think it would affect me so much." She laughed. "I actually thought it might be good for me to see it."

Trout pulled the car onto Winnie's road. "Do you want to pull over for a while before we go see them?"

"Yes."

They parked on the side of the road. Trout kept the engine running and the heat blasting. Barbed wire fences cut through the yellow fields in all directions. The white sky pressed down on them. Without sun or clouds, the flat sheet of colorless sky felt too close, felt suffocating. Heaven slowly relaxed as she warmed up. She held her dress against the heater and took deep breaths. After a while, she smiled and nodded at Trout. He pulled onto the road.

That last minute, driving up toward Winnie's driveway, felt like taking off in an airplane. Dread, fear, and excitement coursed through Trout. He wanted Winnie's house to be right there, and he didn't want to see it at the same time. He was anxious to see

Lotus and Gordon, and at the same time, he wanted to turn back right then and never set eyes on either one of them again. And then, there it was, Winnie's L-shaped adobe with the falling-down fence skirting around the land. Trout pulled slowly into the driveway. There was Winnie's same old truck. And there was a yellow Cadillac parked beside it. Could that be Gordon and Lotus's? Could they be driving a *Cadillac*?

Trout parked the car and turned to face Heaven. She looked squarely back at him.

"Are you sure you're okay?"

She nodded carefully, her lips in a thin line. They climbed out and walked slowly toward the house. Trout stepped in front of her to knock on the wooden door, but just before his fist fell, it opened.

14

Tuesday

Trout recognized the man standing before him. Apart from a few more wrinkles and much grayer hair, and although he had traded the fringe, leather, and beads for blue jeans and a wool sweater, Winnie looked much the same.

"Hey, hey!" he said brightly and threw his arms around Trout, squeezing him into a rib-crunching hug. Caught off guard, Trout did his best to return the death grip. Winnie's crinkly, blue eyes fell upon Heaven. "Precious," he crooned and gave her a much gentler hug, patting her back as though she were a baby in need of a burp.

"Winnie!" Heaven said, although it sounded like a question. She looked over Winnie's shoulder at Trout, who nodded that yes, it was Winnie. "Winnie!" she repeated. "It's good to see you."

Winnie stepped back and appraised them. "My, my, my. Look at the two of you, all grown up. Makes me feel like an old man!" He clutched at his heart dramatically.

A voice called from the back of the house, a deep rasp that sounded like thousands of cigarette butts shifting in the ground, "Is that my kids?"

Trout froze and felt Heaven grab his hand.

Winnie rubbed his hands together excitedly and did a funny little dance, something between a jig and an old man shuffling quickly toward the nearest restroom. "Come on!" he said and motioned for them to follow. He led them down the hallway to the third door on the right.

Inside the room was a bed, and on the bed lay a man. Trout and Heaven stepped inside. Winnie lingered in the doorway for a moment and then walked off down the hallway. Beside the bed was a chair, and the woman on it turned slowly to face them. Heaven gasped. The likeness between their faces was even more dramatic than Trout thought it would be, but that was as far as the resemblance went. Lotus had become curved over, her upper body caving in on itself like a pill bug about to roll up. She held a hand-rolled cigarette delicately in her right hand. Her dirt-brown hair was riddled with gray hairs that sproinged out of her head like broken bed springs. She wore thin, silver-rimmed glasses that made her look older. Her perpetually tanned skin had grown rough and lined from years of sun and smoking. Her thin, small body was lost inside plain, baggy clothes. Her sharp eyes fell first on Heaven, then Trout, who was trying to pull himself up as tall as he could. He stood a bit in front of his sister, guarding her. Lotus took a drag off her cigarette and squinted at the two of them.

"You're big," she said.

Heaven stepped forward. "Mom." Her voice held trepidation and hope.

Lotus laughed. The ashes of her cigarette fell onto the bed. "Mom. Nobody's ever called me that before. All of a sudden you want to call me 'Mom.'" Her laugh was manic, ha-ha-ha-ha-ha, rolling out of her in a staccato monotone. Lotus looked at the man on the bed, who seemed like he was about to laugh with her but instead coughed a wicked, phlegmy hack.

Trout turned his attention to Gordon, or who he took to be Gordon. The man was barely recognizable as his father. Cancer had chewed his body into an emaciated, hairless, dull ghost of the man he used to be. He lay propped up on several wilted pillows, his arms on top of the covers like bare, winter twigs. His eyes were the only lifelike things about him, and they were fixed on Trout and Heaven like two bright light-bulbs bulging out of their sockets. Like babies' eyes, Trout thought. They look like a baby's eyes. Trout hadn't known what to expect, but nothing in him was prepared to see his strong, capable father looking so vulnerable and small. Gordon lifted a thin arm. It floated up like it was filled with helium. He beckoned Trout and Heaven with it.

"Come here. Don't be shy. I'm not contagious. Lemme see the two of you."

Trout and Heaven walked carefully to the bed as though the slightest bump or noise might break Gordon into a million pieces. Lotus scooted her chair back as they approached. Trout got the feeling that she did it more out of not wanting to touch them than consideration. Gordon stared up at them with electric blue eyes. Several long moments passed. Trout stared back. He felt himself shrinking back in time. Eighteen, fifteen, fourteen, and then he was twelve again and looking into his father's eyes with fear, anger, and adoration. Gordon shifted his eyes steadily back and forth between his two children.

Heaven reached out to touch Gordon's leg. "Hi," she said gently.

For a brief second, Trout thought he saw a mist of wetness cloud Gordon's eyes, but then it was gone. Gordon smiled at Heaven, and then a thought seemed to come into his mind, and he lifted his head a little to look past them. "Where's Jade?"

"He didn't come," Trout said.

Gordon nodded, his old shut-the-door nod that meant he understood what you said and didn't want to talk about it anymore.

"How are you?" Trout asked, aware that it was a stupid question but unable to think of anything else to say.

Gordon began to slowly ratchet his way into a sitting position. "I'm shit." He coughed again. That cough was enough to make Trout want to run out of the house and never look back, it was so full of sickness and death.

Lotus slid her chair back a little farther. It made an awful screech on the hard, dirt floor. "Now, babe, don't go feelin' sorry for yourself," she said.

"Aw, fuck," Gordon answered, and turned his head away from Lotus. He made it halfway to sitting and then gave up and collapsed back against the pillows.

Trout glanced at Heaven, feeling worried about her all of a sudden. Unless his memory was skewed, his parents seemed to have become even more crass and rough with time, caricatures of their former selves, even. Lotus began rolling another cigarette. She propped her feet up on the bed. Trout noticed that she still wore beaded moccasins. Where the hell did she buy those things?

Gordon scooted over and patted the bed beside him. "Come on. Siddown, and tell me what you've been up to. I feel like I hardly know you."

Heaven sat gingerly on the bed. Trout dragged an old armchair over from the corner and sat on it, facing Gordon, his profile to Lotus. Out of the corner of his eye, he could see Lotus scrutinizing his face.

"So how old are you now, Heaven?" Gordon asked. Trout's fingers itched to help his father into a more comfortable position, he was splayed so crookedly on the pillows.

"Sixteen," said Heaven.

"Uh-huh. Do you have a boyfriend?"

Heaven blushed and nodded. "His name's Michael."

"Uh-huh. So you gonna marry him?"

Heaven's eyes widened, and she looked at Trout. He could see her fumbling for an answer.

"She's sixteen," Trout said. "She's not marrying anybody right now."

"Are you married?" Gordon asked Trout.

It struck Trout that he really could be married, even have kids, and his parents wouldn't know. Gordon and Lotus might be grandparents for all they knew. "No."

Lotus wiggled her foot so the moccasin slid off, and she scratched her bare foot with the other shoe. Her toenails were yellow and thick. "I didn't think you would be," she said.

Trout didn't know whether to take this as a compliment or insult, so he said nothing.

"What about Jade?" asked Gordon. "Is he married?"

"No," said Trout.

Heaven perked up. "He has a girlfriend, though. Her name is Holly. She lives with us. She's wonderful."

"And he couldn't come today?"

"No," said Trout.

Gordon began to work his way into a sitting position again. "Well, that's okay. Can't say I blame him."

Trout and Heaven watched the grueling ascent, fascinated and mortified. Gordon had always been so strong. Watching him struggle just to sit up was almost surreal.

He made it up and took a few moments to catch his breath. "So. You came to see your old man die."

Lotus laughed mechanically.

Trout sat on the edge of the armchair, his hands clasped in front of his mouth, his body tense and ready to run.

"We didn't come to watch you die," said Heaven.

Trout stood up suddenly. "Look, if you want us to go, we can go." He wanted them to say yes. He didn't want to be there. What was he doing there? Why was he putting up with their sarcasm and attitude?

Gordon looked taken aback. He looked over at Lotus, who was squinting through her glasses and picking at her toenails, seemingly oblivious to all of them. "No, no. I don't want you to go." His hands groped searchingly about the bed as though he had lost something. The gesture was so helpless and old man-like that a wave of pity washed over Trout, and he sat down again.

"We brought you something," Heaven said and looked at Trout to see if it was a good time for the gifts.

Trout nodded.

Heaven reached into the bag by her feet and withdrew the folded t-shirt. She handed it to Gordon. Gordon took the shirt and unfolded it. He held it up before him. The Virgin stared serenely back from her frame of roses.

"Hey! That's really cool!" He showed it to Lotus, who glanced up briefly from her toenails but didn't say anything. "Wow! Thank you, guys. I'm gonna put it on right now." He pulled his thin, thermal underwear shirt off to reveal a hairless and scrawny chest. His ribs showed like the hull of a decaying ship. Trout looked away.

They had bought a size extra large, thinking of the Gordon of seven years ago. With his newly wasted body, Gordon looked like a child wearing his father's clothes. He didn't seem to notice, though. He smoothed the shirt over his chest, obviously pleased, and Trout was glad they had thought to bring him something.

Heaven took the wrapped mirror from the bag and gave it to Lotus. "This is for you."

Lotus tossed hair out of her face and took the present with a suspicious look. She made a big deal out of opening it, as though whoever had wrapped it had made it especially difficult to open. Then she held the mirror up. She looked at the woman in the sari, cocked her head questioningly, and then flipped it over to the mirrored side. She stared at her reflection for a moment that was brief but long enough for Trout to see the flicker of hatred cross her face, and then she put it, mirror side down, on the floor.

"Thanks," she said and squashed her cigarette out in a large seashell that was filled to the brim with soggy, brown butts.

"Aw, makes me feel like we should've gotten something for you guys," said Gordon.

"That's okay," said Heaven.

Winnie appeared in the doorway wearing a stocking cap and a ski jacket. "I'm going into town. You kids need anything?"

Lotus picked up the tobacco pouch beside her and shook it. "Drum."

"Yeah. Anything else?"

"A new asshole," Gordon said and then laughed, which led into a fresh coughing fit. Lotus joined him, ha-ha-ha-ha-ha-ha-ha, and Winnie, too, thought this was very funny and let loose a few robust, loud guffaws.

"What size?" asked Winnie. They laughed some more while Trout and Heaven exchanged glances. Heaven smiled good-naturedly, but Trout couldn't bring himself to do it, so he buried his mouth in his coat instead.

Winnie left, and Lotus sighed and stood up. She shifted her weight back and forth, picked a few hairs off her sweater, and then walked quickly out of the room.

Gordon's eyes followed her. "This is hard for her," he said after she left. "It's just been so long, you know? And you guys don't keep in touch and … anyway."

Trout wanted to say, 'You guys don't keep in touch, either,' but it seemed point-less. Instead, he crossed his legs, buried his hands in his pockets, and leaned back in the chair. He felt the minutes sliding by. Soon an hour would pass, then the next, then it would be time to go, and he would have to say good-bye to Gordon for the last time. He swallowed.

"How much longer do you have?" he asked.

Gordon closed his eyes, and his brow rose. He shook his head and worked his mouth, and then he opened his eyes and looked directly at Trout. "I don't know. I wish I could tell you. I wish I could tell everybody, so they could all stop hanging on and dealing with this bullshit." His voice grew low and steady. Trout stared back. He felt like a moth near a lightbulb. Sucked in, captivated, regardless of the danger. "I tell you what, Trout, and Heaven, this is the worst fucking ride of my life. I don't want anybody feeling sorry for me. Fuck that! This is between me and the cancer now, me and death, me and the worms in the ground." He drew back, and his face softened. He patted the bed in the direction of his children. "It was good of you to come. Good of you to come see your old man."

Suddenly, Trout felt strong. Something in the intensity of Gordon's voice, something about Gordon's Fuck You attitude even in the face of death, caused a spell to be broken, and Trout leapt through time, out of his twelve-year-old self and back into the adult he had become. He pulled himself up. Was this the worst Gordon had to offer? Sarcasm? Crass self-pity? If so, he was not the invincible giant Trout remembered. This man was frail and old, nothing to be afraid of. A new feeling of power came into Trout. He was not going to spend this last time with Gordon reacting to him, manipulated and confused.

Trout looked squarely at his father. "That's the shits," he said.

Gordon stared back, long and steady, his eyes reflecting the myriad of emotions ruffling through him. Then he smiled and chuckled. "It really is the shits, Trout. Literally."

Trout smiled and breathed easier. "So, whatever happened to your other wife?" he asked.

"I'm tired," Gordon said. "I don't want to talk about this right now. Tell me about you. Tell me all about your lives." He closed his eyes and seemed to sink even farther back into the pillow.

Heaven and Trout looked at each other.

"Well ... " said Heaven. She stood to take off her coat and laid it on the foot of the bed. "I'm in school. I'm a junior. I go to this really cool school called Prometheus. It's right near our house." She rattled on about her life, telling Gordon all about her studies, Michael, painting, her friends. She became animated and talked freely, telling a few funny stories that got Gordon to laugh. She sat beside him on the bed and rested her hand easily on his leg the entire time. Trout stared at her hand, feeling his heart clogging his throat.

Then it was his turn, and he filled Gordon in on his life, omitting a few details, like Laura. Gordon listened, his eyes closed, a small smile on his lips. When Trout finished, Gordon opened his eyes and settled them on his son. For the first time that day, Gordon reached out to touch him. Trout froze, unsure of what to expect, but when Gordon's thin hand fell on his arm, Trout felt every cell in his being rush up to meet it. Every molecule inside of him yearned for that touch, and Trout closed his eyes, afraid he might cry.

"I'm proud of you," Gordon said.

Trout nodded, his eyes still closed.

"I'm proud of you," Gordon said to Heaven, reaching his hand forward until she placed hers inside of it. "I don't even deserve to be called your father, but I'm sure as hell glad I am."

Heaven laid her upper body on the bed, her head beside Gordon's hip, and began to cry. Gordon tenderly stroked her hair. Trout felt ready to crawl out of his skin. What right did Gordon have to experience this sort of intimacy with Heaven? He hadn't earned it! Did he think that just because he was dying, he deserved to be forgiven? That none of it mattered anymore? Who did Heaven think Gordon was? He wasn't worthy of this trust and openness! Wanting to scream, Trout did the only thing he could: he burst into tears. It was just like Gordon to die, thought Trout. Just like him to never be there for his children and then just go and die.

Trout stood and walked to the other side of the room, his back to the bed. He stopped the crying as quickly as it had come, shut if off like a faucet. He dried his face with his palms. The room felt small and crowded. The air pressed in on him. He didn't know how much longer he could stand being in there. Gordon and Heaven lay still on the bed. Gordon's eyes were closed. Trout stared at Gordon's chest, waiting to see if it would move. A minute passed, Heaven lay motionless, exhausted. He stepped to Gordon's side and put his ear close to Gordon's nose. After a few moments, he felt Gordon's breath, weak and barely perceptible, but still there. Trout studied his father's face. Heavy lines creased his forehead and the corners of his eyes. Lines ran down from his nostrils and connected with the corners of his mouth, which were drawn down into a frown. Even asleep, Gordon looked like he was in pain.

Trout touched Heaven's shoulder, and she slowly raised her head to look at him. "I think he's asleep," he said.

Heaven nodded and looked at Gordon. "He looks so sad."

"Let's go into the kitchen."

"I don't want to leave him yet."

"We'll say good-bye. He probably needs the rest."

Heaven stood, and they quietly left the room and walked down the hall to the kitchen. Lotus sat at the long, wooden table, a drawing pad propped on her knees and several pencils spread out before her. She was sketching an aloe plant that sat in a pot on the table. Trout and Heaven came in and sat in two chairs at the other end of the table. Lotus glanced up at them and then continued drawing.

"You draw?" Heaven asked.

"Uh-huh." She held the pencil loosely in her right hand, moving it quickly and confidently across the paper.

Trout raised his eyebrows at Heaven, surprised. "Should I make some tea?" he asked.

"Do you want some tea, Lotus?" asked Heaven.

"There's tea in the cupboard above the stove."

Trout stood and filled a kettle with water, then turned the stove on. Lotus set the drawing on the table. Heaven craned her head forward, trying to see it.

"Heaven draws well," Trout said, leaning against the counter.

Lotus shifted about in her seat, changing positions, looking anywhere but at her children. Heaven looked at Trout. He read her expression. She wanted to experience a meaningful connection with Lotus. She hadn't seen Lotus since she was in the foster home. Lotus and Gordon had visited her twice and promised they would get her back, that it was just a temporary situation, and then she had never seen them again. Just a few conversations on the phone, swimming with empty promises.

Heaven would mention their parents occasionally, less and less as the years went by. Trout and Jade would head off her questions with stories of their childhood, filling her in on what lousy parents Lotus and Gordon had been, replacing her desire to see them with resentment and contempt. Had that been fair? Trout wondered. He had been motivated by a desire to protect his sister, fear that she would want to return to live with their parents, and a strong need to have her on his side, against them. How did Lotus look to Heaven? Did she look as crumpled and pathetic as she did to Trout? As worn out and bitter? The kettle began to sing, and Trout turned the stove off and poured the water into a teapot.

After a few minutes of craning her head forward, Heaven asked to see the drawing. Lotus rolled a cigarette, then silently slid the pad across the table to Heaven. Heaven picked it up and held it before her.

"It's really good," she said and held it up for Trout to see. It was good, but Trout didn't want to say so. Instead, he opened the cupboard and took out three mugs.

"When did you start drawing?" he asked.

Lotus shrugged. "A while ago. After Gordon went into rehab."

"Gordon went into rehab?" Trout and Heaven asked at the same time.

"Yup. A couple years ago."

"What for?" Trout asked.

"Booze."

Trout set the teapot on the table and searched the kitchen for honey. He found it and sat down. Lotus rested her head in her hand. Exhaustion radiated from her like heat from an adobe wall in the summer. Trout felt tired just looking at her. They sipped their tea and stared out the window. Snow was falling in large, heavy flakes.

"We should probably go soon," Trout said to Heaven, "before the roads get bad."

Heaven nodded. She was running her fingers over Lotus's drawing.

"You can have that," Lotus said.

"Wow," said Heaven. "Thank you. It's beautiful. I don't know what to say."

"It's just a stupid drawing," said Lotus.

They finished their tea, and then Trout slid his chair back and stood up. Heaven stood reluctantly. She carefully tore the drawing from the pad and rolled it up.

"We're going to say good-bye to Gordon," said Trout.

Lotus nodded and began to roll another cigarette.

They returned down the hallway. Trout felt time slowing down. This was it. This was the moment he had been dreading ever since Boonray had told them about Gordon's cancer. As they entered the room, Trout half expected Gordon to be dead. He lay motionless in the same position they had left him in, lost inside the Virgin t-shirt. Heaven approached the bed. She put one hand on Gordon's shoulder and said his name. When he didn't respond, she said it again, and Trout's heart sped up. Gordon's eyes opened slowly. He looked curiously at Heaven for a moment, and then recognition fell upon his face, and he smiled.

"I thought you were an angel," he said. "I thought I'd finally died."

"We have to go," said Heaven. Her voice broke on the word 'go,' and her eyes filled with tears again.

Gordon put his hand on her arm. He looked over at Trout, who stepped forward to the bed. "I sure am glad to see you guys," said Gordon.

"We are, too," said Heaven and looked at Trout.

Trout stood and stared at Gordon, wishing the perfect words would come into his mind.

"Tell Jade hello for me," said Gordon. "Tell him he's a little shit for not coming up here."

Trout nodded. He touched Gordon on the shoulder. "Good-bye."

Gordon heaved himself into a sitting position with surprisingly more ease than before, as though he didn't want to miss this opportunity.

"Come here," he said and held out his arms.

Trout leaned into them and embraced his father carefully, afraid to hurt his fragile body. Gordon patted him on the back and then held his arms out to Heaven. Trout stepped back and watched them hug. Big tears rolled down Heaven's face.

Gordon shook his finger at them. "You kids be good. Don't do drugs. All that shit I never told you." He gazed at them for a long moment. "You'll be okay. I know you will. I'm not worried about you." He smiled. "Thanks for the shirt. I think I'll have them bury me in it. What the hell."

Heaven laughed and wiped the tears from her face. "Bye, Gordon."

"Good-bye," Gordon said.

The weight of that word hung between them for a long moment, and then Trout stepped around the bed to lift Heaven's coat. He helped her put it on, and they both stopped to touch Gordon one last time, then turned and left the room. As soon as they were in the hallway, Heaven broke down. She cried her way into the kitchen, where Lotus sat staring out at the snow.

"We're gonna go" said Trout, one arm wrapped around Heaven's shoulders.

"Okay," said Lotus. She didn't move from her seat.

Trout and Heaven lingered for a moment, not sure whether or not they should go to her, then said good-bye and walked out the front door.

The world had become a blank canvas. White snow fell from the white sky and frosted every surface white and smooth. They walked to the car in silence, Heaven clutching Lotus's drawing. They climbed inside, and Trout started the car. Heaven stared at Winnie's house.

"Hold on," she said and opened her door. Trout watched her run through the snow and disappear inside. She returned a minute later, a slight smile on her face, and got into the car.

"What did you do?" Trout asked, backing the car out of the driveway.

"I had to say 'I love you' to Gordon."

Trout said nothing as he plowed through the fluffy snow.

"It didn't feel right, not saying it. I felt like I needed to say it before he died. Are you mad?"

"Mad? Why would I be mad?"

"I don't know. I just thought you might be."

"No. I'm happy. I thought about saying it, but it just didn't seem right."

"I'm sure he knows."

Did he? Trout wondered. Did he even love Gordon? He wasn't so sure. He had thought he did, once upon a time, but that was so long ago, and everything had changed so much.

They reached the end of the road and slid a little on the turn. Trout held the wheel firmly. The windshield wipers were on high speed. Heaven didn't look up as they drove past their old land, then Bob's, then Cookie's. Just before the road turned to pavement, they saw Winnie's truck headed toward them. They slowed, and Trout rolled down his window. Winnie pulled up beside them.

"So, you kids off?" he yelled through the snow.

"Yeah," said Trout. "We want to get back before the roads freeze."

"Smart," said Winnie and tapped his forehead. "Well, don't be strangers!" He beeped his horn and waved at them. They waved back and then pulled away.

"You need anything?" Trout asked. "Are you hungry?"

"A little. I'll just eat these jelly beans."

She opened the bag, and they chewed the candy as they absorbed the sights of the town through the blurred windshield. They reached the hill that led out of Cielo. Trout leaned forward. He didn't like descending this hill in the snow.

"Oh no!" Heaven exclaimed.

"What is it?"

"We forgot to give him the dirt."

"Oh. Maybe we'll come back."

"Yeah. I'd like that."

Halfway down the hill, they hit a patch of ice, and the front wheels began to slide. Trout, nervous because this was where Tom had gone off the road, overcompensated, and they slid into the shallow ditch.

"Shit," he said. He reversed and tried to get out, but the wheels spun uselessly in the snow. He reversed again and realized he was just digging himself in farther. He turned off the engine. "Shit."

Heaven held up a yellow jelly bean. "This one is buttered popcorn flavor."

Trout took it and put it in his mouth. "That's disgusting!" He grimaced but ate it anyway.

Heaven laughed. She pointed at the grimace on his face and laughed even harder. At once, everything seemed funny to Trout. The entire situation struck him as hilarious, and Heaven laughing beside him, pointing at his face and waving different colors of jelly beans, was too much to bear. They sat in the car and laughed so hard and long that when Trout started the car, he was certain that all their laughing had heated the snow around the tires, melted it, and released them. Sure enough, the car heaved itself out of the ditch, and they skated down the hill, laughing at their dumb luck.

When they got home, there was a message from Ruth. They had stopped at the store for steaks, and Heaven started cooking while Trout settled on the couch with the phone. Ruth answered with her usual, surprised hello. Trout sometimes thought that Ruth would never get used to living in town with electricity and a phone.

"Hi, it's Trout."

"Oh, good! I'm just sitting down with a brandy. Mark and James won't be back for a while. I was hoping you would call before they got back."

"You're drinking brandy?"

"Yes. Shhhhh. I know; it's not like me to drink before dinner, but something about the snow falling and having the house all to myself, it feels like a special occasion!"

"Well, cheers!"

"Cheers! So? How did it go?"

Trout heaved a heavy sigh that seemed to carry much of the day's intensity out with it. "It went well. He looks pretty bad, though. Worse than I thought he would."

He recounted the events of the day for her, leaving out the part about Heaven's breakdown. He had forgotten about it until Ruth asked if they had stopped at their old land. He could see Heaven in the kitchen, washing asparagus and singing along with the radio.

Ruth asked about the funeral.

"I didn't ask," he said. "I assume Lotus will tell us when he dies, and then we can go from there."

"Yes, yes. That makes sense."

They said good-bye, and Trout sat on the couch after he'd hung up the phone. Would Lotus tell them when Gordon died? He wasn't so sure. After all, she hadn't told them that Gordon was sick. Trout felt that he needed to know. It wasn't so much that he wanted to go to the funeral as just *know* when Gordon died. So he could let go, maybe, or quit wondering about it.

He got up and went into the kitchen. "What can I do?"

"Set the table, Little Hairy Maid."

"Hey!" He shook a spatula at her. "Don't call me that!"

"What do you prefer? Tina Turner?"

"You guys can all quit it with the Tina Turner joke now."

"Oh, Trout, you should've seen yourself! I have never seen anything quite like it in my life."

They sat at the kitchen table. Heaven had lit candles and opened a bottle of wine.

Trout looked at the table and at his plate of food. They had splurged and gone for filet mignon. "Wow. This is really something. We should eat like this more often."

"Well," said Heaven, "we deserve something special after today."

"I agree." He raised his glass. "To emotional trauma."

"Yes. To getting our asses kicked by life."

They clinked glasses and began to eat. Trout basked in good feelings. He felt very close to Heaven at the moment and closed his eyes, breathing in the warm, meat-scented air of the kitchen.

"Ruth asked about the funeral," said Trout.

"Oh."

"I know. I hadn't even thought about it."

"Do you want to go?"

"I don't know. I don't even know if Lotus wants to have one."

"She should."

"Would you want to go?"

Heaven pondered this as she cut her steak. "Yeah, I would. I think that would be appropriate."

"I'll go with you if she has one. If she tells us about it." He paused and took a sip of wine. "I wanted to talk to you about today, about what happened when we went to the land. We don't have to talk about it right now, but I just wanted to see how you were feeling."

"I feel fine. I mean, not *fine*, but I'm okay. I'll talk to Karen about it, see what she has to say."

"Okay."

"Trout?"

"Yeah?"

"Thank you. Thanks for doing what you did. It really helped."

"I was pretty scared, to tell you the truth. I didn't know what to do. I just feel so bad that I took you down there."

"It wasn't your fault, really. I thought I could handle it. I just hadn't been back there since it happened."

"Did you think it was weird that Gordon and Lotus didn't talk about that?"

"Not really. I mean, what are they gonna say?"

"Yeah. I think it was a good visit, considering."

"Me, too."

They finished dinner, and Trout cleaned up while Heaven ran herself a bath. He stood at the sink washing dishes when, for some reason, the words to an old George Fair song came into his head. Trout sang:

"I just came to say,
I'll be back again someday,
But right now I got to be movin' on.
Once I was a child,
But it's been a long while,
The magic I believed in is gone."

Heaven heard him from the bathroom and joined in.

"And oh, I like the idea of being free.
And oh, I like the idea of you loving me.
But my sweet little honey, if the truth be told,
My heart's gettin' tired and my body's gettin' old.
I just can't pretend anymore,
And I got to be movin' on."

They were eating ice cream in the living room, in the middle of watching a movie, when they heard a car pull up followed by the sound of a door slamming. Jade's voice came booming up the walk, singing a reggae song. He sang off key and loud enough to wake the neighborhood. Trout tried to catch Heaven's eye, but she was absorbed in the movie. The door swung open, and Trout and Heaven sat staring at the empty doorway. A moment later Jade jumped through. "Boo!"

"Hi, Jade!" said Heaven. She patted the seat beside her. "Come sit down. We're eating rocky road and watching a weird, French movie."

Jade took off his jacket and flung it across a chair. He eyed them contemptuously. "Rocky road. That's what we are."

"What's going on, Jade?" Heaven asked.

"Oh, you know, same old. What's going on with you guys?" He spun around and pointed both fingers at them, gun style.

Trout realized Jade was drunk.

Heaven hit the pause button on the remote. "Are you okay?"

"Me? Little old Jade? I'm *fine*! Why wouldn't I be okay? Are you concerned about me or something?"

Trout and Heaven stared at him silently.

"What's the matter? Don't you have anything to say to me? Don't you care how my day was? How my rathole day in this shithole place was?" he yelled as he walked into the kitchen. The sound of the fridge opening, followed by a beer.

Trout sighed and looked at Heaven. She looked tired. It was after ten, and they both had to be up early. The last thing he wanted right now was a scene with Jade.   "What should we do?" he asked her.

Heaven raised her hands in disbelief. "What's the matter with him?"

"I don't know."

"I hear you talking about me!" Jade yelled. He sauntered into the living room. His eyes had that crazy Jade look in them, the look that meant what was coming next was anybody's guess. He pointed his beer in their direction. "Yeah, I know. I know what you're thinking." He tapped his temple. "You think I'm crazy. Loony! Nuts! *Loco*! Whatever. I don't give a shit." He tilted his head back and drained the beer.

"Jade, man, calm down," Trout said. Even as the words were leaving his mouth, he knew it was the wrong thing to say.

"What?" asked Jade. His torso pitched forward like a bull, then back like a rooster, forward and back. His left hand gripped the bottle as if he meant to crush it. "What did you say, Trout?" The light from the TV flickered across Jade's face, making his expression difficult to read.

"I said, calm down!" Trout felt himself growing angry.

"Stop yelling!" shouted Heaven.

"Stop yelling!" Jade mimicked in a pathetic whine.

Heaven pinched the bridge of her nose and squinted her eyes up, ready to cry.

Trout put his hand on her shoulder. "All right, Jade, cut it out. You're obviously drunk."

"Drunk? Whoa! He thinks I'm drunk! Trout, if this is drunk, you need to get out more."

"Okay, Jade, enough. We're tired. We're not up for this."

This scene. It was like so many scenes from Trout's life: Gordon, Lotus, Jade. Every time it happened, he felt as scared and confused as every other time before. It was like he never got used to it, never had time to prepare himself. He'd always hoped that the last time was the last time.

Jade loomed in the kitchen doorway, gigantic. "*You're* tired, Trout? Why? What did you do today that made you so tired? Went driving around, la-dee-da, I think I'll take a day trip to the country. Huh?" His voice rose to a yell. "You know what I did today, Trout? I *worked*. That's right, I worked. Just like I do every day and like I've been doing every fucking day for the last seven years, so you and Heaven can go to school and drive around in the country!"

Heaven buried her face in her hands. Trout wrapped his arms around her shoulders and shot Jade a warning look.

"What?" asked Jade. "Are you afraid Heaven can't handle this? You don't need to protect her anymore, Trout! She's sixteen! Get over it, man! You can't fucking … take care of everything all the time, you know?"

The alcohol had caught up with him. He started weaving, then turned and went back for another beer. Trout leaned in close to Heaven. The pocket she had created with her head curled against her knees was warm and humid with tears. He felt trapped, and he hated feeling that way. The house had grown too small. Jade was in every room. At least, the potential for him was there.

"Are you all right?" Trout asked.

"No! I'm not all right! I can't deal with this right now."

Trout nodded. She was right. She had been through a lot today.

"Why are we so messed up?" Heaven asked through her sobs.

"We're not. We're not messed up, Hevy. Jade's just mad, that's all. He's just mad that we went to see Gordon. He'll get over it."

"Why would I give a shit about that?" Jade asked.

Trout looked up to see Jade standing on the other side of the coffee table, holding a fresh beer. Everything on his face said he cared a whole lot that they had gone to see Gordon.

"Do you?" Trout asked.

"No." His face revealed his lie.

Trout stared at Jade for a long moment, not sure if Jade was really seeing him or not. Finally, he turned to Heaven and said, "Let's go to bed."

Heaven nodded and rose from the couch. She didn't look at Jade as she bumped past him and down the hallway to her bedroom, Trout right behind her. They went inside her room and closed the door.

"Why does he do that?" Heaven exclaimed.

"He doesn't mean it. He's drunk."

"He sure seems like he means it!"

"I know, Heaven. It's okay. It'll be okay."

He left to give her privacy. Back in the living room, Jade sat on the couch staring at the blue screen on the television. Trout sat beside him. Jade's head swung around as though it were loosely attached to the end of a stick. He stared at Trout with unfocused eyes.

"I'm sorry," he slurred.

Trout patted Jade's knee. "Don't worry about it. It's been hard for all of us."

"I jus' ... I jus' dunno what to do. You know? I jus' ... " He shook his head and stared at a spot on Trout's forehead.

"Come on," said Trout, "let's get to bed."

"Naw, you go. I'm gonna stay up and ... watch some TV." He waved at the television.

"Okay," Trout said and stood up. "Good night."

"'Night."

Trout went into his room and shut the door. He could feel the thinning fabric of his family around him, could see through the threadbare places, almost put his hand through in some spots. They were unraveling, just like they had nine years ago when the house burned down. Not again, he thought. He wasn't going to let it happen again. He fell into bed, exhausted, and slept fitfully, dreaming of the same dark thing chasing him through the tired lands of his soul.

15

Thursday

By Thursday, it was as if the scene with Jade had never happened. Trout and Jade finished the patio job and joined the rest of the crew at the straw bale house. Courtney was teasing Trout about his date that night with Laura. The others picked up on it and joined in, making lewd comments to Trout that he smiled at good-naturedly but didn't find funny. He was measuring boards for the staircase when Courtney's boyfriend, José, came over.

"You wanna go climbing this weekend?" he asked.

"Yeah, maybe," said Trout.

"I thought we could go to Los Alamos if the weather's good."

"That sounds good."

"So, what's this I hear about a date with Laura?"

Trout dropped his measuring tape. "Uh-huh. I'm taking her to dinner."

"That's cool. Where at?"

"La Casa Sena."

"Oh yeah, with the singing waiters."

"Uh-huh. You think that'll be good?"

"Yeah. She's cool. Don't be nervous."

José gave Trout a thumbs-up and walked away.

Trout finished up for the day, and he and Jade collected their things.

"You be good tonight!" Courtney yelled after them as they were leaving.

"So you ready to get some action?" Jade asked as they climbed into the car.

Trout shot Jade a look.

"Sorr-ry!" said Jade.

Most of the snow from Tuesday's storm had melted, and the gray slush that coated the roads made a shushing sound as the tires slid through it.

"So how did Gordon look?" Jade asked.

Trout glanced over at his brother, whose eyes were fixed firmly on the road. Jade hadn't yet mentioned the trip to Cielo two days before. "He ... looked ... like he was dying." He couldn't put it any other way.

Jade nodded. "You think he'll go soon?"

"Probably. I don't know about these kinds of things, but he looked pretty bad."

"Did he ask about me?"

"Yeah."

"What did you tell him?"

"That you couldn't come."

Jade was silent for a minute. "How did Lotus seem?"

"The same. But older. And meaner."

"Do you think you'll go up there again?"

"I'm thinking about it. I felt like there was a lot I didn't say."

"Like what?"

"I don't know. We didn't really talk, you know? He was so tired, and then he fell asleep. He went to rehab."

"Really? What for?"

"Alcohol."

"Wow."

"I know."

"When would you go up there again?" Jade asked.

"Soon. He really looked like he could die any second."

"The bastard."

The words sounded strange coming out of Jade's mouth, like it wasn't what he meant to say at all. He sounded like he was quoting somebody else, what another person's reaction might be. They pulled up to the house. Trout felt more nervous with each passing minute. In an hour and a half he would be picking Laura up for their date.

He showered off the day's grime and dust and then stood before his closet, debating what to wear. He wanted to look nice but not uptight. He settled on a thin, gray sweater and jeans, then took the jeans off and put on a pair of black slacks. He went out into the living room where Jade was talking on the phone. He pointed at his clothes with a look that meant 'Do I look okay?' Jade nodded and gave him the thumbs up. It was 6:15. Trout didn't want to pick her up too early. He tinkered about the house, straightening up.

Jade hung up the phone. "That was Boonray. We're going to go hear this band if you guys want to meet up with us later."

Trout imagined taking Laura to meet up with Jade and Boonray. He could already hear the embarrassing comments they were sure to make.

"Maybe," he said.

At 6:45 he put on his jacket and stood by the door. "I'll see you later."

Jade came over and mussed up Trout's collar. "Break a leg, man. Oh, Heaven called while you were in the shower. Can you pick her up at the gallery later?"

"Why can't you?"

"Because! I really want to hear this band."

"Yeah, but Jade, I'm gonna be on a date. Can't Michael bring her home?"

"His car is in the shop. Laura won't mind."

"All right. What time?"

"Whenever. She's just helping him hang the show."

Trout sighed and walked out the door.

On the drive over, the gas light came on in the car. He pulled over for gas. This was going to make him late. He checked his reflection in the side-view mirror as he filled the tank.

"Trout?"

He turned around. A tall, lanky man with long, blond dreadlocks and a Rasta cap was walking toward him. Trout stared. There was something very familiar about the man's face, but he couldn't think of where he knew him from. Then it dawned on him.

"Max?"

"Yeah!" Max opened his arms and gave Trout a weak hug. Trout smelled patchouli and, underneath, strong body odor.

Max stepped back and grinned. "Whoa! Trout."

Trout stared into Max's eyes. They did not seem connected to the eyes of the seven-year-old boy he had known from Cielo. There was something eerie about them. They reminded Trout of photos he'd seen of sharks' eyes—vacant and hollow. Max wore a scraggly beard. His dingy clothes didn't fit quite right. A large green rucksack was perched on his back, an old army sleeping bag tied atop it with rope. Max grinned at Trout and nodded his head slowly up and down. Trout felt that he should say something, but he was so taken aback by the dullness of Max's eyes that he just stood there, silent.

"So, what are you doing?" Max asked.

A clock sprang into Trout's mind. "I'm actually on my way to meet somebody. I'm late."

"Yeah. Me, too."

Trout stared into those blank, gray eyes. They didn't seem to be looking back at him. "What are you up to, Max?"

"Uh … hu-huh. Wandering."

"Wandering?"

"Yeah." Max swept his arm out as if to show Trout the entire parking lot of the gas station. "Out there."

"Do you live in Santa Fe?"

"I live … everywhere."

"Yeah." The nozzle clicked off, and Trout hung it back on the pump. "Listen, I've got to go. You should call us while you're in town. Me and Jade. We live together." Max nodded slowly.

Trout reached into the car and found a pen and paper. He scribbled his number on it and handed it to Max. "Here. You could come over for dinner or something."

Max took the paper and rubbed it between his thumbs and forefingers. Then, he slowly folded it and put it in the pocket of his red jacket that was too small for him. "Trout," he said.

Trout waited, but Max didn't say anything else. "It's good to see you, Max." He gave Max another hug, his arms bumping against the metal frame of the rucksack.

"You, too. Trout." Max's eyes wandered away and fell on something in the distance. Trout turned to see, but nothing was there, just a line of street lamps receding into the night.

"Bye," Trout said and got into his car. As he drove away, he glanced in the rearview mirror. Max was standing in the same spot, staring off at nothing.

He sped to Laura's and got there right at seven. His mind had been so preoccupied with Max that he had forgotten all about being nervous until he shut off the engine and looked at her house. Should he have brought flowers? No, too corny. He took a deep breath and walked down the path to her door. He knocked and waited. He could hear music playing inside, Van Morrison. The music went down a few notches, and then the door opened, and Laura stood before him.

All week Trout had been conjuring her face up in his mind, trying to keep the details etched in his memory. Now his heart leapt in his chest. She was even more beautiful than he remembered. She wore a dark red skirt and a black, velvet top. Her hair fell in thick curls past her shoulders, and her lips were curved into the generous smile he remembered.

"Hi!" she said and stepped back from the door. "Come on in."

She lived in a small guesthouse behind a larger house. It was an old adobe with wood floors and low ceilings. Nichos dotted the wall, and she had filled them with shells and stones. Trout felt a strong sensation of coming home.

"This is nice," he said.

"Yeah, I got lucky. My rent's only $275."

Trout raised his eyebrows. Santa Fe was becoming more of a popular tourist destination each year. People were beginning to move there from all over the world, and because of that, rents had been steadily climbing. "You did get lucky."

"Come on, I'll show you around."

She led him through the house. She had either straightened up or was very tidy. A cat brushed up against Trout's legs. He looked down at a small calico that mewed up at him.

"That's Diego," Laura said and picked the cat up. "Do you want to hold him?"

"Oh, I'm allergic."

"Oh no! Well, he'll stay away from you, then." She set the cat down and picked a few hairs off her shirt. "That's too bad, that you're allergic to cats."

"I know. I really like them, but I've never been able to have one."

"They say short-haired cats are better than long, if you're allergic."

Trout nodded. He felt the old, familiar tickle in his nose and dryness in his throat coming on. He did not particularly want to have an allergic reaction five minutes into his date. "Should we go?" he asked.

Laura nodded. She went around the house turning off lights, then put on her coat. "Hey, I thought I could drive us," she said.

"Sure." Trout was a little relieved. He hadn't had time to clean the car out, and it didn't seem clean enough for her outfit.

She led him to a blue Dodge Dart parked on the street and opened his door for him.

"Thank you," he said, feeling a little foolish, then got inside and reached over to open her door for her.

She climbed in, and Trout's stomach did a nosedive at sitting so close to her. She turned the key, and there was a single click. Nothing happened. She turned it again. Click. Still nothing.

"Hmmm," Trout said, "that doesn't sound good."

"No, it doesn't."

"Maybe we should take my car, and I can look under your hood when we get back." He turned bright red. He couldn't believe he had actually said that.

But Laura laughed. She tried to start the car again. "You know, I've really been neglecting my car lately."

"Uh-huh."

"I think it feels lonely, unloved. Maybe if we just give it a little love, that'll help."

"Um …" Trout was not at all sure what she was talking about.

"Trout, would you mind just getting out and giving the car a kiss?"

"What?"

"Just a little kiss. On the hood. Please?"

Trout stared blankly at her. Did she really want him to kiss her car?

"Come on, Trout. I think it'll help."

"Okay," he said and climbed out of the car.

Feeling like an idiot, he walked to the front of the car, leaned over, and kissed the cold hood. Laura smiled at him from the driver's seat. He took his right hand and gently caressed the hood a few times. Just then, the engine roared to life, and Laura started clapping. He climbed back in the car.

"See? I told you it would work."

Trout laughed. "How did you do that?"

"I didn't do anything, Trout. You did! It just needed some attention. Cars have feelings, too."

"No, really. How did you do that?"

"I don't know what you're talking about. Where am I going?"

Trout gave her directions as she drove to the restaurant. He couldn't help but sneak glances at her. Her hair had fallen a little in her eyes, and she kept brushing it back with her hand. Even at rest, her face had a smiling expression. She parked near the plaza, and they walked past the closing shops.

"I love it here," she said. "It's so beautiful."

They looked around at the small downtown, the squat, adobe shops and the plaza with its radiating walkways leading to the obelisk in the center. Trout held the door into the restaurant for her. He had thought ahead to make reservations, and he gave the hostess his name.

"Your last name is Ajna?" Laura asked. "Wow. That's really beautiful. Do you have a middle name?"

"I only tell that on the fourth date," he said, grinning, as they sat down.

"Well then, I'd better be on my best behavior so you'll take me out again."

Trout smiled and tried to relax. He read the menu, asked Laura if she wanted wine, and ordered a bottle, wondering if he was he doing it right. She was obviously enjoying herself. She looked around at the other diners and at the waiters taking turns singing old show tunes as they made their way around the room.

"How's school?" Trout asked.

"Great. I love Chinese medicine."

"Yeah? What do you like about it?"

"I love the theory of it. It's so in harmony with nature and our own bodies."

"I've never had acupuncture."

"Oh! You should let me practice on you sometime."

"Yeah, maybe."

A beanpole of a waiter came over to their table singing "Greased Lightning." He got down on one knee in front of Laura and sang to her. She laughed and clapped her hands over her mouth. The waiter sang a few more lines and then left. Laura leaned over the table to whisper, "I never realized how dirty that song is!"

Trout found himself regretting his decision to bring her there. It was fun to watch the singing, but it made it more difficult to talk. He watched her watching the waiters, smiling and laughing. She was having fun. Maybe later they could go somewhere to talk.

"So where does the name Ajna come from?" Laura asked as their food was set down on the table.

"My dad. He ran away from home when he was a teenager. He didn't want his parents to find him so he changed his last name. It has something to do with the third eye. Chakras. All that crap."

"What was it before?"

"I don't know. He wouldn't tell us."

"Was he afraid his parents would find you, too?"

"Yeah. Or that we would try to find them."

"So you have no idea who your grandparents are?"

"Not on that side. I know Lotus's parents."

"Who's Lotus?"

"My mom." The food was delicious, but it stuck a little in his throat when he said that. "Her parents live in Georgia. Her dad's a preacher. They're pretty strange. Hardcore Baptists. Lotus doesn't talk to them at all."

"How sad, not to talk to your parents."

"What are your parents like?"

"They're really sweet. They're older. My mom's sixty-four, and my dad's sixty-eight."

"That is old. For parents, I mean."

"They had me later. I have older siblings. They thought they were done having kids, so I was a surprise."

Trout loved hearing about families like Laura's. He could see her parents puttering around the house, baking and tending the fire, so happy, so different from his family. Sometimes he thought his family must be the only messed up one out there, but then he would think about Boonray's family, or Esperanza's. Even Holly had a pretty sad story from what Trout had heard.

He watched Laura eat. She went about it enthusiastically. "You don't seem nervous at all," he said.

She looked up at him and swallowed. "Really?"

"Yeah. I keep being afraid I'm gonna do something really stupid, like spill my wine or choke on my food, but you just seem completely natural."

"I'm nervous."

"Oh, good! I mean, I'm not happy that you're nervous, but I thought I was the only one."

She laughed. "That's sweet of you to say."

He was curious about her, her childhood, what her life had been about until now and what it was about now. He asked her questions, and she answered them all. She seemed so open and innocent. He found himself feeling increasingly drawn to her and also more and more anxious that she definitely was not going to like him once she knew him better.

The conversation then turned to him. Trout pushed his plate away and took a sip of wine.

"Fire away," he said, trying to appear as nonchalant as possible. The waiters were singing "One" from A Chorus Line.

"Let's see," she swirled her wine playfully. "Well, what are your parents like?"

Trout shifted in his seat, not sure how much to tell her. "They're ... well, you already know they were hippies. So that probably tells you a lot."

"No, it doesn't, actually. I didn't grow up around that scene at all."

"Oh, well, let's see, then. What do you want to know?"

"What was it like? What were your parents like growing up? Did they take you skinny-dipping? Did they play music?"

Trout smiled, but it was a pained smile. This was the version people always assumed. Happy, colorful hippies dressed up as clowns, running naked through grassy fields with their mandolins and stilts, carrying their kids on their shoulders and tossing organic veggies up to them. But the reality, for most kids he knew born into the hippie scene, was that those happy scenes were the exception. Most hippie kids he knew had either learned to parent themselves early on or succumbed to the layers of apathy and addiction surrounding them. He didn't want the childhood he had. He didn't want to taint Laura's pretty, perfect world with stories of adultery, drugs, alcoholism, neglect, and abuse. He searched his mind for ways to soften the truth.

"My parents were pretty 'out there.' I didn't have a childhood anything like yours. Lotus was very young when I was born."

"Why do you call her Lotus instead of mom?"

"I don't know. That's what Jade always called her, and I just copied him. She wasn't really like a 'mom,' so it just seemed natural to call her by her name."

The waiter cleared their plates and offered them dessert. Trout suggested they go somewhere else for dessert. As he waited for the bill, he stalled in the telling of his story. Laura sat patiently, a soft smile on her lips.

"I grew up in the mountains near here, a town called Cielo. It's a small, Hispanic village where a bunch of hippies decided to settle. We didn't have running water or electricity."

"Wow. How did you cook and wash your clothes and stuff?"

"We had a woodstove that we cooked on, and we got our water from a creek on our land. We did everything like the pioneers did, washing our clothes by hand and stuff.

I think my parents had this fantasy that they were pioneers of a sort." He couldn't help but smile grimly at this thought.

"Anyway, I don't really know what to tell you. It wasn't a happy childhood. I mean, there were some nice things about it. I loved living in the country. My neighbor had horses, and he and I used to go riding all over the hills. But ..."

He trailed off, and the waiter brought the check. Trout counted out the money and then helped Laura with her coat. He walked behind her out of the restaurant. He didn't want to be rude, but how was he going to avoid talking about his childhood? Surely he couldn't hide it from her forever. But if she just got to know him first, to see that he wasn't like that. They got outside, and Trout suggested a small café nearby.

"It seems like you don't want to talk about this," she said as they walked.

"There's just not much to tell. I left home when I was thirteen, with my brother, and we lost contact with our parents. They weren't really into being parents, so I think they were kind of relieved when we left."

"What about your sister?"

"What?"

"Heaven. Did she stay with your parents when you and Jade left?"

"That's a whole different story. Can we talk about something else?"

"Okay."

But they didn't talk about anything else. They walked in silence to the cafe, Trout feeling worse and worse along the way. By the time they reached the café, he was sure she would never want to see him again. He was coming across as such a jerk! But he couldn't tell her that Heaven had been taken away by the state when she was seven, after she'd been raped by one of her parents' friends. Trout might be out of practice with dating, but he knew not to talk about stuff like that on the first date. Or the second or third. He didn't know when to talk about stuff like that.

They sat at a small table with a lamp hanging down between them. Trout had to keep peering around it to see her face.

Laura smiled. "Stupid place to hang a lamp, huh?"

"I was just thinking that."

They shared some cake and drank coffee. Trout wanted to touch her, to feel her skin. He nervously placed his hand on the tabletop. Should he creep it over or just grab her hand? What was the right thing to do? He slid it across the table and carefully interlaced his fingers with hers.

"That's nice," said Laura.

"So, I'll tell you some more about my family," he said, afraid he was coming across as aloof.

"I understand if you don't want to."

"No. I just ... I don't want you to think I'm weird."

"Trout." She looked firmly into his eyes. "I don't think anything about you is weird. I don't think there is anything you could tell me that would make me think you are weird. My family is nowhere near as normal as it sounds, believe me."

"It's more than just not being normal, though, Laura. The stories about my past aren't funny or enjoyable to listen to. I don't feel any nostalgia when I talk about it. Actually, I try not to think about my childhood as much as possible."

She squeezed his hand. "I am so sorry that all happened to you, Trout," she said.

"Don't," he said.

She looked affronted, stitched her eyebrows together. "What do you mean?"

"I mean, that's just life, you know? That's just the luck of the draw." He released her hand. He knew he sounded like Jade, but he didn't care.

Laura looked at him with a puzzled expression on her face. Trout, unable to apologize at the moment, asked for the check and paid without a word. They left, and he could tell Laura was confused. They got into the car, and once again, it wouldn't start.

Trout turned to face her. "Look, I'm sorry. I just can't stand people feeling sorry for me."

Laura didn't say anything for a moment, just stared out the windshield at the streetlights. Then, "I don't feel sorry for you, Trout. I feel empathy, which is a very different thing. I don't pity you because of what you share with me; it makes me feel closer to you."

Trout leaned across the seat and kissed her. They kissed for several long moments, and then Laura pulled back and grinned.

"Get out again, and kiss my hood," she demanded.

He climbed out and kissed the hood, keeping his eyes on hers the whole time. Immediately, the engine roared to life, and they smiled at each other through the windshield.

When they got back to her house, she invited him in.

Trout paused. "Just for a minute; I have to pick up my sister."

He had forgotten about the cat until he got inside and started sniffling. He could tell Laura felt bad, but there was nothing either of them could do about it. They sat on the sofa, and Laura kept pushing Diego off until finally she locked him in her bedroom, where he mewed and scratched at the door.

Trout smiled at her. "I should go."

"I had a really nice time."

"Me, too." He leaned over to kiss her, and then maybe half an hour passed, maybe twenty minutes, maybe only a moment. He pulled away and stared hard into her eyes. "Bye."

"Bye."

He left her apartment reluctantly, with a backward glance at the closing door, the red skirt swirling away, a soft light going on in the bedroom window. He sighed and picked a yellow daisy from the sidewalk, tucked it under her windshield wiper, and drove away chuckling. How had she done that trick with the car?

He pulled up in front of Michael's gallery a few minutes later and stared through the window at the bustle of activity inside. He could see Heaven standing off to the side, wearing her long black coat, watching Michael hang a painting with another woman. Trout didn't want to go in. He was filled with happy memories of the date. He was sure that if he opened the door, they would all float out into the night, never to return. Honking seemed rude, so he waited. He kept the engine running and the lights on until finally Heaven turned to see him sitting out there.

"Hey!" she said, coming out. "What are you doing sitting out here? Why didn't you come in?"

He smiled.

"You had a good date."

He nodded sleepily.

"Let me grab my purse. Do you want to come in for a second?"

"No, I'm too tired."

He watched her say good-bye to Michael. Michael waved at Trout through the window, and Trout waved back, the flick-your-wrist-once-to-the-side kind of wave, the I'm-not-your–friend-but-we-have-to-associate-with-each-other kind of wave.

Heaven wanted to hear all about the date. It made Trout feel good that Heaven was excited about it. She really wanted him to be happy, he could see. They pulled up to the dark house, and Trout reluctantly opened the door. Somehow, that made the date seem truly over. Conrad jumped all over them when they got inside.

"Hey, buddy!" said Trout. "Haven't you gone for a walk today? Where's Jade?"

He fed the dog and peered around for a note from Jade but found none.

Later, as he was flipping through some homework, Heaven beside him on the couch, painting her toenails, he remembered the phone call from earlier that week. He set the book down and watched Heaven carefully brush a soft pink polish onto her small nails.

"How's the apartment hunting coming?" he asked.

Heaven froze for an instant and then kept painting. "What are you talking about?"

"Aren't you looking for an apartment for you and Michael?"

"Well, we're discussing the possibility, remember?"

"Oh. 'Cause this woman called the other day about an apartment she has. She said you called her."

"How come you didn't give me the message?"

"Um … because you agreed to hold off on the apartment idea for now."

"Yeah, I am. I just thought I'd start looking and see what's out there, to see if it's even a realistic idea or not."

"Oh."

Heaven kept her face close to her toes. Once again, the panicky feeling began to come over him, the feeling that his family was falling apart, and there was nothing he could do about it.

He stood up. "I'm gonna take Conrad for a walk."

"Okay." She was annoyed at him, he could tell.

He grabbed Conrad's leash off its hook by the door, and Conrad came running. They set out into the night.

It was cold and clear. Trout's breath puffed before him in white clouds that vanished quickly. He walked to the park, and Conrad pulled at the leash, wanting to run, but Trout kept walking. They walked along the river, toward downtown, and then Trout turned and headed uphill. He reached Ruth's house ten minutes later. The porch light was on. On a hunch, Trout walked around the house to the back porch, where he found Ruth bundled on the porch swing, her pipe tucked in her mouth.

"I hope you're not here to sell me anything, 'cause I'm a broke, old lady," she said as Trout walked up.

He smiled, and she tossed him a blanket. He sat beside her and let Conrad loose to explore the yard.

"What's up?" Ruth asked. She had that wise old lady look she got when she had been sitting alone for a while. Her eyes glowed softly, and her face had relaxed so much her wrinkles were barely perceptible.

"I just had to get out of the house. I thought I'd come see you."

She nodded and passed him her pipe. Trout puffed, gazing up at the stars with Ruth. He felt better already. They didn't speak for a while, and then Ruth asked, "Did you have a bad date?"

Trout shook his head. "No, actually. It was a pretty good date."

"Are you going to see her again?"

"Definitely."

"So what's going on?"

He groped for words for his feelings.

"I don't know, Ruth. I feel like my family has been falling apart ever since I was born. Since Gordon and Lotus met each other and even before that. I feel like we're doomed. Like we're cursed or something. Do you think that's possible?"

Ruth shook her head. "I don't believe in curses. I do want to ask you something, though."

"What?"

"What would happen if you let Jade and Heaven make their own mistakes? If you let Lotus and Gordon go? What would happen if you just worried about Trout for a change?"

"Um … they would fuck everything up."

"Huh." Ruth reached over and took her pipe back from him.

"I get it. I get what you're saying—I feel like I have to control everything, keep people from getting hurt."

"I didn't say anything. You said that."

"Sneaky, you are," said Trout.

"What?"

"You're sneaky. And you're a wise advisor, like Yoda. Sneaky, you are."

"I get it."

"You know who Yoda is?"

"I been to them talkies." She shoved him playfully. "I'm hip! I may be an old lady, but I'll still go out of my way to see Han Solo in his tight, black pants."

"Ew!" said Trout. "You can't tell me things like that!"

Ruth laughed and handed him the pipe. They puffed the leathery smoke and watched Orion trace his great, heroic arc across the sky.

16

Saturday

Snow once again crisped the air and danced high above their heads as Heaven and Trout climbed into the car to make their second trip to Cielo. They had received news through Boonray that Gordon was still alive. Jade, still refusing to come, slept in.

"Do you think it'll snow?" Trout asked, peering up at the sky.

"Who knows?" said Heaven. "I cannot figure out New Mexico's weather. Sixteen years I've lived here, and it's still a mystery."

Things had felt stiff and stilted between them since Trout had brought up the apartment hunting a couple nights before. He knew he had done it poorly and had been searching for a way to apologize. He longed for the familiar ease between them that appeared less and less frequently. Heaven opened her journal.

"Do you want to drive?" Trout asked.

Normally, Heaven would have jumped at the opportunity, but today she shook her head and said she'd rather write.

They arrived in Cielo after lunch. The town looked vulnerable and exposed on its mountaintop, with the white sky swirling behind it. Lotus answered Winnie's door after several long minutes, her silver glasses perched on her nose, her small frame lost inside a bulky, green sweater.

"Hi," said Trout.

Lotus looked past them into the driveway and craned her head around.

"Just you two?" she asked.

"Yep," said Trout, glancing at Heaven.

Heaven smiled and squeezed the drawing pad she had brought to her chest. Lotus stepped back, still staring out the door, and let them in.

"Looks like it's gonna snow," she said. The hard edge she had shown last visit was tempered. She seemed old and fragile. Trout wondered if something had happened.

The house was cold and dark. Lotus closed the door softly and walked toward the back of the house. Trout and Heaven followed. Gordon's breathing was dry and rasping like someone filing away at old metal. He was propped up in the bed, so his back was arched, his head tilted backward. Lotus moved forward and adjusted some of the pillows.

"It helps him breathe," she explained.

Trout and Heaven hung back, watching the wasted body before them struggle to hold on, fighting for a tiny bit of air. Gordon looked even thinner than before.

Heaven set her things down on a chair and brusquely pulled off her coat. In a matter-of-fact way, she stepped up to the bed and carefully arranged the blankets, then touched Gordon's shriveled hand.

"Hi, Daddy," she said.

Trout was startled by the familiar address.

Gordon's eyelids lifted, and he tilted his head to see her. He smiled. "Hi," he croaked.

Even from across the room, Trout could see what looked like love and tenderness in Gordon's eyes as he gazed at Heaven. Probably thinks he's finally dead, Trout thought. Lotus took her seat by the bed and got busy rolling a cigarette. The tobacco crackled loudly in the still room. Trout was reluctant to remove his coat. He wondered why the house was so cold.

As if reading his mind, Lotus said, "The wood got wet. I didn't want to leave Gordon to get more. Winnie's on a trip somewhere."

Trout nodded. He couldn't take his eyes from Gordon's face. He'd never seen death up close. It was spooky. He took a few steps forward to the bed and stared down at his father.

"You look like shit," he said.

Gordon grimaced. "That's funny."

Heaven gave Trout a reproachful look. "You don't look like shit, Gordon. You look … " Her voice trailed off.

Lotus puffed vacuously on her cigarette until it lit. "He looks like shit," she agreed.

"I'm gonna go get some wood," Trout said suddenly.

Lotus stared at him. "Where?"

"I don't know. Somewhere. It's freezing in here! Jesus Christ."

Lotus swung her feet off the edge of the bed and rubbed the soles of her bare feet on the dirt floor. "I'll come with you."

Trout paused. "No, that's okay. I'm good by myself."

"I know you are, Trout, but I want to go with you. I need to get out of this stinkin' house." She scowled at him as she passed, and Trout turned to follow.

"You all right here alone?" he asked Heaven over his shoulder.

She nodded somberly and stroked Gordon's hand. She looked like a nun, Trout thought, sitting there, so pious and serene. He waited by the front door as Lotus slipped on her moccasins. She puffed on her cigarette and eyed Trout suspiciously until he opened the door, and she shuffled past him out into the yard. She handed Trout a set of keys and walked toward the yellow Cadillac. Wordlessly, Trout climbed into the driver's seat and pulled onto the road.

"No Jade again, huh?" asked Lotus. She was smoking her cigarette with the windows rolled up. Trout rolled his window down partway and breathed in the fresh air.

"Nope. When did you get a Cadillac?"

"Oh, three years ago. My dad died and left it to me."

"Grandpa died?"

"Yep."

"Why didn't you tell me?"

Lotus didn't answer.

"What about grandma?"

"She's dead, too, one month before him. One, two, boom, boom. I got a car." She turned in her seat to survey the car, which was littered with paper bags, coffee mugs, clothes, and papers. The windows on the passenger side were all cracked. Trout thought to himself, looking at the cracks, that just once in his life he'd like to own a car with each of its windows in one piece.

He slowed when they passed their old land, thinking Lotus might want to say something, but she didn't even look at it. Just squeezed the soggy end of her cigarette and squinted at the road ahead. Because this made him angry, he pushed the gas pedal hard once they passed the land, so she jerked back.

"Where am I going?" he asked.

"There," Lotus said and pointed to Bob's old trailer.

Trout pulled into the drive and parked. The driveway was empty and the house dark. He got out. "I don't think anybody's here."

Lotus made her way to the side of the house where an overhang sheltered high stacks of dry firewood. She began piling logs into her arms. Trout watched.

"What are you doing?" he asked.

"Wood. Help." She motioned to the trunk of the car, which Trout reluctantly opened.

"Whose wood is this?"

Lotus shot him another mean look and went back for more. Trout followed, glancing around him for signs that somebody might be home after all.

"Lotus, whose wood is this?"

"It's our wood, Trout. Now, are you gonna help me or not?"

"I just don't want to be stealing somebody else's wood."

"Hey!" Lotus threw down her logs and stuck a spindly finger in his face. "Are you callin' me a thief?"

"Maybe." He stood up tall. "It depends on whose wood this is."

"This … " she motioned to the woodpile, then the house, "wood belongs to my friend Hodge, all right?" She stared at him for a long moment, then turned back to the woodpile and began gathering the logs she had tossed. "So, don't go callin' me a thief, you son of a bitch."

Trout walked to the car, anger boiling inside of him, until he realized how funny her insult was.

"Hey, Lotus, don't you think it's kind of funny that you called me a son of a bitch?"

She slammed the logs into the trunk and then climbed into the driver's seat. She held her hand out the window and flicked her fingers, motioning for Trout to give her the keys. He dropped them into her palm, and just as he was reaching to open the passenger door, she drove off without him. He watched her speed away. He knew he could run after her, calling for her to stop. He also knew she wouldn't.

After the car had disappeared, he turned back to the house and tried the door-knob. "Hello?" he called. Nobody answered, so he stepped inside.

It looked even more cluttered and run-down than when Bob had lived there. Trout searched through the mess until he found a pen and paper. He took them and wrote a note that read: LOTUS AJNA WAS HERE. SHE TOOK WOOD. He went outside and pinned it beneath a log in the woodpile and began the walk back to Winnie's. When he got there, Lotus was nowhere in sight. Heaven crouched by the woodstove, tending the newborn fire.

"You walked?" she asked.

He nodded and sat by the stove, rubbing his hands briskly together to warm them up.

"He still alive?" He motioned to the back bedroom.

"Barely."

Trout sat listening to the fire whiz and pop. "How long do you want to stay?"

"Just a while longer. Don't you wanna see Gordon?"

He had thought he did when they drove up, but that was before he saw how Gordon looked today. He hesitated, then said, "Yeah, I'll go see him."

The door to the first bedroom was closed, and Trout assumed Lotus was in there. She's probably having sex with Winnie these days, he thought. He rapped on Gordon's door and quietly entered.

Over the course of the week, Trout had formulated some of his thoughts into sentences. He ran them through his head now, wiggled them about on his tongue, imagined hanging them on the sweet, cold air that filled the room. He sat upon the bed, feeling numb and bewildered. He gazed out across the room, his chin propped in his hand.

"You look just like Lotus's dad," came the raspy voice.

Trout turned to see Gordon peering at him out of sleepy lids. Prescription bottles littered the table beside him, and Trout assumed he was heavily medicated.

"Did you know that?"

"No," Trout said. "I don't remember what he looked like."

"You should see a picture." He coughed dryly. "Just like him." Gordon closed his eyes for so long Trout thought he had fallen asleep again until Gordon suddenly said, "She ever tell you that?"

"Lotus? No."

"Yeah, well, she hated him. He was a real asshole. That's why she always had it out for you. You remind her of him."

Trout stared at Gordon's closed lids. Why had he never thought of that before? Lotus was always meanest to Trout. She used to tell him he was self-righteous and judgmental, words she'd used to describe her father. She would say things like 'get off your high horse,' and 'little moral, perfect Trout.'

Instead of bringing him relief, this insight brought more anger. His grandfather had been a Baptist minister who wore a three-piece suit to the beach and thought homosexuals should be in prison. If there was any resemblance between Trout and his grandfather, it was purely physical. He felt the sting of injustice at being punished all those years just because he looked like someone else.

Trout sat by Gordon's bed for a long time, watching Gordon's eyes periodically open and blearily look around him, sometimes registering that Trout was beside him, sometimes looking right through him. Eventually, Trout stood and wandered out into the house. He found Lotus and Heaven in the kitchen, drawing each other. They sat at either end of the table, drawing pads propped on their knees, faces serious, pencils scribbling. Trout got busy making tea and eyed each of their drawings out of the corners of his eyes. They were good. Heaven's was better, but Lotus's wasn't bad. He sat at the table and poured three cups of tea. He set a mug in front of each of them and sat down to watch them draw. Heaven, deeply absorbed, moved her pencil rhythmically across the page. Lotus drew fast, as though in a race, her nose wrinkled and her eyes squinted. She set down her drawing pad down and began rolling a cigarette.

"He dead yet?" she asked.

Trout didn't say anything but reached over and took a rolling paper from the packet. He sprinkled some of Lotus's tobacco in it, watching it fall like brown snow, rolled it carefully, then licked the edge and sealed it. He struck a match and lit the end of his cigarette, then shook out the match without offering it to Lotus.

"Let's see," Lotus said to Heaven.

"It's not done yet."

Lotus stood and walked outside. Heaven sighed and set down the pad.

"It's good," said Trout.

"Yeah, it'd be better if she didn't keep moving."

"I like the way you didn't try to make her look prettier."

Heaven gave him a confused look. Lotus came back in and began pulling things out of the cupboards.

"I thought I'd make us some spaghetti," she said.

Trout and Heaven exchanged surprised looks.

"Can I help?" Heaven asked.

Lotus handed her an onion and a knife. Trout sucked on his cigarette. It was dry and tasted the way horses smelled. He wasn't sure why he was smoking.

When the food was ready, the three of them sat together and ate. It wasn't bad, thought Trout. Simple, but good. Lotus motioned for Heaven to hand her the drawing, which Heaven did. Lotus peered at it but didn't say anything.

"Can I see yours?" Heaven asked.

Lotus slid her pad across the table, and Heaven gazed admiringly at the drawing.

"I love it," she said in a breathless, airy voice.

Lotus didn't respond. Her table manners were as atrocious as ever, Trout noticed. She had one foot on the table and leaned back in her chair, holding her plate under her chin and sucking her food up loudly.

"So, are there any funeral arrangements?" Trout asked.

"I got it covered," Lotus said.

"Can we go?"

She shook her head. "He doesn't want that. He wants to be cremated, and he wants his ashes dumped in the acequia."

"Is that legal?"

"Who cares? It's what he wants."

They finished eating, and Trout rolled another cigarette while Lotus and Heaven did the dishes. He didn't feel bad. He had always done the dishes as a kid.

Saying good-bye was not so hard this time. Gordon didn't seem sad like he had last time, and Trout felt more used to the idea that he was dying. But Heaven sobbed and rested her head on Gordon's hand until Trout gently pulled her away.

On the drive back Heaven looked at him accusingly. "You're mean to them."

"What?"

"You're mean to Gordon and Lotus."

"Not any meaner than they are to me."

"That's not true. They're old, and Gordon's dying. You should have more compassion."

"Please don't tell me how I should be, Hevy."

"I just think you should be nicer to them is all."

"They don't deserve me being nice to them."

"Trout! Listen to yourself! You're being so stubborn. Don't people ever deserve a second chance?"

"Not them."

Heaven fell silent and stared out the window. Trout spent the rest of the ride home absorbed in his thoughts. He was remembering the time Lotus had scratched his neck after he caught her at Forest's and the time she slammed his head into the van window. He could remember so many times she'd struck him, scratched him, screamed at him, cursed him, and wished him dead.

So that's why, he thought to himself: I look like her dad. Funny how that works. Just like Heaven looked like Lotus, and Jade looked like Gordon. Sometimes, Trout caught himself feeling things for his parents when he looked at his siblings. Could this be why he was so afraid of Jade's drinking, he wondered? Heaven fell asleep, and Trout pulled over to wad up his coat and prop it between her head and the door, then pulled onto the road for the dark ride home.

17

Sunday

Trout got out of bed at five, tired of grasping for sleep. He went into the kitchen to make coffee and found Heaven sitting at the table in her robe.

"Coffee's made," she said curtly.

"What are you doing up?"

She looked at him as if he had asked her who she was. "Trout, it sounded like we'd opened a bar in our living room last night. I couldn't sleep."

"Me either."

"I really think I should be able to stay at Michael's. If you guys can't keep it quiet enough for me to sleep, I need an alternative."

"I asked them to keep it down. I wasn't making any noise," he said defensively.

"Yeah, but it doesn't make a difference. They just keep on whoo-whooing, and AAAHH!! I can't stand it anymore!" She scowled at him, then stood with a huff and walked away.

A few moments later, he heard the shower start running. It was true, it had been loud in the house. Jade and his band mates had barreled in after a show, wired on alcohol and adrenaline, and set up their after-party in the living room. Trout knew that living with Jade meant tolerating the occasional late party—after all, Jade paid half the rent—but Heaven was left without much of a say. Maybe the right thing *was* to let her stay at Michael's. He shook his head and tried to put it out of his mind.

Later that morning, Trout felt proud holding Laura's hand as they waited for a table at his favorite breakfast restaurant.

"You look beautiful today," he said.

She blushed and smiled shyly, then turned to look at a bunch of posters pinned to a bulletin board behind them.

"Look at this!" she exclaimed and pointed to a green-and-black flyer.

In large, hand-drawn letters, it read: The Psycho Puppies from Outer Space. Halloween night. Club West. Beneath the letters was a crude drawing of a deranged-looking dog in a flying saucer.

"Yeah," said Trout. "God, that looks terrible."

"Isn't that Jade's band?"

"Mm-hmmm."

"We should go! That would be fun."

"Have you heard them before?"

"Yes. I heard them at your party, remember?"

"And you still want to go see them?"

She shoved him playfully.

"So, what did you do yesterday?" she asked once they were seated.

"Studied," he lied, not wanting to tell her about the trip to Cielo. "How about you?"

"I studied also." She laughed. "We're so boring!"

"Listen, I'm sorry I was such a jerk the other night."

"I didn't think you were a jerk at all."

"Well, thank you. But I think I acted like a jerk. I get really sensitive around the topic of my family. I wish it wasn't that way, but it is."

"Trout, it's okay. You weren't a jerk. *I'm* sorry for pushing you to talk about it. It's just... you have this sweetness about you. I can't explain it. I haven't met anyone like you before. I feel close to you even though we just met. I want to know everything about you. I'm sorry if I come across as nosy. It's not like that."

Trout sipped his coffee. "I think I know what you mean. I feel the same way about you. I like wondering what you were like as a teenager and as a little girl. I wonder what you'll be like as you get older."

She grinned.

"What would you like to know?"

"Why don't you tell me what you were like as a little boy?"

"I was ... "

Running. Gordon couldn't find his wrench and was sure I'd lost it. He had turned to me, his hot, whiskey breath burning my nose, and said, "You're a goddamn liar. You have ten seconds to bring me my wrench, and if you don't, I'm gonna make you wish you'd never been born."

So I ran. I didn't know where the stupid wrench was. Jade probably took it. He and Boonray. They were always doing the bad stuff, and I was always getting blamed. Not perfect Jade. I ran and hid in the goat shed. It stank like goats in there, all leathery and milky, even though we'd sold the goats years before. I ducked in there and hid, my breath fast and dry, peering out through the cracks between the planks. From the house,

I heard Gordon calling, "TROUT! GET YOUR ASS BACK HERE! YOU'RE IN BIG TROUBLE NOW! WHEN I FIND YOU ... " Like that was really going to make me go home.

I stayed in the goat shed so long I fell asleep sitting against the wall. I don't know what time it was when I awoke, but it was late. It was night. The air had grown thin and was peppered with the calls of crickets. Fireflies traced their scattered patterns over the fields that I traipsed across, my bare feet crackling the dry grass. I snuck into the house as quietly as I could, terrified I'd wake Gordon. He was asleep next to Lotus, one arm flung across her, snoring. I crept into my bed and pulled the covers up over my head. "Please God," I prayed, "please don't let him be mad in the morning."

In the morning, of course, Gordon didn't remember a thing. His wrench was right where he'd left it, on the floor of his truck. He tousled my hair as I passed him on the way to make my breakfast. When I pulled away from him, he teased me, saying I was getting too grown-up to want to be affectionate with my dad. I gave him a look that I hoped said everything, but he just dug into his potatoes and hummed a George Fair song. Asshole, I thought.

" ... quiet, I guess. Smart. Bored in school. I got into a lot of fights."

"You did? Bad ones?"

"Some." He pointed to the faded scar on his cheek. "That's from when a boy knifed me."

"You were *knifed*?" Laura looked appalled and impressed at the same time.

He nodded casually. "That wasn't the worst, though. The fights I mean. The worst was the anticipation of them, knowing they were coming. I could never relax, always waiting for the next one."

"Why were you in so many fights?"

"I got picked on. I was the only blond kid in my class. I stood out."

"Wow. What a crazy experience."

"So, what were you like as a kid?" he asked.

"I was ... I don't know. Normal, I guess. I was kind of ugly."

"You were?"

"Yeah. I had frizzy, red hair and freckles. I wore glasses. I wasn't very coordinated and got teased for that. But I did okay. I had friends and everything."

"The ugly duckling turned into a swan."

"I guess you could say that."

He tossed a sugar packet at her, and it fell into her lap. She giggled and tossed it back. They did this for a while until their food came.

"What do you want to do after this?" she asked.

"I thought we could go for a walk around the plaza."

"I still call it the square."

"Don't."

"No?"

"You will be teased mercilessly by every local who ever hears you say that. Plus, you won't fit in."

"Is that what's most important?"

"What?"

"Fitting in?"

Trout was silent. He ate his potatoes.

"I'm sorry," said Laura.

"For what?"

"Did I just offend you?"

"Not at all. I was just thinking about that, about fitting in. See, when I was a kid, it was all about fitting in. Now look at us. We're two normal people, eating potatoes."

"It's nice to be an adult," Laura said.

After breakfast, Trout took her to see the Cross of the Martyrs, a large, white cross at the top of a high hill that looked out onto downtown Santa Fe. "We used to come up here when I was a teenager," he said. "We'd smoke pot and hang our heads backward over the ledge, like this." He demonstrated, dangling his lean torso backward until the world looked like a fishbowl to him.

"Try it," he said and pulled himself up, but Laura was gone. Trout called her name, but she didn't answer. When she didn't reappear after a minute or two, he began to feel anxious. "Laura? Laura! Come out; this isn't funny!"

Nothing. Trout circled the cross.

"LAURA!"

"BOO!" she jumped out from behind a tree.

"That's not funny!" he said angrily.

She gave him a startled look.

"You could have been kidnapped or something!"

"Relax, Trout! I'm okay."

"Don't do that again, all right?"

"All right, I won't."

She hugged herself, and he was sorry he'd gotten angry. He put his arms around her and turned their bodies so the wind was at his back.

"It's just that sometimes weirdos hang out up here. I didn't know where you'd gone."

"I'm sorry," she said. "I see how that freaked you out. I won't do it again."

They walked back down the curved pathway to the street. Trout felt like kicking himself for overreacting the way he had. He knew it was just like the way he treated

Heaven when she was a few minutes late or forgot to call. He wondered if the world as he saw it would ever stop being full of danger.

They wandered the streets, and Trout realized they were in front of the gallery where Michael's show was.

"My sister's boyfriend has his paintings hanging in here." He stared at a large painting lit up in the window. Bright, neon orange, red, yellow, and white swirled together like a nebula, with jagged, green lines hacking through like radioactive lightning bolts.

"Let's go in!" said Laura, already opening the door.

Trout followed and heard a squeal. Heaven ran toward him and threw her arms around his middle.

"I knew you'd come see the show; I knew it!"

He grinned and introduced her to Laura. Michael approached, wearing a pressed, tan suit and a carefully practiced smile. He extended a hand to Trout, which Trout shook and then introduced him to Laura.

"So what do you think?" asked Michael.

Trout nodded. "Quite a space here."

"Isn't it something? The owner is great, just great."

Michael stood with his arms crossed, surveying the gallery like a landowner. Heaven had her hands looped through his right arm. Trout scowled at the floor.

Laura wandered through the gallery, stopping to look carefully at each painting. Trout joined her, and at a particularly hideous painting, he gave her a look that meant 'this is sooo bad,' but she didn't seem to notice and kept walking. Heaven and Michael stood by the door, arms draped around each other. Trout gritted his teeth and followed Laura sullenly. When she finished the loop, she walked back to Heaven and Michael.

"Great work!" Laura said. "Really original. I love your use of color."

Trout's eyes widened involuntarily. What was she thinking?

"Hey, we're going to get some lunch. Do you guys want to come?" Heaven asked.

Trout said no, and Laura said yes at the same time. He smiled at Heaven and said yes, yes they'd come. Trout and Heaven walked behind Laura and Michael, who had struck up a conversation about art. Trout glared at them.

"Are you okay?" Heaven asked.

"Yeah. Why?"

"No reason."

Michael chose a semi-fancy restaurant and announced that he was buying. It turned out that Laura had majored in art history in college. The discussion at the table centered on painting, and Trout's mind wandered to Heaven's painting of the bluebird.

"Hey," Trout interrupted, "why doesn't Heaven have a show at that gallery?"

There was silence, and Heaven blushed.

"I'm not ready," she said.

"Sure you are!" said Trout. "You're a fabulous painter, Heaven. Better than ... most people I've seen. You could get a show easily, I bet."

Michael put his hands together, elbows on the table, lips skewed to one side. "There's a lot more to it than being good, Trout."

"Yeah? Like what?" He glanced at Laura, who was spreading butter on a roll.

"Experience for one. You have to have shown places before."

"Well, how does she get her first show?"

Michael wrapped his arm around Heaven's shoulders. "That's what art school is for. Heaven will have loads of opportunities to show her work while she's in school."

"Oh, please," said Trout. "You can't tell me every painter who shows in a gallery has gone to art school."

Michael looked at him blankly. "Of course not, Trout." His tone bordered on condescending.

"So how else do people get shows, besides art school?"

Michael looked exasperated. He looked at Heaven, and she looked at the napkin on her lap.

"I'm not ready, Trout," she said.

He knew better than to push her, so he let the subject drop like Laura's limp roll dropping onto her plate, half smeared with butter. Laura wiped her fingers on her napkin and excused herself to use the restroom.

Heaven watched her walk away and then turned to Trout. "She seems nice, Trout! And very beautiful."

Heaven looked so small sitting under Michael's arm, so vulnerable and young.

When Laura returned to the table, she looked refreshed, her eyes brighter. "This is a nice restaurant," she said, sitting down.

Heaven leaned over and whispered into Michael's ear. Michael nodded.

"So," said Heaven, addressing Trout, "I was thinking Michael could come with us next time we visit Gordon and Lotus."

Out of the corner of his eye, Trout saw Laura's eyebrows go up.

"I don't think we should talk about this right now," he said to Heaven.

"It's fine with me," said Laura.

"Okay. I don't think that's a good idea, Heaven. Gordon and Lotus don't know Michael."

"That's the point. I want Michael to meet my dad before he dies."

"I'm sitting right here," said Michael.

"Yeah, no kidding," Trout said. "Heaven, what makes you think we're even going back up there? When? We were just there yesterday." He caught his contradiction too late. He couldn't look at Laura. "Look, Hev, can we talk about this later?"

Heaven shrugged and looked away. Michael flagged the waiter for the check.

The four of them walked back to the gallery. Heaven and Michael said good-bye and went inside. Trout and Laura walked back to the car.

"I'm guessing Michael's not your favorite person," Laura said.

"Everyone says that."

"Yeah, well, it's pretty obvious."

They reached the car and climbed inside.

"I'm trying to like him," Trout said. "Heaven's crazy about him. She wants to live with him. Don't you think that's weird?"

"No."

"Come on, the guy's twenty-one and dating a sixteen-year-old. He wears a suit."

"Well, I don't know the details, and I happened to like his suit. But girls mature a lot faster than men, so Heaven and Michael are probably on par."

"Not Heaven. She's different."

"What do you mean?"

He shook his head. "That's Heaven's story, not mine. She's not ready to live with anybody."

"Just you?"

"Yep. Just me."

They pulled up to her house, but she didn't invite him in. They sat in the car with the engine running.

"Why did you lie to me about what you did yesterday?" she asked.

Trout closed his eyes. "I'm sorry."

"Don't do it again."

"Okay."

"I'm serious, Trout. I won't go out with you if you lie to me. About anything."

He looked at her and nodded.

"I'll see you later," she said and climbed out of the car.

Trout watched her walk down the path and into her apartment. She didn't look back.

"Shit," he said and drove away.

18

Thursday

The next few days passed in a strange fog, waiting for the phone call from Lotus or Boonray or whoever was going to tell them that Gordon had finally died. Trout couldn't shake the image of Gordon's hollow face staring at him from the soggy pillow. *She hated you because you reminded her of him.* He hadn't told anybody about that conversation. He wasn't sure why, other than that it felt extremely private, as if he had finally found something precious he'd been searching for his whole life: proof that there was nothing wrong with him after all. It had been a case of mistaken identity, nothing more.

Each day that passed without news of Gordon brought Trout more anxiety. By the time Thursday rolled around, he was useless at work. He ruined two boards by cutting them too short. James suggested he take the rest of the day off, and he did so willingly. He decided to surprise Heaven and pick her up from school. He waited out front in the car, but Heaven did not come out. Finally, he went into the school's office and asked for her.

"She didn't come to school today," said the secretary.

"What? I watched her leave the house with my own eyes."

He immediately began to panic. The neighborhood they lived in wasn't the safest. Why did he even let her walk to school? It was so stupid! He used the school phone to call the police, but they could tell him nothing. He called Michael's and got the answering machine.

"Heaven!" he called into it. "If you're there, pick up! Come home right away! Why didn't you go to school today?" He felt scared, yelling into the empty void of the telephone.

"Did she call or anything?"

The secretary shook her head. "I'm sure she's fine, Trout."

"How?"

"Just … she's fine. I'm sure. I know about these things."

"Do you know where she is? Is there something you're not telling me?"

"No. Calm down."

"Don't tell me to calm down! MY SISTER IS MISSING! Okay? You don't know about Heaven; she's different!" He stormed out of the office and immediately began to look for clues. A hat or scarf, her bookbag, maybe she had been grabbed just as she got to school. He drove the route she usually walked, scanning the ground for signs. When he got home, he ran inside to check for messages. One, from Laura.

"Hi. It's Laura calling for Trout, and I was wondering if we could get together this weekend. I hope you're doing well, and hi, Jade and Heaven!"

He picked up the receiver and dialed Ruth's number. She urged him to be calm. "She's probably fine, Trout. Did you call her boyfriend?"

"No answer."

"Well, I'm sure they're off somewhere together. Come over if you like. I'll wait by the phone."

He got in the car and drove to Michael's gallery. "Hello?" he called. A woman emerged from the back.

"Can I help you?"

"Yeah, I'm looking for Michael. Or my sister, Heaven. Have you seen them?"

"Oh, so you're Heaven's brother! She's quite the painter, I hear."

"Yeah, um, have you seen her or Michael today?"

"Michael came by this morning and said he was going out of town."

"Did he say where?"

"No."

"Do you know when he'll be back?"

"No, I don't."

"Well, do you know if Heaven was with him?"

"Sorry."

"Thanks," Trout said and walked out. He tried to control his fear as he drove to Michael's, searching the streets for Heaven. He pounded on Michael's front door, calling her name. He peered into the windows, but the shades were drawn. He realized he had no idea who Michael's family was, how to find him. Stupid idiot! he thought. This guy could've been a total psychopath this whole time. Who knows where he's taken Heaven? He drove back home, intending to call the police again.

He arrived to find another message. He breathed a huge sigh of relief when he heard Heaven's voice. "Hi, it's me. Um, I'm going out with some friends after school. I'm gonna eat dinner with them, so I'll be home after that. Love you guys!"

Trout stared at the answering machine, dumbfounded. He paced around the kitchen for a while and then tried to study, but he couldn't concentrate. He was useless. He called Michael's every half hour. Finally, just after eight-thirty, Heaven strolled casually through the door. Trout sat on the sofa, fuming.

"Where were you?"

She gave him her best innocent look. "What do you mean?"

"Don't screw around, Heaven. I know you didn't go to school today, so where were you?"

Her face turned red. "I was with Michael," she said softly.

"Do you have any idea how worried I've been? I've been driving all over the city calling people. I called the police, Heaven! Goddammit, you can't do this!"

"I'm sorry."

"No! Sorry isn't good enough this time! First of all, you are not allowed to ditch school. Second, I don't want you taking trips with Michael without my permission. And third, if you go anywhere, and I mean ANYWHERE, I need to know where you are, who you're with, and when you'll be home. Do you understand me?"

He had made her angry. She stood with her chin quivering, staring defiantly into his eyes. Trout immediately regretted the way he'd acted.

"Look," he said, "let's just sit down and talk about this. I don't want to fight."

She agreed, and they sat down on the sofa.

"So, where were you?"

She scratched at her head and didn't say anything.

"Heaven? Did you hear me?"

"I was with Michael."

"I know, but where did you guys go?"

"Don't get mad, okay?"

"Okay ... "

"We went up to see Gordon and Lotus."

"Why?"

"Because I wanted Michael to meet them. And them to meet him."

Trout was mad, but he tried to hide it.

"I'm not mad, Hevy, but I wish you would have asked me first."

"I did ask you, Trout! You wouldn't even talk to me about the possibility!"

"I just don't want any old person going to see Gordon right now! He's sick, and it takes a lot of energy for him to see people." Trout winced at his lie. He didn't care a rat's ass about how Gordon felt. He was angry because he didn't want Heaven getting closer to Gordon and Lotus than she already was. Was this how Jade had been feeling?

"Michael is not 'any old person.' He's my boyfriend, and he's very important to me. I wanted Gordon and Lotus to see him, know him. Also, Trout, I don't see why I should have to get *your* permission to go see *my* parents."

"You don't, Heaven. I just, this is all a little fragile right now."

"No, I don't think that's it. I think this is all about Michael. I think you just don't like him, and you can't stand the idea of me doing anything special with him."

"What? God, you are so off!"

"No, I'm not. I was really nice to Laura last weekend. Why can't you be nice to Michael?"

"Hev, you were nice to Laura because she's a nice person."

"And Michael isn't?"

"Michael's just ... Michael."

"Why do you dislike him so much?"

"I don't dislike him. I just, we don't connect is all. He's kind of stuck-up."

Heaven stood up suddenly. "That's it. I can't stand this fucking hypocriticalness anymore!"

"That's not a word, Heaven."

"Shut up!" She pulled her coat on and threw her bookbag over her shoulder. "I hate you, Trout! You can be such an asshole!"

She whipped out the front door in tears. Trout went to the doorway and called after her, but she didn't turn around.

"Shit." He went back into the house for the car keys.

He drove the dark streets looking for her. She had probably cut across the park, and that meant he had to drive up several streets before he could turn to get to the other side of the river. There was no sign of her. He checked the nearby payphones, thinking she may be calling Michael. He went to her friend's, Theresa, who lived nearby, but they hadn't seen Heaven. This time, though, Trout wasn't worried. He knew she was on her way to Michael's. She had obviously steered clear of the places she knew Trout would look for her. He gave up and turned the car around. Being home seemed like a dismal prospect, so he drove to José and Courtney's.

"Trout!" said Courtney, opening the door. "Right on! Come on in."

Their dinner dishes sat in the sink, and a game of Scrabble was set up on the table.

"Hey, Trout!" said José. "Wanna play Scrabble?"

Trout sat down and pulled off his coat. The house felt pleasantly warm and smelled like cinnamon and wood.

"You're in luck. I just got up to make Spanish coffees," Courtney said and began pulling mugs out of the cupboard. "What are you up to?"

"Just wanted to see some friendly faces is all."

José finished clearing the Scrabble board and handed Trout one of the wooden letter holders. "You're in luck again, my friend."

Trout held it together for a while. José had suggested they play using only slang words or phrases. Courtney kept them all in fresh supply of Spanish coffees, and before long, Trout relaxed into the warm, tingling sensation that spread throughout his body.

"*Pendejo*," José announced, setting his letters down.

"That would be a good one, except no foreign languages," Courtney said.

"What? That's not a foreign language."

"Yes it is, and you know it."

"Tsss, your *pinche* English is the foreign language."

He took some letters back and rearranged the remaining to spell dope. "Dope. As in 'idiot,' 'moron,' or 'kind bud.'"

"Let's get out the kind bud," Courtney said. "Trout?"

He hesitated. "Maybe just a tiny bit."

Courtney rolled a joint, which they passed around.

"It's mellow," said José. He knew about Trout's reluctance to get high. "We got it from a friend of mine. It's perfect for a nice, after-dinner buzz that won't give you a hangover the next day."

"How are things going with Laura?" Courtney asked.

"Don't you talk to her?" said Trout.

"Yeah, but I want your version."

"What does she say?"

"I'm not telling! I won't tell her what you say, either."

"Well … I don't know."

"Uh-oh," said José, "that doesn't sound good."

"Yeah." Trout felt all the emotions of the week rushing back. The Spanish coffee combined with the pot had given rise to a sensation of floating in water. He felt like laughing and crying at the same time.

"Do you want to talk about it?" asked Courtney.

"I don't think she likes me very much."

"Why? I can't imagine anybody not liking you."

"Thanks. But I can be a jerk; you guys know that."

José and Courtney glanced at each other.

"I don't think you can be a jerk, Trout," said Courtney.

"Me neither, man," said José.

"Well, I can be. I lied to Laura, and she's pretty upset. I just totally acted like a jerk with Heaven, and she ran out of the house to be with her boyfriend. Now *there's* a jerk, lemme tell you."

As he spoke, he realized he was a little drunk. It felt good. Freeing. He suddenly wanted to say everything, to get it all off his chest.

"Look, here's the deal. I'm, like, this little hippie kid growing up in the mountains with no running water or electricity, with these assholes for parents who drink, smoke, do drugs, fuck anybody they want, and basically can't stand their own children. And then along comes Laura with her *perfect* little Midwestern background and her *perfect* family. I don't mean you Courtney, you're not perfect. I mean, that didn't sound right, but it's a compliment. Believe me."

"I'm pissed off, I realize! I am so PISSED OFF! It's like, I feel angry all the time! I get mad at Heaven, at Jade, at myself, at Laura. Nobody can do anything right, they're all just fucking everything up all the time! I just want to be happy, you know? I want everybody to be happy, and nobody fucking wants to be happy. They just want to fuck everything up, and it pisses me off!"

At some point during Trout's speech, José and Courtney had started laughing. They were doing their best to suppress it, but as Trout finished and stared into their faces, the laughter broke free, and José and Courtney sat holding their sides and laughing convulsively.

"What's so funny?" Trout asked.

"You!" said Courtney. "You're fucking hilarious, man!"

Trout squinted at them, trying to comprehend the joke.

José wiped tears from his eyes. "Trout, man. Stop being so down on yourself! Everybody feels that way! We're all pissed off at the life we're given. Our parents, our siblings, ourselves."

"Yeah," agreed Courtney, "and there's a big difference between acting like a jerk and being a jerk. We can all act like jerks, but you're not a jerk, Trout."

Their laughter subsided, but not before Trout himself was smiling.

"I guess you're right. I think I scared Laura away, though."

"I wouldn't be so sure," said Courtney. "She's not as perfect and innocent as she seems. She's tough, and she's been around the block a few times. It'll take a lot more than one lie to scare her away, believe me."

"I'll believe it when I see it." He laid his letters down. "Square. Not as in the shape, or what Laura calls the plaza, but like, 'that guy's a square.'"

"Good one," said José.

Trout felt tremendously better. Maybe José and Courtney were right. Maybe he was being too hard on himself. He breathed a deep sigh of relief and forgot about everything for the rest of the evening.

He left José and Courtney's feeling carefree. He drove home along the dark streets, resisting the urge to drive by Michael's house and check on Heaven. He walked in the front door of his house and heard voices in the kitchen.

"Hey," said Jade as Trout walked into the kitchen. "You remember Max, right?"

Max sat at the table next to Jade, his bulky dreadlocks draped over his shoulders. Boonray and Holly sat across from him. Max raised a hand toward Trout.

"Hey, Max! We ran into each other the other night."

"He called," Jade said. "We invited him over. Man, it's been a long time!"

"Yup," Max said and nodded his head slowly. An open beer sat on the table beside him. He ran his hands nervously along his thighs.

"Max was telling us about his trip to Central America," Holly said.

Trout opened a beer and pulled a chair up to the table. Max's vacant eyes settled on him without expression. Trout felt the same uneasy feeling rise in him that he had felt with Max at the gas station. "Oh, yeah? When were you in Central America, Max?"

"Oh, sometime."

Boonray and Jade looked at each other and smirked. Trout could tell they found Max's emptiness amusing.

"So, what are you doing in town?" Boonray asked.

"Seeing."

"Seeing what?" asked Jade.

"Things." Max paused for a long while and stared at the refrigerator. "Lots of things ... Dogs."

"We got a dog," Jade said and whistled for Conrad, who came loping over from his corner. Jade ruffled Conrad's ears. "Hey, buddy! Hey there!" He made growling sounds, which got Conrad excited, and the dog crouched down low and growled back, wagging his tail.

Max raised one hand and stared intently at Conrad. He slowly moved his hand forward toward the dog and opened his eyes wide. Conrad continued to try to entice Jade into roughhousing with him.

"Ha-ma-lay-lee-hak-hum!" said Max in a loud voice.

The others stared at him, speechless. The dog looked up to find Max's flat hand inches from his face. Conrad cocked his head and wagged his tail. Max leaned forward and craned his head toward the dog, his hollow eyes open wide.

"Shay-um-ha-nee-hay!" he said.

Conrad whimpered and tucked his tail between his legs.

"I don't think he likes that," said Jade.

Max gave no indication that he had heard. He began to rise off the chair, his dreads dangling down like dead snakes. Trout exchanged uneasy glances with Boonray and Holly. Jade's body was tense, as though preparing to leap up and shove Max back into his seat. Conrad backed toward Jade, whimpering softly. He gave a low growl and then barked at Max. Max moved slowly closer to the dog, hunched over, his hand still thrust forward.

"Pa-pa-pey-NO-NAH-NAH-NEY!" Max commanded.

Conrad burst into a full bark and began to back up, his head pitched forward toward Max.

"Cut it out, Max," said Jade.

Max continued staring at Conrad.

"Hey, Max," said Trout, "I think you should leave the dog alone." He reached out to touch Max's curled back.

Max straightened up and returned slowly to his seat, keeping his eyes, which had a wild look to them now, fixed on the dog. He took a long sip of beer and wiped his hands on his thighs. He held his chin high as though he felt proud of what he'd just done. Jade ran his hands along Conrad's ruffled back and soothed him with his voice. Everybody except Max exchanged incredulous looks with one another while Max stared at the refrigerator.

Trout began to wonder what they should do with him. "Hey, Jade, could I talk to you about something?" he asked. He started walking toward the living room and motioned for Jade to follow. Once in the living room, Trout addressed Jade in a whisper. "What the hell is the matter with him?"

Jade tried desperately to suppress his laughter. "I don't know, man, but he's fucking insane!"

"I know. I'm thinking we shouldn't let him stay here."

Jade, who was always helping the underdog, protested. "Aw, Trout, he's not dangerous or anything. No big deal if he spends one night on our couch. He's harmless."

Jade grasped the side of Trout's arm as though to reassure him, but it had no effect.

"Have you heard from Heaven?" asked Trout.

"No. Why?"

"I just don't think it's a good idea if she comes home late by herself and Max is in the living room."

Jade looked serious for a moment. He chewed on his thumbnail and then met Trout's eyes squarely. "Wow, Trout. You are really fucking suspicious; did you know that?"

"Yeah, well, maybe that's a good thing. Especially when it comes to my little sister."

"Whoa, she's my sister too."

"Then why don't you act like it? Jesus, Jade, we don't know anything about this guy! We can't just let him sleep here!"

"Trout! What are you talking about? That's Max!"

"No, that's not Max."

"Who is it then?

"I don't know, but he gives me the creeps. It's like there's nobody home in his eyes."

"I know. It is kind of weird."

They both stared off at the kitchen doorway for a moment. Then Jade once again clapped Trout on the arm.

"Don't worry about it. I'll take care of it. Don't you have school in the morning?"

"Yeah, I should get some sleep."

Trout popped his head into the kitchen to wish everybody a good night. Holly leaned on the kitchen table, massaging her own scalp. She waved a few fingers at Trout. Boonray gave him a quick nod of the head, but he was so absorbed in watching Max that he barely looked at Trout. Jade gave Trout a reassuring wink, and Max's eyes took so long to transition from the fridge to Trout that Trout was already turning to leave when he felt Max's stone eyes brush over him like the falling wings of a dead insect. He shuddered as he walked to his room.

He tossed fitfully, trying to find sleep. Images of Heaven in the snow by the river kept playing through his head, her eyes rolled back, her mouth open, terrified screams escaping from her mouth like the cries of a wild animal caught in a vicious trap.

19

Friday

The next morning, Trout awoke before anybody else. He took a shower, dressed, and walked through the living room, into the kitchen, and then stopped in his tracks. He turned slowly back toward the living room, not sure if he wanted to see what he thought he'd seen.

A mess of blankets and pillows lay on the couch where Jade had obviously made a bed for Max to sleep on. But Max was gone. And from the looks of it, he had taken their stereo and television with him. "Shit," Trout whispered. His eyes scanned the living room. Jade's guitar stand stood empty in the corner. The VCR was gone.

Trout stormed back to Jade and Holly's room and flung the door open. Jade looked up, his face scrunched into a scowl.

"Nice, Jade," said Trout.

"What?"

"He fucking stole our TV and VCR. And our stereo. And your guitar."

"What?" Jade began to get out of bed. Holly stared blearily at Trout.

"Max! You let him stay here, and he robbed us! I thought you said you were taking care of it!"

Jade pulled on a pair of pants and followed Trout into the living room.

"Shit," he said, looking around.

Trout went back to Heaven's room and quietly opened the door. She was fast asleep in her bed. Relieved, he closed the door and went back to the living room.

Jade stood with his hands on his hips, shaking his head. "I don't believe it. That shithead!"

"Why did you let him stay here last night?"

"I thought it'd be okay, man. Besides, he'd had a lot to drink, and he was acting … weird."

"So you let him stay? Jade, if somebody's acting weird, you don't let them stay at your house!"

"I'm sorry, Trout! What do you want me to say? I didn't think he'd *rob* us!"

Holly came out in her robe, followed by Heaven.

"What's going on?" Heaven asked.

"We were robbed," Trout answered. "By Max."

"What?"

"Yeah. Jade let him stay here because he was acting weird, and he took a bunch of shit."

"How'd he carry it all?" Jade asked.

They all stared at each other for a moment, and then Trout and Jade rushed to the door and flung it open.

"FUCK!" Jade screamed. "He took the car?"

"Oh my God," Holly said. She sat on the couch and then looked at Max's blankets and stood back up with a disgusted look on her face.

"What should we do?" asked Trout.

"Call the police," Jade answered and picked up the phone.

They stood staring at each other while Jade dialed.

"I *knew* we shouldn't have let him stay here," Trout said.

"We didn't know," Holly said softly.

Jade gave the details to the police and then hung up the phone. "They're on their way. Trout, I'm really sorry. I never would've let him stay here if I'd thought ..."

"It's not your fault, Jade. You thought you were doing a good thing."

They made coffee and waited for the police, surveying the house, checking for what else might be missing. They called out to each other as they discovered more missing items.

"He took the beer."

"He took the fucking change jar! It was nothing but pennies!"

"And the cheese."

"He took my tarot cards!"

"He took the peanut butter ... "

"No, I ate that yesterday."

"Oh."

"The camping stove is gone."

"Oh! He took my ring! I left it on the table last night! He asked to see it! What a dickhead!"

"He took the basketball."

"And the Oreos!"

"I don't believe it."

"What?"

"He took Conrad's collar!"

They all gathered around the dog, who was happily wagging up at them with a bare neck.

"Oh my God."

"What a sicko!"

"Why would you steal the collar off a dog?"

"I don't know, but if I ever see that guy I'm gonna—"

There was a knock at the door, and Heaven opened it for the squat police officer standing on their porch. Heaven let him in, and his eyes ran professionally over the living room. They gave the officer a list of everything that was missing.

"He took a dog collar?"

"Yeah! Right off of the dog!"

The officer raised his eyebrows. "That's pretty weird."

While Jade gave the officer the information about the car, Trout pulled Heaven aside.

"I want you to be really careful, okay?"

"Why?"

"Just be careful. Max is strange, and I'm not sure what he's capable of. So I'll walk you to school today."

"I'll give her a ride," said Holly.

"Great. I'll come with you guys. Just in case. And we'll arrange to have you picked up from school. I don't want you walking around alone for a while."

Heaven nodded, and then she and Holly rolled their eyes at each other.

Trout felt strange all day at school. He had ridden his bike and missed his first class. He kept thinking he saw Max out of the corner of his eye, then he'd turn to look, and there'd be nothing or a shadow on the wall. He called Heaven during her lunch break, slipping out of his design class.

"Michael's picking me up," she said.

"Don't wait for him outside. Have him come in and get you."

"Okay, Trout." Irritation buzzed in her voice.

"I'm sorry, Heaven. I just worry about you."

"I know. You worry too much."

He winced. "I'm going out with Laura tonight. Are we still on for Cielo tomorrow?"

"Yeah, but how are we gonna get there?"

"Oh shit, I forgot. Maybe Holly will lend us her car."

"She has school in Albuquerque tomorrow."

"Well, we'll figure it out one way or another. I love you, Hev."

"You, too. Bye."

"Bye."

Trout rode home in the cold wind. His nose was red and running when he pulled into the empty driveway. He had half expected to find the old Toyota sitting in it. Jade wasn't home from work yet. Trout showered and began to dress for his date. It was then that he realized his nice, wool jacket was missing, too. His anger toward Max had been mounting all day. Now, he pounded the wall where his jacket normally hung and screamed with frustration. He wondered if Max's parents still lived in Cielo. Maybe Max had gone up there, and they could pay him a visit tomorrow.

He had Laura pick him up.

"Where's your car?" she asked as he climbed into the passenger seat.

Trout began to tell her the story of Max, but she interrupted him.

"Wait, you need to get out and kiss the hood again."

"Laura, I'm really not in the mood."

"No, I'm serious, Trout. It won't start unless you do."

He shot her an irritated look. "It's a funny joke, really, it is. I'm just tired and hungry."

"Trout, you don't have to kiss the hood, but you do have to get out for the car to start."

He sighed and climbed out. She started the car, and he climbed back in.

"It's a weird thing about some of these Darts," she explained. "They have this mechanism where the car won't start if there's somebody in the passenger seat unless their seat belt is buckled. Since the seat belt is broken on that side, the car won't start if somebody is sitting there."

"Huh. It's like a sensor."

"Mm-hmmm."

They drove to the restaurant in an awkward silence punctuated with cordial exchanges. Trout yearned to feel the easy closeness they had shared on their first date.

Over dinner, they talked about Max and everything that had happened.

"Hey," said Laura, "Courtney said you stopped over there last night."

Trout tensed up. How much had Courtney told Laura?

"Yeah."

"She said you guys had a really nice time."

"Mm-hmm. Courtney makes a mean Spanish coffee."

He waited to see if the subject of his lie would come up, but it didn't.

After dinner, Laura suggested they go to her house for tea. Trout hesitated, thinking of the cat.

"I learned some points for allergies," Laura said. "Why don't you let me try them on you and see what happens?"

"Great. An allergic reaction *and* needle-prodding. You sure know how to show a guy a good time."

She laughed. "Come on. I'll let you drive my car. It's really fun!"

At her house, Trout sat on the couch, feeling his nose begin to clog and his eyes begin to water. Laura came in with a small black box and opened it beside him. Trout examined the contents: paper boxes with Chinese writing on them, clear plastic tubes, cones of incense, a canister of needles.

"Ready?" she asked.

He nodded, and she tapped a needle into his arm.

"How's that feel?"

"I don't feel anything."

She wiggled the needle.

"OW!" Electric pain snaked up his arm.

"Oops, sorry. Is that okay now?"

"Yeah."

She put a few more needles in him, wiggling each one until he felt the electric snake. "That's the chi," she explained.

She left the room to make tea, and Trout let his eyes wander over the room. Photos of smiling people in wooden frames hung on the wall, stood on the bureau, the mantle, and the piano.

"I just noticed you have a piano," he called.

She came in and set a tray on the coffee table with a pot of tea, mugs, honey, and milk. Trout felt annoyed by everything being so perfect.

"Hey, you sound less stuffed-up!"

He sniffed. "You're right! I think this is working! So, do you play?"

"The piano? A little, eensy-teensy bit."

"Will you play for me?"

"NO."

"Ever?"

"Well … it's negotiable."

"What does that mean?"

"It means I'll play for a price."

"Oh, torturing me with needles isn't enough for you?"

She laughed and poured tea. "Just relax, close your eyes. Let the treatment work."

Trout closed his eyes. He felt the electric snake wiggle up his arm again, then he felt Laura plucking out the needles.

"That wasn't very long," he said, opening his eyes.

"It was twenty minutes. You fell asleep."

"I did?"

They laughed.

Laura pulled the last of the needles out. "You never told me your dad is dying. I'm so sorry."

"No, don't be. I mean, thank you ... He's got cancer. I went to see him for the first time a couple of weeks ago. I hadn't seen him in seven years. I'm sorry I didn't tell you. It's just ... I just found out, and—"

Next thing he knew, he was crying. His head fell to his hands, then onto her shoulder. He shifted, like a slideshow, from crying about Gordon, to crying about himself, to crying about sadness in general, to just crying without thought. Laura stroked his head. His hands gripped her knee, the sofa. He cried until there was nothing left to cry about. Laura curled around him and hugged him tightly.

He sat up and smiled. He told her all about his parents, what it was like to grow up inside the crazy whirlpool of constant partying. About Gordon and how he got mean when he drank, how he fixed cars with a cigarette dangling out of the corner of his mouth, his shirt off, and the green, six-armed deity roasting in the sun. How he was sometimes nice to Trout and other times totally removed and detached. About Lotus and how she was in a bad mood unless she was getting attention from men, how she couldn't stand her children and treated them like they were in the way, *her* way, a bother. About Jade and his wildness, how Trout had looked up to him growing up but had also been afraid of him. About Heaven and how she never spoke to people, how she would wander the land all by herself, talking to the animals. He told her about Ruth and Mark, about Cielo, about the fire, the house burning down. He told her about Heaven being taken away by the state. How Gordon and Lotus hadn't gotten her back, and then they had moved to the commune in Abiquiu. He told her about the events of the night that he and Jade finally decided to leave for good. About driving away in Boonray's truck, moving to Santa Fe, and getting Heaven back on their own. About being a teenager in Jade's care, helping Heaven all those years, taking care of her. Finally, he told her about his recent trips to Cielo, Gordon's cancer, that he was dying, could already be dead. She listened intently. Trout found himself laughing at some parts and getting a few laughs out of her, as well.

He took a long, deep breath. "I feel no allergies whatsoever."

She looked proud.

"You are going to be a fantastic doctor," he said.

His hand reached out and touched her face. He gently tilted her head up and kissed her.

"Thanks for telling me all that," she said. "I needed to know. I can't explain why."

Their lips met softly at first, then tenderness gave way to the desire that had been building between them. He gently pushed Laura back onto the sofa and lay down with her. Outside it began, quietly, to snow.

20

Saturday

"Just cut it out," Trout said and brushed Heaven's hand from the stereo knob as she flipped restlessly through the stations.

Heaven shot him a look and then turned to roll her eyes at Michael in the back seat. Trout slowed at the usual bend in the steep hill.

"A friend of our parents rode his motorcycle over the cliff here," Heaven said to Michael and pointed at the deep ravine that severed the land to their right.

"Was he okay?" Michael asked.

"No. He died."

Trout held the steering wheel tightly until they were well away from the bend. That spot always freaked him out. The car crested the hill, and Cielo unfurled before them.

Cielo looked like it belonged on the set of a Western. Gordon always said that the town was twenty years behind the rest of the country, but Trout thought it was more like forty.

"I'd love to come painting up here," Michael said, gazing at the squat houses and jacked-up cars.

"Yes!" said Heaven. "We should!"

Trout tried not to laugh as he envisioned the paintings Michael would create from Cielo. He saw atrocious, neon abstracts with vague suggestions of fuzzy dice and skinny dogs.

"We should stop if anybody's hungry," Trout said. Even though Lotus had fed them last time, he knew they couldn't count on it.

"I'm fine," said Michael.

"Me too," Heaven said.

Trout drove on through town and bumped along the dirt road beside the *acequia*. Heaven pointed things out to Michael as they passed: Garcia's Grocery, the church, Cookie's house, Mark and Ruth's old road, the falling-down barn, Bob's old trailer, and their empty square of land.

"Could we stop?" Michael asked as Trout bumped past the black willow of their old property.

Trout eyed Heaven. She was chewing her fingertips.

"Naw, I think we should get up to Winnie's. They expected us a half hour ago."

"There's really nothing to see," Heaven said. "The house burned down. You can see everything from the road."

"Yeah, but I want to walk around on it. Smell the earth. See all the hiding places that Heaven used to go to."

"Maybe some other time," Trout said, turning onto Winnie's road.

Trout felt annoyed that Michael was with them. It was really the only way they were able to get to Cielo that day. Nobody else had a car they could borrow, and Heaven had been pleading for Trout to allow Michael to come. Michael wore a putrid cologne that stained Trout's nostrils and stuck to his hair and skin. He felt annoyed with himself for giving in at all.

He had awoken early that morning at Laura's. As he waited for her to wake up, he suddenly knew what he wanted to say to Gordon. He had found pen and paper and written his father a letter that was now tucked safely into his coat pocket. He wasn't sure if he would read it aloud to Gordon or just paraphrase it, but he was sure he didn't want Michael to be there when he did. He began to think that he would probably leave the letter with Gordon to read later. If Gordon was in the same shape as last time, though, he wouldn't be able to read a thing, and Lotus would have to read it to him, and Trout certainly didn't want Lotus's weasely eyes touching his letter.

He pulled into Winnie's driveway and shut off the motor. Trout had insisted he drive, under the pretense that the roads to Cielo could be dangerous. The truth was that the drive up to Cielo made him anxious, and he couldn't stand riding as a passenger. They climbed out of the car. Michael pulled his overcoat tight around him and surveyed the house and land, the falling-down fence, the rusted, old truck and the yellow Cadillac parked side by side. Trout looked at Michael, thinking that no matter what he was wearing or who he was with, he looked out of place anywhere but his fancy gallery. He looked like he belonged in a Santa Fe travel brochure.

The door opened, and Winnie waved an enthusiastic hello. Heaven waved back and tugged on Michael's coat sleeve. He did a corny pretend stumble and followed Heaven, laughing like they were running down the beach in Mexico, not toward an old hippie's dilapidated house in the mountains, inside of which her father was dying of cancer. Trout sighed and locked the keys in the car.

"Dammit!"

"What?" said Heaven, looking back.

"I just locked the keys in the car."

"It's okay," said Michael with a liquor-ad grin. "I have an extra in my wallet." He patted his pocket, then grinned excitedly at Heaven and jostled behind her into the house.

Trout shuddered and stared at the keys dangling from the ignition. He wanted, more than anything, to break the stupid window, but he tucked his hands into his pockets and followed Heaven and Michael inside. Winnie was taking their coats and hats. Heaven handed hers over graciously, as though Winnie was the nice butler who looked after her country cottage. The gesture reminded Trout of something Michael would do, and he cringed at the thought of Heaven adopting any of Michael's bourgeois manner-isms. He made a mental note to get on her case about it later.

Trout was glad to hear a fire blazing in the woodstove.

"Come in, come in," Winnie said.

Trout shut the door and unbuttoned his coat. He looked around for signs of Lotus. An ashtray on the kitchen table overflowed with wet, brown cigarette butts, and a half-finished drawing of a dead bird sat on one of the chairs. Trout wandered over and picked up the drawing pad. He knew Lotus would be pissed if she caught him looking at it. He flipped through. Mostly still lifes—fruit, plants, dishes—but here was one of Gordon. Trout held it at arm's length and admired it.

"Wow," said Michael from behind him. "That's really good. Who did it?"

"Lotus," said Trout, setting the pad down. "Heaven's better."

Michael reached for the drawing.

"Don't," Trout said. "She doesn't like people looking at them."

"Should we go see Gordon?" asked Heaven.

Michael and Trout followed Heaven down the hall and into the second bedroom. Gordon sat propped up in the bed, his head tilted back a bit and his mouth open. Trout didn't think he was asleep, but he didn't look quite awake either. He was probably heavily drugged. Michael pulled back toward the doorway. Made braver by Michael's fear, Trout joined Heaven by the bedside. Gordon opened his eyes and peered up at his children. He looked better. His face was a little filled out and had more color. His eyes were brighter, and there was a new twinkle to them. Trout pulled up a chair, sat down, hooked his fingers through his belt loops, and adopted an air of casualness in the face of death. That would show Michael.

Heaven motioned Michael over, and he walked softly to the bedside.

"This is Michael," she said to Gordon.

"I thought you guys came up here the other day," Trout said.

"We did, but nobody was home."

"Where'd you go?" Trout asked Gordon, surprised.

Gordon's eyes twinkled. "For a drive. I had to get out of this stinky house."

Michael extended his hand, and Gordon shook it. Trout could tell that Gordon didn't like Michael either. Good. He knew Gordon would think Michael was too slick, too money. Poor Heaven. She held Michael's arm proudly. The moment of her man meeting her dad, and here her brother sat scowling on the whole scene like a dirty wood-stove belching black smoke. He stood up, suddenly disliking his own company, and left the room under the pretense of needing air.

From the kitchen, he peered out the window and saw Lotus in the field, leaning against the fence, wrapped in an old serape. He put on his coat and went out to join her. She stared at the ground where a rabbit carcass shifted and twitched as insects dug under and through it.

"I keep finding dead things," she said.

A shudder passed through Trout. He looked over at her. She looked sicker than Gordon. Her skin was grayer than usual, and she seemed to have lost as much weight as Gordon had gained. Her eyes looked huge in her thin face, and her wrinkles seemed to have multiplied.

"What, did the cancer abandon Gordon's body for yours?" he asked.

"That's not funny."

"Yeah, well, you look like hell."

"Thanks, fucker."

Trout felt strange, warm feelings arising in him. Exchanging insults with her felt almost affectionate.

"No, seriously. Gordon looks better today."

"It's the strange beauty that comes over you right before you die."

"Whatever."

She shrugged and poked at the rabbit's head with her shoe.

"So, Gordon told me that you always hated me because I remind you of your dad."

"He did, huh?"

"Is it true?"

Lotus brought her shoe down on the rabbit's head and leaned on it. Trout heard a delicate crunch as the skull was crushed, followed by a faint smushing sound. She turned and walked away, following the line of the fence away from the house. He watched her. He knew better than to follow. He turned and walked back to the house, a euphoria coming over him that was at once familiar and strange. Familiar in that he had experienced similar euphoric feelings every time he stood up to his parents but strange because he hadn't experienced it as an adult before.

He whistled a happy tune and closed the door behind him. He put water on for tea and watched Lotus through the window. She continued to follow the fence, squatting down to pee on the northern edge of the property, and then circled back toward the house. Trout pulled two mugs from the cupboard and dumped some dried peppermint into the teapot. When Lotus opened the door, he was seated at the table, tea steaming in front of him, Lotus's drawing pad on his lap.

"I like this picture you drew of Gordon," he said as she pulled off her shoes. He said it to piss her off, and it worked.

She stomped into the kitchen, not making much of a racket with her frail frame, and tore the drawing pad from his hands.

"What do you want?" her eyes blazed on him like he was an animal she'd cornered and meant to kill. He knew he had her. Heaven and Michael were in Gordon's room; Winnie was in his room with the door closed, and it was getting colder by the second outside. There was nowhere for Lotus to be except here in the kitchen with him, unless she jumped into her car and drove away, but he didn't plan on letting that happen. He pushed the chair across from him back with his feet.

"I want you to sit down and have tea with me. I want us to talk like two normal people. That's all."

She closed the drawing pad and stuck it in a drawer. "Bullshit. You want to attack me, tell me what a shitty mother I was to you. You want to hurt me." She stood over him with wide eyes and flyaway hair.

"Lotus, you look like you're about to testify at your father's church. Or receive an exorcism."

She sat down and crossed her arms. Trout poured her a mug of tea and slid it gently across the table. "I'll tell you everything, Trout. I'm not ashamed. What do you want to know?"

He took a deep, slow breath. "I want to know why you hate me so much."

His eyes stayed steady and calm. She glared into them.

"I don't hate you, Trout. It was you who always hated me."

"I don't think so."

"Yes, I think so. You hated me from the second you were born. I never knew where you came from. If I hadn't seen you come out of my vagina with my own eyes, I would swear you weren't my baby. You bit my nipples till they bled. You cried whenever I touched you. You stared at me with hatred in your icy, blue eyes. Yes, you did. You hated me right away. I could never do right by you."

"How could I have hated you, Lotus? I was a baby!"

"Don't ask me, but you did."

She began to roll a cigarette.

"So you're saying that you hated me because I hated you?" he asked.

"Pretty much. You wanted us to be at war with each other all the time. I just protected myself from your venomous wrath."

"Venomous wrath? Okay, wait. I need for this conversation to make sense! I only hated you after years of your abuse! I mean, I hated you at times but not overall hatred. I still wanted you to love me, to start being a mother. You never wanted to be a mother!"

Now he was fired up, and she stared at him coldly, blowing thin streams of smoke into his face. The old, stoic ice queen was back.

"That's true. I never did want to be a mother."

"Why did you become one, then?"

"By accident. But it turned out to be the ticket out of my parents' life. I told them I was pregnant and that I had to get married to the father. They were irate but started making arrangements for a hasty, discreet marriage. You should have seen the looks on their faces when Gordy pulled up on his hog, his long hair in a ponytail, his arms all tattooed. They about had a heart attack. He didn't even get off the bike. I climbed on the back with my bag and waved, and we drove off.

"I thought I'd get an abortion. I didn't even tell Gordy I was pregnant for a while. But when I did, he started crying and said he wanted to keep it. You know what a crier he is. I actually liked being a mom for a little while after Jade was born."

She trailed off and stared out the window, her eyes far away. Trout didn't want to move or take a breath, so precious was this information. He quietly rolled a cigarette for her. He thought maybe if he could keep her smoking, he could keep her sitting there and talking.

"What happened?"

"Huh?"

"You said you liked being a mom for a while. What happened?"

"What happened is that Gordy became addicted to crystal meth, and then being a mom pretty much sucked. I had this baby that I had to take with me everywhere. I had no money. I couldn't do drugs the same way because I had to keep track of this other person. He wanted to eat all the time, always reaching for my tits like I was a fucking cow. Soon, I didn't give a shit anymore. I was so fed up with the constant demands Jade put on me that I secretly wanted him to die or get kidnapped. I just wanted my life back! I started leaving him with different people, hoping somebody would want him and steal him. They always tracked me down and gave him back to me, though. It got harder and harder to find people to watch him, 'cause they all knew I wouldn't come back for him.

"Then Gordy went into rehab, and I was pregnant again. I went to live with my parents. God, that was fucking miserable. They dressed Jade up in these little churchy outfits and called him Jacob. They told me that if you were a boy, you would be named

Matthew, and if you were a girl ... I forget. Mary or Rachel, probably. I told them, either way I was naming you Truchas. Ha-ha-ha!"

"Shit, Trout! I didn't want you! I wanted to be free, to be young. I was twenty-three years old! Can you understand that?"

Trout almost nodded but caught himself. He kept his poker face on, afraid one wrong move would clam her up.

"No, I didn't think so. My parents loved you from the start but refused to call you Truchas. Gordon joined us after you were born, and he started calling you Trout. He was clean and all into being a dad all of a sudden, so I just handed you over to him. As soon as I looked in your eyes, the instant you were born, I knew you and I were not gonna get along. Gordy liked you just fine, though, so he hung out with you and Jade most days. We left Georgia and came out here. That's when life really turned to shit. I met Forest and fell in love with him. Gordy was screwing whoever, left and right, maybe Forest too; I don't know. I started taking the pill so I wouldn't have to have another baby, but I got pregnant again anyway. I wasn't sure who the father was until Heaven was born, and I knew she was Gordon's baby right away. She was so beautiful. Having a baby girl was a whole different thing for me. I loved her in a way I could never love my sons."

"That didn't last long, though," said Trout, thinking of all the days he'd spent taking care of Heaven because Lotus was too drunk or irritable or had disappeared for a few days.

"Yeah, well, what can I say? I just wasn't supposed to have children, but I screwed up. I screwed up, Trout, and you can spend your whole life pissed off at me, or you can get over it already."

Michael came into the kitchen with an apologetic expression. "Heaven wanted some time alone with her dad."

"We're kind of in the middle of a private conversation," Trout said.

"Oh, get over it," said Lotus. "Where's he gonna go? Winnie's room? I'm sure Nickel can deal with our shit."

"What did you just call him?"

"What?"

"Did you just call him Nickel?"

"Fuck if I know." She lit the cigarette Trout had rolled and thumped her mug on the table the way an obnoxious drunk at a bar will signal to the bartender that he needs a refill. Trout poured her more tea and waited, ignoring Michael examining the cupboards as if they were fascinating pieces of art.

"How could you tell we weren't going to like each other as soon as I was born?"

"I told you; I saw it in your eyes."

"Yeah, but what, exactly, did you see in my eyes?"

Lotus leaned forward and narrowed her eyes. "Judgment. You judging me."

"What? Lotus, that is the craziest thing I've ever heard! A baby isn't capable of judging anything!"

"Ha! What would you know? Babies are capable of a lot more than you might think. And I was right. You did judge me. My entire life. You were always so fucking righteous with me."

Michael cleared his throat and slid off into the living room, where there wasn't any furniture, just a bunch of pillows and rugs. Trout wondered if Michael was sorry he'd come.

"Lotus, don't you see? I look like your father! I have the same eyes as him. So when you saw my eyes, you felt the judgment from your father, not from me! But then you pushed me away and were so mean to me all the time; of course I judged you and was righteous! You were a fucking bitch!"

"Bullshit! You hated me from the beginning! It was like a past life thing or something!"

Heaven came to the doorway and stood looking at them.

"Where's Michael?" she asked.

"I'm in here," Michael called from the living room.

Heaven went to join him.

Trout heard them murmuring softly to each other, no doubt commenting on the argument in progress in the kitchen. He knew he wasn't going to get anywhere trying to convince Lotus that her hatred of him preceded his of her, but he had found out what he wanted to know. Gordon had been right; she did hate him because he reminded her of her father, not because of who Trout was. He breathed a long sigh of relief. "I feel much better," he said to Lotus. "Thank you."

"Jade's here!" cried Heaven.

Trout heard the sound of a truck door slamming. Lotus's eyes flew open, and she practically ran back to Gordon's room, probably to warn him, or maybe suffocate him with a pillow so he could be spared having to face his oldest son. Jade and Boonray strode into the house, looking tall and powerful in their lumberjack hats and coats, stomping snow off their construction boots.

Heaven flew into Jade's arms. "I'm so glad you came! He keeps asking for you, and I didn't know what to say anymore!"

Jade hugged her, grinning, and saluted Trout with his chin. Winnie came out, his hair all messy and his eyes blinking off the nap he had just woken up from.

"Winnie!" Jade cried and released Heaven to wrap Winnie in a bear hug.

"It's my protégé! Come back to me!" Winnie called, lost inside Jade's broad arms. "How ya doin'? My God, look at you! You've gone and grown up on me!"

"Yeah, well, that's what we do. You shrank!" They teased each other for a good few minutes. Boonray came to sit in the kitchen with Trout and set to work rolling himself one of Lotus's cigarettes. He pulled a plastic bag from his pocket and sprinkled a little pot in with the tobacco, then sealed the cigarette with his tongue. Winnie got excited when he smelled the pot, and everybody got good and stoned except for Trout and Heaven, who sat side by side and fed the fire. Michael had fallen asleep by the woodstove.

"What were you guys talking about?" Heaven asked.

"I finally got Lotus to say why she always hated me."

"Did she say why she always hated me?"

The sorrow in Heaven's voice sliced right into Trout's chest, and he put his arm around her, tears in his throat.

"She didn't hate you, Hev. Just me."

"What makes you so special?"

He laughed. "It was something about her dad and how I look like him. She didn't hate you; she just didn't want to be a mother."

"Nice."

"I know. What did you and Gordon talk about?"

"Mmmm … nothing, really. He tried to explain why they left me in foster care, but then he fell asleep."

Jade stood up from the table and stretched his arms over his head.

"Well, here I go," he said and slowly and purposefully walked out of the room and down the hallway.

"He's sleeping," said Heaven.

"Well, too bad!" Jade called over his shoulder.

He hadn't been in this house since he was seventeen, the night of Winnie's party. Trout wondered what it was like for Jade to walk down that hallway. Trout closed his eyes. He wished he had shared his letter with Gordon before Jade arrived. Now Jade was going to get Gordon good and pissed.

He could hear them talking. Lotus was laughing her high, hyena laugh she used when she was feeling defensive. Michael snored loudly. Heaven laughed and lay down beside him. Trout closed his eyes and thought back to the night before, with Laura. A smile crept over his face as he basked in the warmth of the woodstove and thought of Laura's red hair and blue eyes. He lay down, as well, and began to slide into a pleasant afternoon nap. He could hear Boonray and Winnie talking in the kitchen. The teakettle hissed. Heaven was humming softly and stroking Michael's hair. Trout felt overcome by a feeling of family. How funny, he thought. Now Gordon's dying, and we'll never be a family, all together, again. This is it. This is the first time in nine years we've all been together, and it will be the last time, too.

"Heaven?"

"Hmm?"

"I just realized that we're all here, in the same house, for the first and last time."

"I know. I thought about that, too."

He blinked up at the *vigas*, suddenly not willing to give any of this afternoon away to sleep. "What do you think they're talking about in there?" he asked.

"Who knows? Could be anything."

"I kind of want to go see."

"You should give them their privacy."

"I know. But I'm curious. Do you think they're getting along?"

He was feeling very much like a little kid again, whispering with Heaven on the floor, speculating as to what their parents were doing. Heaven scooted around Michael and came to lie next to Trout.

"I don't hear any yelling," she said.

"Me either."

She laid her head on his arm.

"Do you remember all the stories I used to tell you?" he asked.

She laughed. "Yes. You made up such good stories! I remember all the characters you used. There was Mr. California, the squirrel; Mr. and Mrs. Jenkins, the rabbits; Sam Salami the Salamander … "

"We had fun."

"We did. Thank God for you. I don't know what I would have done without you. I'd probably be in a mental institution playing Yahtzee with myself."

"If it hadn't been for you, I'd probably be a drug addict. Me and Jade would be in prison, writing you letters."

"That I wouldn't get to read because I'd be a pyromaniac."

"Wait, I couldn't write you letters from prison because I would only be in prison if you hadn't existed. But you do, so I'm here."

Soon, Trout couldn't stand it anymore. He got up and walked quietly down the hall. The door to Gordon's room stood open a crack, and he peered in. Jade sat on the bed, crying, his shoulders hunched forward. Lotus sat in her chair, staring at the floor. Gordon was softly patting Jade's hand. Trout yearned to go in, to hear their conversation, but he knew Jade wouldn't want him in there.

He returned to the living room and lay back down, disturbed.

"What are they doing?" asked Heaven.

"Nothing."

"They're not fighting?"

"No. Jade's crying."

"Oh."

Trout fed the fire and wondered what Jade was saying to Gordon. He resented the fact that this was his third visit, and he hadn't been able to think of a single thing to say to Gordon, other than to comment on how terrible he looked, but here Jade came, breezing in, and spilled his heart for an hour.

Trout went into the kitchen and sat down next to Boonray.

"Did Jade tell you what he was going to say to Gordon?"

Boonray looked very stoned.

"No, man. I don't think he knew."

Trout made up his mind. He went back to Gordon's room and swung open the door. Jade looked up and wiped his eyes.

"Can I come in?" Trout asked, even though he knew nobody would say no because that would mean acknowledging that a tender moment was happening, and God forbid Gordon and Lotus should be involved in any tender moments.

Gordon stared at him, sleepy-eyed. "Get your sister," he said. "I have some things I want to say."

Trout's heart sank as he went to fetch Heaven. The moment he'd been waiting for all day, when he could read his letter to Gordon, looked like it was never going to come. When they had settled themselves about Gordon, some on the bed, some on the chairs, Gordon propped himself up on his mound of weary pillows and stared at his children like they were something he'd just won at a local bingo hall.

"I'm so glad you're all here together. I didn't think I was ever going to see your brother again. Jade, remember everything I said. I meant every word. Trout, Heaven, Jade, I know I haven't been the best dad. I've been a drunk, mean, screwed around on your Mom, but I always loved you."

"And you hit us," Trout said.

"Yes. Yes I did. And I'm sorry for that, also. You see, the closer I get to dying, the clearer I see everything I did wrong. But I also see everything I did right. And having you kids was just about the best thing I ever did. Now, I been thinking about what I have to leave you when I die. Lotus is taking care of all the dead stuff, what to do with this mangy old body and all that, so that's out of your hair. Jade, I want you to take my guitar. I know it's not much, but I figure you can get some use out of it."

He pointed to the corner where a worn guitar leaned against its case. Next to it sat two cardboard boxes. "Trout, you've always been the studious one, so I'm leaving you my books. They're in those boxes there. And as for you, Precious," Gordon picked up a paper bag from the nightstand. He reached inside and withdrew several pieces of large, handmade jewelry. "I want you to take my rings and necklace. These were made by a Navajo named Guapito."

"Guapito?" Trout asked. "I didn't know he was a jeweler."

"Oh yeah, all them Navajo folk are."

Heaven took the jewelry, blinking back tears.

"I don't have any money to leave you," Gordon continued. "As you know, I ran away from home when I was fifteen and haven't seen my folks since, not that I would have got much from them, anyway. But I hope you'll take what I have to offer and remember your old man by it."

Trout resisted the urge to roll his eyes. He knew Gordon was trying to get them to feel sorry for him. Well, he wasn't going to do it. He gritted his teeth and looked at Jade and Heaven, both on the verge of tears. They were buying all of this! His anger toward Gordon mounted. Did he really think that just because he was dying, his children were going to forgive him everything? He looked Gordon squarely in the eyes.

"I don't care about an inheritance," he said. "I never figured on getting anything from either one of you. But I'll tell you something, Gordon. I am not going to forgive you just because you're dying. You're right; you weren't the best dad. You weren't even close. You were a shitty father. You know what? You two weren't even parents! You were assholes I was cursed to live with until I was old enough to get away!"

"Trout!" Heaven admonished.

"What, Heaven? What are you protecting them for? They didn't give a crap about you! They let you get raped and then didn't lift a finger to try and get you back!"

Heaven started to cry. Gordon glared at Trout, his jaw set. Lotus rolled cigarettes furiously, her small eyes flashing from person to person and then back to her tobacco.

"Look," said Trout, "I'm not trying to hurt you or make you feel guilty. I'm sure I couldn't even if I tried. I just need you to tell the truth. I can't sit here and pretend that there is all this love and tenderness between us. I'm sorry you're dying, Gordon. It's the shits, really, it is. But I'm even sorrier for the way you lived your life. I, for one, cannot forgive you for what you did to us. I'm sure you don't remember most of it as you were usually drunk as hell when you beat us—"

"He didn't beat you," Lotus said coldly.

"Yeah, he did."

"He hit you. He didn't beat you."

"Oh. Excuse me. I didn't realize there was a difference."

Lotus got to her feet and stuck her tired, old finger in Trout's face. Trout felt like he knew the tip of her right index finger better than her face.

"All right, Trout, that's enough. Gordon is dying here, and I have been taking care of him day and night. I'm not gonna stand here and listen to your shit anymore. If you have something nice to say, say it. Otherwise you can get the hell out."

Gordon laughed weakly. Trout stared back at Lotus, daring her to push him further.

"Must've been tough, taking care of Gordon," Trout said. "I know that taking care of people doesn't come naturally to you."

"Get out!" Lotus yelled and shoved him in the chest.

Trout stumbled backward, not because of Lotus's strength, but because he was surprised that she'd actually shoved him. Like he was still a little kid.

"Fuck you," he said and turned and walked out of the room. He went outside and walked toward the road, not sure where he would go, just feeling the need to walk. He heard the door of the house close and Heaven calling after him. She ran to catch up.

"Are you all right?" she asked.

Trout nodded and then immediately shook his head.

"I'm sorry," Heaven said. "I'm sorry I said you were mean to them. I didn't want to ... " she paused, "acknowledge how mean they are to you. To us."

"Yeah, well, now you know."

Heaven handed him his coat, and he put it on. They walked up the road, away from Winnie's driveway, in the opposite direction of the road that led to town. Trout realized he'd never walked up this road before. Strange. He thought he knew all of Cielo. He fingered the letter inside his coat pocket.

"I just don't know what I'm doing here, Heaven. What do I want from these people? An apology? Did I think that because seven years have gone by, they somehow learned to be kind? How to be grown-ups? I mean, what are we doing here?"

Heaven didn't say anything, just studied the ground. The road had quickly deteriorated into two deep, rocky ruts overrun with weeds. They navigated it in silence until the ruts turned into faint paths that eventually became meadow, and then they were standing in the middle of thigh-high, October grass. The wind whipped around them, and a snowflake fell on Trout's eyelash. He pulled his coat tight.

"Let's go," said Heaven, raising her voice above the wind. Trout nodded but didn't move. He turned and looked out over the slim valley below. He pointed to a square in the distance.

"There's Forest's house."

"Let's go," Heaven repeated and started walking.

Trout followed. His cheeks were growing numb with cold.

Michael was waiting for them in the driveway. "I was worried," he said to Heaven, his arms outstretched.

Trout scowled at him. "She was with me."

He walked past them and into the house. He walked past Lotus at the kitchen table, her head bent over her drawing pad, and went to stand in the doorway of Gordon's room. Jade had his feet propped up on the bed. An unlit cigarette dangled from the corner of his mouth, and he was busy rolling a second one. He winked at Trout in the doorway and then licked the rolling paper shut and leaned over to place the cigarette between Gordon's lips. Jade struck a match and lit both cigarettes. Gordon inhaled deeply and sighed. Trout opened his mouth to say something and then decided against it. Gordon peered over at him.

"I saw you about to say something."

"No, I wasn't."

"Come here," said Gordon, and patted the bed beside him.

Trout hesitated and then went over to stand beside the bed. Jade finished rolling a third cigarette, lit it, and handed it to Trout. Trout contemplated it before taking a drag.

"These things will kill you," he said to Gordon.

"Good."

Trout's hand wandered into his pocket and again fingered the letter. He felt the afternoon slipping away.

"I understand your anger, Trout," said Gordon. "I really do. I had a lot of anger toward my dad. I hated both my folks. Man, you think you had it bad? My dad used to whip us. Honest to God. I got tied up in the barn so many times. I'd be left out there for hours, knowing what was coming. My dad would come in only when he was good and drunk. And you know, drunk people are strong. Everybody thinks you get all floppy and uncoordinated when you're drunk. Well, that's only if you're a happy drunk. A mean drunk gets strong as hell. Like they're on PCP."

"Yeah, I know," said Trout.

"I'm just sayin'. You had it easy. Try growing up with my dad, and we'll see how you do. Or Lotus's dad."

"No thanks," said Trout. "You were enough."

"The thing is, Gordon," said Jade, "it's hard to be pissed at you when you're like this. I mean, me and Trout, we came up here with a lot of stuff to say. But you're, like, all dying and sentimental. None of that other stuff seems important now."

"Well, what have you got to say? Now's your chance." Gordon put his thin arms behind his head and puffed cheerily on his cigarette.

Trout and Jade glanced at each other.

"It's cool," Jade said. "We're cool."

"I'd like to know," said Trout, "why didn't you ever come looking for us?"

Gordon handed his cigarette to Jade, who stabbed it out in the seashell ashtray. He shrugged. "I guess I assumed you didn't want to be found."

"Because you ran away from your parents," Trout said.

"That's right."

"You thought that's just the way it is."

"Pretty much. Kids stay with their parents too long in this country, anyway. I always knew you guys would leave when you were ready."

"And Heaven? What about her?"

"We did try to get her back, Trout. The state wouldn't let us have her."

"They let Jade have her."

"Yeah, I think they thought it was a better environment for her. Given everything."

"You guys didn't show up in court for the hearing. You missed your visits with her. Lotus was drunk and called the social worker an asshole."

Gordon laughed. "He was an asshole. He wouldn't let us take her to the park! To swing!"

"Because she was raped twenty feet away from your house! While you were harvesting your pot crop at the neighbor's!"

"Shit! Happens! Trout!"

"Not that kind of shit!"

"What do you want me to say? I'm sorry? For what? You wouldn't even be here if it weren't for me, Trout! I gave you life! I don't owe you anything else."

"Gordon," Jade said, "you don't really mean that."

Gordon looked at Jade, and it was as though it took his eyes a few moments to register who he was looking at. Then he laughed. "Naw, I don't mean it. LOTUS!"

Lotus came scurrying in. "What is it?"

"Get Heaven in here. I want to say good-bye to everyone."

"Okay. What about Nickel?"

"Who?"

"Never mind." She slumped out of the room.

Trout heaved a big sigh and hung his head down. He felt tired. Lotus reentered the room followed by Heaven, whose forehead was knotted with worry.

"What is it?" Heaven asked.

"Nothing," Gordon said. "I just don't know how long 'till I crash. I'm pretty tired these days. Come here. Scoot over, Trout."

Trout stepped back from the bed so Heaven could sit beside Gordon.

"Jade," said Gordon, "roll me another cigarette."

"I got it," said Lotus and went to take the tobacco pouch from Jade's hand.

"Just … let him do it!" Gordon said. "He's a big boy. Let our kids do something for once. It's not like they been here taking care of their old man! While he's *dying!*" Gordon laughed. Trout felt ill.

"Look," Gordon said. He patted Heaven's hand and gave her what Trout thought was supposed to be a loving look. Then he looked at Jade, Lotus, and Trout in turn. "I want everything out in the open before I die. So, I'm gonna say what I have to say, and then you're gonna say what you have to say, okay?"

They nodded.

"Heaven, you're the youngest, so I'm gonna start with you. You were a weird kid. You know that. I mean, not to us you weren't weird, but to everyone else. Lotus and

I tried to just let you be yourself. We wanted you to be free to figure out who you were and how the world works, so you had a lot of freedom as a kid. Much more than most. And all in all, I think that was a good thing, but there was a price to pay. We couldn't be there for you all the time, and so we let you run around and encounter life's beauty. But one day, you encountered life's evil. Acting through Colin, we think."

"We *know*," said Heaven.

"And I'm so sorry I wasn't there. I should have been there for you. But if Ruth and Mark hadn't taken you to the hospital, you wouldn't have been taken away from us."

"She would have died," Trout said.

"Trout, cut it. The thing is, Heaven, we don't know what might have happened. But I do know this: Lotus and I were devastated when you were taken away. We tried as hard as we could to get you back, but the State don't like people like us. And we came to realize you were being taken care of in the foster home. And we were real broke then and intended to get you back when we had things a little more together, when we had a home again, but then Jade and Trout left and got you, and we knew you'd be okay. We just knew it, as only parents can. And now look at you! You're so beautiful! You're smart and talented. You know, things happen for a reason. I wish I could take back that … abomination. That …"

"Rape," Heaven said. "It was rape. You can say it."

"There could be a lesson in it for you that we don't understand yet."

Trout stepped up beside Heaven and took hold of her tense shoulders. "That's enough, Gordon."

Gordon turned to look at Jade. "Jade, you're the oldest, so I'll do you next. You were always my favorite. No offense, Trout and Heaven, but every parent has their favorite, and Jade was—is—mine. You were everything I wanted in a son. And what happened that night at Winnie's party was a travesty. But what can I say? From one man to another, you know how to pick your women! You couldn't understand it back then, and I don't know if you're old enough to now, but when you get to be a certain age, and there's a chance to make love to a seventeen-year old? You don't pass up that chance. I wasn't thinking, man! Had I stopped and thought about it, I never would have done anything to hurt you. I didn't realize you and Espi were so tight. But you know all of this. We've talked. What I really want to say is, nothing can make up for lost time. I understand that now. I've missed you, buddy. I wish we could have had more time together. And I'm sorry for that. Thank you for coming up here, Jade. It really means a lot." He patted Jade's hand.

"And Trout," Gordon said, resting his eyes on his middle child. "You and I have had a hard road to go. You're so like me, so much anger toward your dad. You'll work it out. Believe me. And yes, maybe I spanked you a little too hard here and there, but I did it out of love. I love you. I love all of you. Come here. Give your old man a hug."

Trout, Jade, and Heaven looked at one another, and then each took a turn bending over Gordon and giving him a hug. Then the three of them gathered in a semi-circle at the foot of the bed.

"Goodbye, Gordon," Heaven said quietly. Trout couldn't help but notice that her voice contained no trace of sentimentality. He looked over at her. There was just the barest glimmer of the old, mute Heaven staring back at Gordon, but on top of that was a hard resolve Trout recognized from his own face. Suddenly, Heaven looked more like Trout than anyone else. He smiled.

"Goodbye, Gordy," said Jade.

"Goodbye, Gordon," said Trout.

Gordon smiled and nodded. Then he waved one hand for several long moments, closed his eyes, and went to sleep.

His children stood and looked at him in silence, and then they turned and filed out of the room.

Michael sat at the kitchen table and smiled at Heaven as they entered from the hallway. "You okay?" he asked her.

Heaven shook her head and began to cry.

"Let's get out of here," Jade said. "Where's Boonray?"

"He went to the grocery store," said Michael. "He said he'd meet us there."

They took their coats off the rack near the door. An unspoken question about saying goodbye to Lotus floated in the air until Jade wordlessly opened the door and walked outside, buttoning up his coat. Heaven followed, Michael's arm around her. Trout paused to look at Lotus's drawing pad on the table just before he walked out. Whatever was on there had been erased. A trail of gray smudges was all that remained.

21

Saturday

They were silent as they drove away from Winnie's, apart from the sounds of Heaven crying. Trout and Jade sat up front with grim faces. Michael kept his arms wrapped around Heaven in the backseat. Nobody turned to look as they passed their old land, or Bob's trailer, Cookie's house, or anything else for that matter. It was as if their eyes were focused on a tiny point far ahead that was the future, and if they stopped looking directly at that point, they would lose it and be stuck forever in that town. Trout was reminded of how he'd felt when he and Jade had left as teenagers.

Trout pulled onto the side of the road in front of Garcia's and shut the engine off. Nobody moved.

Finally, Jade spoke. "Can we never speak of them again, please?"

Trout nodded.

Heaven said, "I can't believe they thought it was my fault I got raped."

"They're assholes," said Trout. He turned to look at his sister. "Don't ever forget that. They are assholes. They never deserved you."

Michael gave Heaven a squeeze.

"I don't see Boonray's truck," said Trout. "Should we wait for him or just head back to Santa Fe?"

"Wait," said Jade. "I told him I'd keep him company on the drive."

"Let's go inside and get something to eat," Trout said.

Trout was surprised to see Mr. Garcia still sitting behind the counter after so many years. He nodded as the four of them walked inside, and Mr. Garcia nodded back. The shop had been redone. Shiny coolers ran the length of one wall. New shelves ran up and down the store, allowing customers to pick things out for themselves rather than asking Mr. Garcia to fetch everything from behind the counter.

They split up and began to wander the store, picking up bags of chips and donuts and then setting them back down. Jade ruffled through cold burritos in one of the coolers. Heaven ran her hands over stacks of candy bars. Trout heard the door open and looked up. Over the top of the shelf, he could see a water-stained, brown cowboy hat. Cowboy boots clicked across the wood floor, and then a man turned the corner and headed straight toward Trout, whistling and holding onto the top of his hat. He looked up, and Trout squeezed the bag of chips he was holding so hard it exploded with a loud pop. Heaven gasped nearby. Colin looked in the direction of the sound, and before Trout had time to relish the idea of doing it, his fist flew through the air and landed hard on the side of Colin's jaw. Colin lurched sideways into the shelf, scattering bags and boxes across the floor. Heaven, Michael, and Jade rushed over. They stared dumbfounded at Colin, holding onto the shelf, and at Trout, his arm pulled back for the next punch. Heaven turned and fled from the store. Michael followed.

"You! Mother FUCKER!!" yelled Trout. "YOU SHOULD BE DEAD!"

Trout's entire body burned with hatred. He waited for Colin to get steady on his feet so he could hit him again. He wanted to send him down again and again until he was too broken to get back up.

"Hey!" called Mr. Garcia, walking as quickly as he could toward them. "*¡Fuera! ¡No se puede pelear!*" He carried a baseball bat.

"Come on, Trout," Jade said.

"No." Trout's blue eyes were fixed on Colin, whose arms shielded his face.

"Trout." Jade stepped around Colin and gently lowered Trout's arm. "There's nothing you can do," he said softly.

Colin lowered his arms and stood up. He squinted at them. "Trout? What the hell was that for?"

"*¡Fuera! ¡Fuera!*" Mr. Garcia yelled. Get out! Get out!

Trout couldn't think straight. All the emotion that had been building over the past weeks had become a storm inside of him. A truck pulled up outside. Jade and Colin turned at the sound of Boonray's voice.

"Boonray!" Colin called and backed out of the store.

Trout followed with Jade between them, Jade's hands up like a referee at a boxing match. Boonray stood by his truck, wiping grease from his hands with a dirty rag.

"What's up?" he asked as Colin strode quickly toward him, holding his jaw.

"Your buddy Trout clocked me a good one."

Boonray tossed the rag into the cab of his truck and eyed Trout. "You hit my dad?"

Trout looked around. Heaven and Michael stood a ways down the road, talking heatedly. Jade was leaning against Michael's car, lighting a cigarette and trying to act casual. Mr. Garcia stood inside the store with his bat, watching them. The town felt deserted.

Trout looked at Boonray. "This doesn't concern you. Anyway, he's not your real dad."

"What the hell is wrong with you?" asked Colin, his narrow eyes shifting between Trout and Jade. "You boys think you can come up here and prance your shit around?"

"Hey Colin," said Jade, "we didn't mean anything by it. Trout here just has a grudge, and you got in his path on a bad day."

"A grudge?" asked Colin. "What the hell you got a grudge for?"

Trout stared at him in disbelief. Was he actually going to make Trout say it?

"What do you think?" he asked Colin.

"Is this about your dad?"

"What? No! It's about what you did to my sister!"

"Now wait a minute," said Colin, backing up, his hands in front of him. "You don't know what you're talking about."

Suddenly Colin was on the ground, his cowboy boots flying up behind him. Nobody had seen Michael coming. Michael sat on Colin's back, pinning his arms to the ground with his knees, looking completely surprised.

"Is this the guy?" Michael asked. "Is this the one? Did I get him?"

"Get off of him!" Boonray yelled and shoved Michael.

Trout wasn't sure which happened first, but suddenly, Michael was punching Boonray, and Trout was wrestling Colin on the ground, and Jade was holding Heaven back. It was a blur of feet and legs and dust and tires, and then Colin's head slammed into Trout's nose, and blood came spewing out. He reached reflexively for his nose, and Colin flipped him onto his back and pinned him down, landing a hard punch on the side of Trout's head. Heaven yelled, and then she was pummeling Colin's back with her fists, shouting for him to get off. Colin punched Trout again. Jade grabbed Colin around the neck, and Boonray lunged at Jade. Trout rolled out from beneath Colin just as Boonray wrestled Jade off. Colin crouched on his hands and knees, coughing. His cowboy hat lay on the ground a few feet away. Heaven walked over and kicked a huge load of dirt up into Colin's face.

"That's for my brother!" she yelled.

Colin leaped to his feet and staggered away, coughing, his hands clutching his face. Boonray and Jade continued to wrestle next to the truck. Trout and Michael broke them apart with difficulty, and they leaned against the truck, heaving side by side. It wasn't the first time they'd fought each other. Trout watched Colin stagger inside the store. Mr. Garcia tried to prod him back out with the bat, but Colin pushed past the old man and disappeared into the back.

Trout felt his anger slipping away. That hadn't felt good at all. There was no feeling of revenge. Just perpetuation. Mr. Garcia opened the door and yelled that he was calling the cops. An empty threat as there wasn't a police station for miles, but he might get Lucio and his buddies, and that could be bad news.

"Here," Michael said and handed Trout a t-shirt from the back of his car. Trout thanked him and held his nose with it. "We should go," Michael said.

Heaven was crying and hugging Trout, whose face throbbed too much to hug her back. His left eye was quickly swelling shut, and he thought his nose might be broken. He climbed into the back seat of Michael's car and tilted his head back. Heaven climbed in beside him. Michael stayed outside helping Jade to his feet. Jade shook his head and motioned at Boonray, who said, "No," and then Jade and Michael walked to the car. Michael climbed into the driver's seat. Jade opened the passenger door and stuck his head inside.

"I'm gonna stay with Boonray," he said.

Boonray had gone into the store, presumably to look for his dad.

"Suit yourself," said Trout.

Boonray and Colin came out of the store. Colin, clutching a wet bandana to his eyes, got into his own truck and drove away slowly. Boonray walked over to them and gave Jade a hug.

"Sorry, man," he said.

"It's all right," said Jade.

Boonray sighed and stepped back. "I'm gonna go talk to Colin. I need to clear some shit up with him. I'll catch up with you tomorrow."

Boonray squatted down and looked at Trout through the window. He rapped twice on the glass, and Trout waved back. Like this, things were made okay between them.

"Lemme drive," Jade said to Michael, reading Trout's thoughts exactly. It was later in the evening than they had meant to be heading out, and the early-winter roads were slick with a thin layer of mountain ice.

Michael shrugged him off. "I can drive in the snow."

"Yeah, but this isn't snow; it's ice. It's different."

"I know," Michael said. "I grew up here, too, you know."

"You did?" Jade asked, surprised. He climbed into the passenger seat and closed the door. "I thought you were from, like, California, or New York."

"Where did you go to school?" Trout asked, glad they'd found something to talk about besides this terrible day. Why had he never met Michael before, if they were the same age? Everybody in Santa Fe seemed to meet eventually.

Michael backed the car onto the road, and they rolled quietly out of Cielo. Nobody turned to look back.

"I went to St. Mike's"

"Oh," said Trout and Jade together. Private school. Religious.

"I graduated early and went straight to school in Chicago. I moved back just before I met Heaven."

"Isn't that a little weird for you? Dating somebody who's in high school when you've already finished college?" Trout couldn't help himself.

"Trout!" Heaven admonished.

"No," Michael answered. "It was weird when I first met her. She was sixteen, and I was twenty. But, you know, we were in the drawing group together, and I got to know her before I asked her out, and, well, she's really mature for her age. Or I'm really immature. Either way, I think it works."

"How's your nose, buddy?" Jade asked, turning in his seat to look at Trout.

The car hit a bad patch of ice and went into a skid. Trout flew against the door. His head slammed into the window. Jade yelled, "OH SHIT!" and clutched the handle above the door. Michael, his lips set in a grim line, held firm the steering wheel and managed to right the car. They rolled down the hill, safe, past the canyon where so many had flown away.

PART III

22

May, 1977

"That's it, Trout. You can do it. One foot in front of the other."

His feet gripped the knotted rope as he balanced his way across. He felt like an idiot. The kids jumped and clapped as he reached the end and stepped onto the ground, a whole six inches below him. He knew it was supposed to be a challenge, and it was for the little kids, but he found it ridiculously easy like most things there.

Donna patted him on the back and instructed everyone to clean up and gather their things to go home. Trout helped Aaron, Donna's son, put away the wooden trucks and blocks. Trout was five years older than the next oldest student at the small school Donna ran out of her house. Donna let him come even though Lotus and Gordon didn't give her any money.

When everybody was ready, they stood in a circle and took turns thanking another person in the group for something they'd done that day. Aaron thanked Trout for helping him clean up the toys. Several other students thanked Trout for helping them with their schoolwork, which was a daily affair. Trout thanked Donna for lunch, as he did every day, and also thanked a little girl named Emily for giving him one of the paper pinwheels she'd made. A pang shot through him when she smiled at him. She was the same age as Heaven and had long, blonde hair.

He walked home along the highway, a straight, two-lane road with sage and wild sunflowers clustered along the shoulders. Red cliffs rose up on either side of him, and the electric blue sky hung vibrantly over the thin valley. Home, these days, was a small commune near Abiquiu called The Family In. Trout had been living there for seven months with Gordon, Lotus, and Jade. It had been started just a few years earlier by a man named Badger, who had taken an immediate liking to Gordon upon meeting him in the Taos co-op and had invited them to live there.

Trout turned off the highway and onto a dirt road that dipped down toward the river. When he neared the commune, his feet stopped, and his mouth fell open. Boonray's truck was parked in front of the coyote fence next to the garden. Trout broke into a run. Surely this was the first time he'd ever felt excited to see Boonray. He ran past the spindly, dry garden, up the walkway overgrown with weeds, through the opening in the fence that used to be a gate before it broke off, across the empty, dirt yard known as the Play Room, and into the Family Room.

The Family Room was a large, circular building that housed the main meeting area for the commune. Trout thought he'd find Boonray and Jade in it, but there were only a couple of kids playing with dolls on the rug. They looked up at Trout and smiled when he came in.

"You guys seen Jade?" he asked.

"I think he went to the river," said the younger.

Trout ran back outside and followed the winding paths that led to the Chama River. He ducked beneath the low-hanging branches of Russian olive and salt cedar, his feet nimbly navigating the uneven flagstone paths that wove through and around various one-room, adobe structures and teepees. He heard Gordon's laugh booming out from inside one of these. Trout reached the river and ran up the trail that led to the hot springs, panting and grinning.

There were four natural hot springs near The Family In, two of which had been built up into decent soaking pools. Jade and Boonray sat in the larger of these with a couple of women from the commune. Trout stripped off his clothes and climbed in beside Boonray with a loud whoop.

"Trout!" Boonray cried and immediately put him into a headlock. "You little punk! How you been? You sound just like your brother!"

"Jade said you were getting out!"

Boonray grinned. "Here I am. Free as a bird."

"You look good, Boonray. Older," Trout said.

"Yeah, well, that's what ten months in the slammer will do to you. Make you old. And wise."

"What were you in jail for?" asked one of the women. Her name was Lonnie. She was visiting her sister, June, who sat beside her. June had been living at The Family In for almost as long as Trout's family. Trout could tell that Lonnie thought the commune was weird. He couldn't blame her.

Boonray paused. "I'm trying to think of something really cool to say, but it was just auto theft."

"What would be a cool thing to be in jail for?" Lonnie asked.

"Rev-o-loo-shun!" Jade crooned.

June laughed and stood up. "I gotta go. You staying for dinner?" she asked Boonray.

"Sure!"

"Lotus is cooking. I'll tell her to make a place for you."

Boonray stared at June's figure as she climbed out of the pool. Lonnie narrowed her eyes at him and then muttered to June as they walked away, "The men here are fiends!" to which June laughed merrily.

"That's Gordon's new wife," said Trout when the women were out of earshot.

"No shit? Where's Lotus?"

"She's here," said Jade. "They're still married. Gordon's just all on some polygamy shit. Everybody here is."

"Wow!" said Boonray. "So, like, how many wives can you have?"

"As many as you want," Jade said. "There's no rules."

"Far out."

"Actually, it's kind of lame," Trout said. "People fight a lot. They say they're not jealous, but I think they are. Lotus especially."

"It's true," Jade agreed. "Lotus got mean. You think she was mean before, man, she's a bitch now."

Boonray laughed. "Where's your sister?"

They fell silent.

"What, they didn't get her back?"

Trout shook his head.

"So she's still in a foster home?"

"Yeah," said Jade. "We haven't seen her in a year."

They sat quietly, listening to the sound of the brown river rushing by. Thunder rolled in the distance.

"You know she said it was Colin who did that to her?" Jade finally asked.

"I heard that," said Boonray. "I guess there's no way of knowing, though."

"Well," said Trout, "she said it, so that's good enough for me."

"He's a total prick," said Boonray, "no bones about that. But I just can't see him doing something like that, you know?"

"Well, it doesn't affect you and me, brother," Jade said to Boonray. "We're still good."

The three of them laid their heads back on the moss-covered stones and stared out at the river.

"Tell us about jail," Trout said.

Boonray talked, and the two brothers listened. They were filled with respect as Boonray described what his day-to-day existence had been for the past months: the routine, the friends and enemies he'd made, the work duty he'd had to do on the side of the highway in a bright orange jumpsuit. Every story he told reminded them that he'd never said a word about Trout and Jade being with him when he'd stolen the Mercedes. He'd told the police Trout and Jade had walked home from Garcia's that day, and he had followed the Hollywood producer on his own, leaving his truck on a side road and coming back for it later.

"That sure was a nice car," Trout said.

"Yeah," Boonray agreed. "Totally worth ten months in jail, being able to drive it for a day."

They laughed.

Trout sat next to Boonray at dinner that night with Jade on Boonray's other side and the three of them across from Gordon and June. Lonnie and Lotus served. Lotus plopped stew in Trout's bowl so hard it splattered onto his shirt. "Thanks," he muttered. Gordon was loudly telling some story about Boonray beating him at pool years ago.

About thirty people were at dinner that night. When everyone had been served, Badger lowered his head and closed his eyes. This cued everybody to do the same, and then Badger, a muscular, blond man who Trout thought looked like a Viking from a comic book, said, "Lord, thank you for all you provide. We look forward to spreading your message of love in all we do. *Sat Nam.*"

"*Sat Nam,*" everybody answered.

"Are you guys Christians?" asked Boonray as they began to eat.

"We don't know what we are," Jade said.

"We're lovers," Gordon said. "We can be anything we want. We're free."

"Amen to that," Boonray said. "Being free feels pretty good." He smiled mischievously at Gordon. "I hear you're pretty free these days, Gordy."

"My name's Krishna now," Gordon answered.

Boonray tried to suppress his laughter but ended up spraying stew onto the table.

"It's okay," said Gordon, defensively, "you can laugh. I didn't do it so anyone would think I was cool."

"No, no," Boonray protested, "sorry. It's just a contrast, you know? From jail to this."

"We're all in jail," said Gordon. "We're in jail in our hearts and in our minds. Even in our bodies! Until we wake up as a people, as a nation, and see that our institutions are holding us prisoner, we'll just keep consuming blindly, following the laws made by other men blindly."

As Gordon talked, Trout couldn't help but notice that nearly everybody around the table listened with rapt attention, as they did whenever Gordon spoke. He knew why they viewed Gordon with such awe. It was the way he spoke, the emotion he could stir inside them with his ideas and voice. Trout had once felt proud when people looked at his father as these people did, but it had been a long time. He knew there was nothing to

Gordon's words, that it was just talk. They hadn't been at The Family In long enough for anybody here to know that the words went on and on without any follow-through. That was, anybody except Trout, Jade, and Lotus.

Trout looked over at his brother. Jade slouched low in his chair, stirring his stew slowly. He hadn't looked at Gordon with admiration since the incident with Esperanza. He was smirking and trying to get Boonray to see, but Boonray sat staring at Gordon, doing his best to listen politely. Trout could tell Boonray thought Gordon was off his rocker.

Gordon wore a loose-fitting, lavender muumuu that was embroidered with gold thread and slightly see-through. His hair and his beard were long and showed flecks of grey. He'd been putting on weight since they arrived at the commune, and Trout could faintly see hairy rolls of fat under the muumuu. June sat upright beside him, tilting her chin up and leaning into every word he said. She's proud of her "husband," Trout thought and looked over at Lotus seated at the end of the table. Lotus's face was tied up in the scowl that had become her signature expression since arriving at The Family In. She wore a gray sweatshirt, and her hair was unwashed. Trout felt sorry for her until she caught him looking at her and showed him her middle finger.

"Nice," said Badger, who had seen the gesture from the other end of the table. Lotus ignored him.

Trout didn't feel much like eating. Somebody had burned a bunch of incense before dinner, and the room smelled sickly sweet. He caught Jade's eye and motioned with his head that they should leave. Because of the rift between Gordon and Jade, and Heaven's absence, Trout had enjoyed a new closeness with his brother.

Jade nudged Boonray, and the three of them stood up, thanked Lotus for dinner, and carried their bowls into the kitchen.

"Where ya goin'?" Gordon called after them.

"Guy stuff!" Jade called back. "Teenagers! You know!"

They washed their bowls quickly and trounced out to Boonray's truck.

"That soup was foul!" Boonray exclaimed.

"Yeah, we know better than to try Lotus's cooking," said Jade. "Did you eat much of it?"

"Just a bite. It was hard to eat with Gordon's tits staring at me."

Trout laughed. They pulled the truck out and onto the highway. Jade had persuaded Boonray to let him drive. He whooped and pounded the roof as they sped into town.

"I love this truck, man!" Jade yelled. "Where we going?"

Trout was sure Boonray would suggest a strip club or bar in Española, but Boonray surprised him by saying, "Let's get some beers and head out to the lake."

They bought beers and burritos at the convenience store, gassed up the truck, and drove to Abiquiu Lake. They swam in the cold, May water, jumped off the high, red cliffs, and lounged in the evening sun.

"I feel old," Trout said, propped up on his elbows and staring out at the water.

Jade and Boonray laughed hard.

But he did feel old. He puffed on his cigarette, sipped his beer, and thought about how to get Heaven back. "We should get out of here."

"We just got here," Boonray said.

"No, I mean out of *here*. Out of this place."

Jade sat up. "What do you mean, little bro?"

"I mean, are we just gonna stay at the commune with Lotus and Gordon? What are we doing there? They're totally off on their own trip, and that place is so fucked up!"

"It's pretty bad," Jade agreed, looking at Boonray. "There's just a ton of drinking and drugs. It's way overboard. The whole 'married to everyone' thing is a joke. They all fight; nobody wants to do anything. The fact that we actually all sit down for a meal is a huge feat. They're probably having a big argument right now."

"Hmmm," said Boonray. "Drugs, booze, women, don't have to do anything. I don't know, guys. It sounds pretty good to me!"

"It's not," Trout said. "Believe me. Hang around for a while, and you'll see."

When it got too cold to swim, they walked through the dark trees to the truck and drove to a nearby canyon, where they sang loudly and listened to their voices echoing back from the curved walls.

Boonray decided to stay at the commune for a week. He had a bed made up in a small teepee and quickly made a girlfriend out of June, which Gordon was not too happy about. It made Lotus smirk, though, and Jade walked around saying things like, "What goes around comes around," and, "To each his own."

School ended for Trout, and without that daily distraction, he found his mind dwelling more and more on Heaven. He had a terrible, gnawing feeling that she needed him. So the morning when the blue truck drove up and beeped its horn, Trout was already running down the path toward it before Mark and Ruth had finished climbing out. He threw his arms around Ruth's middle and asked, "Did you come to take me to see Heaven?"

"I confess that is exactly why we came," Ruth said. "Let's go talk to Gordon and Lotus."

"No, no, no!" Trout protested, afraid his parents wouldn't let him go. "Let's just go!"

Lotus and Gordon didn't seem to care, though. Lotus gave Ruth and Mark an icy stare and said, "Go ahead. They won't let you see her, anyway." To which Gordon added, "Tell those sons of bitches I want my daughter back!"

Trout filled Ruth and Mark in on the way to Santa Fe.

"After our house burned down and Heaven was taken away, we went to live in Taos. Heaven was in Taos with a different family than the one she's with now, but Lotus and Gordon made the social workers mad. Also, they were supposed to do some parenting classes that they didn't want to do or they missed or something. I wasn't allowed to go with them to visit Heaven. Jade wasn't with us then. He was with Boonray until Boonray got arrested, and then he stayed with some people in Dixon. Lotus, Gordon, and I were living in the van. Well, then I saw you guys, so you know all that.

"Let's see, it started to get too cold to stay in the van anymore, and we'd met Badger by then, and he invited us to The Family In. Gordon and Lotus said they couldn't get Heaven back anyway, as long as we were living in the van, so we moved into the commune. That was ... November. I guess sometime after that, Heaven was moved to a different family in Santa Fe. That's the last I heard. Once in a while, a caseworker comes to see Gordon and Lotus, but nothing's happened yet. I don't think they'll get her back."

"Why not?" Ruth asked.

"Because they're doing drugs. Heroin. Gordon has two wives and wants another. Lotus doesn't care about anything anymore. That commune's a wreck."

"Well, not all communes are like that," Mark said. "Just some."

They stopped for lunch at a taco place on Santa Fe's busiest road. They sat at a round, cement table in the sun. An idea had been growing inside Trout ever since Ruth and Mark drove up that morning. He chewed his crisp tacos and thought about how to suggest it. Unable to think of the right words, he climbed into the truck when they were done and rode wordlessly between them. Ruth held his hand along the way and began squeezing it firmly when they turned off the main road onto a smaller one and even more firmly when they pulled into a small trailer park. Trout's heart sank. Is this where Heaven was living? He had pictured her in a big house with lots of toys and other kids, a big yard, and maybe even a dog.

Mark parked beside a long, blue trailer and shut the engine off. An apple-shaped woman came to the door of the trailer and peered out. She waved and stepped onto the trailer's tiny, metal porch. Ruth opened the truck door, and the woman called, "Patty's not here yet!" Ruth nodded and shut the door again.

"What's going on?" Trout asked, craning his neck to see into the dim trailer.

"We have to wait for the social worker," said Ruth.

Two tricycles sat next to the trailer. One was pink and shiny, the other red and rusted with one wheel smaller than the other. A round, plastic table and matching chairs sat next to a chain-link fence edged by tall weeds and pieces of trash.

A car pulled up beside them, and Ruth and Mark stepped out. Trout followed. The woman who climbed out of the car wore a clean, black suit and carried a pink purse, out of which she immediately pulled a lollipop that she handed to Trout.

"I'm Patty," she said. "You must be Trout."

Trout nodded and stuck the lollipop in his pocket. Patty greeted Ruth and Mark, and they walked to the trailer. Trout could tell that they'd all met before, and he wondered when and where. The apple-shaped woman opened the trailer door and ushered them in.

It was dark and smelled like corn chips. After Trout's eyes adjusted, he saw that they were standing in a surprisingly large living room. The walls were covered in fake wood paneling, and the carpet was brown and orange. A glass-topped coffee table sat in front of a sagging, orange couch, next to which stood a large entertainment center with the biggest TV Trout had ever seen. To his right was a kitchen and dining area, well lit by a window and overhead, fluorescent lights. A bowl of fruit sat on the shiny counter. To his left was a dim hallway. He could hear muffled conversation happening somewhere down there.

Before he thought about it, he started to walk toward the voices. Ruth began to call after him but stopped. Several doors led off the hallway, which was narrow and of the same fake wood paneling. When he got to the last door on his right, he stopped and pushed it open. Heaven sat on the floor with another girl about the same age. They had a board game set up between them. Two small beds were pushed against opposite sides of the room with a small, pink desk between. Dingy, orange curtains covered the small window. Several shelves lined the walls alongside the beds, holding books, stuffed animals, and toys.

Heaven looked up. Her hair was brushed and gleaming, and she had a blue ribbon tied around her head. She stared at Trout. The other girl stared too, a well-chewed ballpoint pen sticking out of her mouth. She had short, curly, blonde hair and blue ink around her mouth.

"Hi," Heaven said.

"Hi," said Trout. "Can I come in?"

Heaven nodded, and the little girl with the pen in her mouth eyed him suspiciously. Trout sat down beside them. His heart pounded in his chest.

"I'm Trout," he said to the girl. She sucked on her pen and stared at him.

"That's Theresa," Heaven said. "She's Becky's daughter."

"Is Becky who you live with?"

"Yeah," said Heaven. "Becky and John. And sometimes Alex."

"Oh. What are you guys playing?"

"Operation," Heaven said. "You try and operate on this guy without touching this thing to the sides. Watch." She leaned over the game and concentrated on grasping a plastic heart with a pair of small tweezers. Trout watched her closely. She looked significantly older to him. Her blue dress was new and made of velvet with a white sash around the middle.

"It's hard," said Theresa, staring intently at Trout.

Heaven succeeded in removing the heart. She held it up and beamed at Trout.

They passed the next hour playing with the games and toys in the room. Heaven wanted to show him everything. "I have a lot of toys here," she said, sitting on the bed, surrounded by the contents of the shelves. Theresa jumped on the other bed and did flips. She was trying to land on her feet but kept thumping down on her back. She jumped higher and nearly landed on her feet, but they slid out from under her, and she whacked her head on the wall. It couldn't have hurt too badly, Trout thought, because the wall was so thin it visibly bowed outward when it met her head. She started crying nonetheless, and Becky bustled in and shooed them into the living room.

Heaven ran to Ruth and climbed onto her lap. Trout sat on the orange couch next to Mark, and Theresa sat on Becky's lap in an armchair across from them. Trout decided to bring up his idea from earlier in the day.

"I was thinking," he looked at Mark, "you guys could adopt Heaven."

Ruth and Mark looked at each other and smiled sadly. Ruth shook her head. "It's not that easy," she said.

Heaven came over to sit by Trout. She wrapped her small arms around him and said, "I want to be with you."

"I know, Hevy, I want to be with you. But I don't think Gordon and Lotus will take care of you."

"You can take care of me," she said. "Kids do it. I'm reading this book called *The Boxcar Children*, and they all live in a train."

"Sakes alive!" Becky exclaimed. "You are not going to be wandering off to live in a train yard! Not when you have a perfectly good home here. Don't you worry, little girl. Everything's gonna work out fine."

But Heaven dug her nails into Trout's arm and looked at him imploringly. It really did smell strange in that trailer, Trout thought. It was dim, and Becky was stroking Theresa's head, laughing and humming. She seemed nervous. Trout's eyes searched Heaven's face, looking for the silent signals they used to communicate with. She closed her eyes and sighed, and it was suddenly clear to him that Heaven was incredibly sad. Maybe she had toys and clothes and school and a regular life, but she was with strangers. He put his arms around her, and they hugged and rested on the couch.

The trailer door opened, and Patty came inside.

"Everything okay in here?" she asked.

"Fine, fine," Ruth said. "Is it almost time?"

Heaven gripped Trout tightly. "Please, please, please," she whispered. "I don't want to be here."

"I'll come get you," he whispered back. "I promise, Heaven. Just a little while longer, okay?"

"Do you swear?"

"I swear. I'll write you letters until then, okay?"

"Okay."

They hugged good-bye, and then Trout walked out with Ruth and Mark. He turned to look at Heaven. She stood in front of the orange couch. The blue ribbon had slipped partway off her head, and she waved at him. He waved back, and then the door closed, and she was gone.

On the ride back to Abiquiu, he devised a plan. He would have to get a job in order to save money. Maybe work at the convenience store over the summer or for Badger, who sometimes worked construction off the commune. He could save enough to buy a car for Jade, and then they could get Heaven and move into their own house. He was envisioning it—he could see the yard with a swing set and maybe a dog—as he fell asleep with his head on Ruth's lap.

23

June, 1977

The river flooded, and people started getting sick. Lotus was curled in a ball on her side, throwing up into a pot by the bed every hour or so. In between, she'd stagger to the outhouse or the woods with diarrhea. Lonnie had taken June to the hospital when June started seeing blood mixed in with her stools, but they'd sent them away, saying there was nothing they could do, just ride it out for a week or so. It was Badger who figured out that the flood had caused the outhouse to leak into the creek they drank out of. Gordon was pissed.

"Who the hell builds an outhouse above their drinking water!" he roared.

"I didn't build it," Badger said weakly from his bed on the lawn. "It was here when we moved in."

Trout was sicker than he could ever remember being. Boonray and Lonnie were the only two who were spared: Lonnie because she never drank out of the creek, instead carrying her own water everywhere while people laughed behind her back and called her "city," and Boonray because, well, who knew?

"I've had all this shit before," he boasted. "I grew up sick as a dog, drinking out of puddles and killing my own pigs for dinner. Ain't nothin' can get me sick now."

Boonray surprised Trout by showing up with gallons of clean drinking water for the commune. He even pulled a thermometer from his shirt pocket and took Jade's temperature. Then he looked at Trout and said, "Aw, what the hell, Troutcito. I'll save you, too," and put the thermometer in Trout's mouth.

Trout was so sick he forgot about his plan to rescue Heaven. Days later, when he no longer felt like a giant hand was twisting around inside his gut, wringing bloody diarrhea out of him, he found himself sitting across from Jade, weakly eating a bowl of soup Lonnie had made. Jade was thin-faced and pale.

"Thanks for the soup, Lonnie," said Jade.

Lonnie was washing dishes on the other side of the room. "You're welcome," she replied. "I made a big batch. Make sure everyone gets some. You all need your strength to pull this place back together."

Trout eyed Jade over his bowl. Jade sucked his soup up in slow, methodical bites.

That afternoon, Lonnie and June packed up Lonnie's car and left for Boston. June was sniffling as she said good-bye to everyone, but when she hugged Trout, he was sure he saw relief in her eyes. Gordon draped a strand of beads around her neck and muttered something into her ear to which she nodded, and Lotus scowled. Then, she kissed Boonray on the cheek and rode off, probably back to college. Boonray walked over to where Trout and Jade stood on the edge of the dusty garden and shrugged.

"Another one down," he said. "What say we go for a swim?"

Their strength came back bit by bit, and in a few weeks, Trout and Jade were working alongside Gordon, Badger, and the other men of the commune as they constructed a new outhouse in a better spot. A renewed energy had infused The Family In after the E. coli outbreak, and once the outhouse was finished, they went on to build a swimming hole in the river, replaster the Common Room, overhaul the garden and get some plants growing, and clean the place up in general. At night, they stayed up late, drinking and doing drugs. Gordon was usually at the forefront of the parties, encouraging everyone to get crazy and then sometimes berating them if they went too far.

Trout was by Jade's side whenever possible. They went around shirtless and had soon turned rich shades of brown. Trout's hair had grown long again and turned a brilliant blond in the summer sun. He wrote Heaven as he'd promised, assuring her that it wouldn't be much longer until he came to get her, but he wondered to himself how he would ever pull it off. He thought about different ways to propose a plan to Jade for the two of them to head out on their own but was reluctant to bring any of them up until he was sure they'd work.

It was hard for Trout to read Jade anymore. He participated in the work with everyone else and seemed happy, but Trout suspected that it was Boonray who was keeping Jade's spirits up. The two of them spent most of their time playing their guitars and talking about "going somewhere." Trout began to grow increasingly afraid that one day, Jade and Boonray would disappear without him.

As the end of June approached, everyone started getting ready for the commune's annual summer party. The commune was cleaned up, the grounds weeded, sweat lodges were built along the river, and buses of people began to arrive for the weeklong event, bringing all sorts of food, musical instruments, and games with them. Dogs and children ran around, flags fluttered from the trees, and laughter and music rang out. Trout walked through, looking at it all as if in a dream. He knew hardly any of the visitors, and it was surreal to see so many strangers cooking in the kitchen, soaking in the hot springs, and going in and out of the outhouse. He watched as Jade and Boonray sought the attention of the same girl, and then he laughed when she rejected them both for another girl. He joined a group of kids around his age who had nicked a joint and spent the afternoon stoned and climbing the nearby cliffs with them. He befriended a family he liked and helped them cook dinner in their van one night, then watched with fascination as the mother read a bedtime story to the youngest son. And he watched Gordon and Lotus in their strange dance of hatred and dependency, each trying to hurt the other more using whoever and whatever came along.

As the days went by, the weeklong event devolved from a camping trip in the mountains to a semi-hostile free-for-all. Most of the families with children left, but a few stayed as the harder drugs appeared, and the quiet hours disappeared. Trout drudged through, finding food where he could and snatching sleep in fragments. He no longer sought Gordon and Lotus out for anything. Since arriving at The Family In, they had ceased any form of parenting, perhaps assuming there were enough adults around to look out for him or that he was old enough now and didn't need them. And he had come to feel that he didn't need any looking out for. If anything, he made it a point to help some of the other kids who wandered around hungry and tired, their parents assuming that somebody else would look after them.

One evening, he was standing ankle deep in the river, taking a piss, when a toddler came floating by, face down. Trout bounded out into the waist-deep water and snatched her from the mild current. She was bright red, coughing and sputtering, and clung fiercely to Trout as he carried her to shore. He looked up to see Jade watching from a few yards away. Jade reached for the baby, his face set in the grim expression he'd been wearing more and more, and wordlessly carried her back to her parents who were soaking in the hot springs upstream, oblivious that their daughter was gone.

Late that night, Trout and Jade made beds up in the hut they usually slept in.

"I'm so tired," Trout moaned, crashing onto his pillow.

"Let's go camping tomorrow," Jade said, turning the kerosene lantern down. "You, me, and Boonray. It'll be good to get away from this scene."

Trout smiled and fell asleep.

He awoke minutes, maybe hours, later. It was dark except for a dim, red glow from the bonfire burning across the grounds. He could hear laughter and yelling from the people around the fire, but that wasn't what had woken him. He listened intently. There was a scuffling sound coming from inside the hut. A man's voice started muttering.

"Can't keep 'em away. I'd have to kill 'em. It's too dark."

Trout sat up and peered into the pitch black of the hut. Jade snored in his bed. The man shuffled closer to Trout's bed. Trout's heart pounded audibly. His hands reached out to the bedside table and groped for matches. He knocked the lamp to the floor with a loud crash, and suddenly, the man had hold of Trout's head. He started screaming, "CAN'T KEEP 'EM AWAY!!! I'LL KILL 'EM!! YOU DON'T KNOW WHAT I CAN DO!!!"

Trout felt a cold sting on his throat.

"JADE!!!" he started to yell. But before his brother's name was out of his mouth, the man fell on the bed, unconscious.

Jade struck a match, and his face sprang out of the darkness. He picked the lamp up and lit it. Trout looked down at the man lying unconscious in front of him. He didn't recognize him.

"Are you okay?" Jade asked.

Trout nodded. There was a log on the floor. "Did you hit him with that?"

"Yeah," said Jade. "Jesus, I didn't know he had a knife!"

Trout touched his throat and withdrew his fingers to see blood. Jade stared, horrified, at the cut on Trout's neck.

"Who the fuck is that?" Trout asked, beginning to shake and tremble. He kicked at the man, who didn't stir, and then picked up the knife and tossed it across the hut.

"He got here today with a few other people," Jade said. "They were smoking PCP."

"What's that?"

"Angel Dust. Fucked-up shit."

Jade reached under his bed and pulled out his duffel bag. He started shoving clothes into it. "Come on," he said to Trout. "We're going."

Trout jumped off his bed and joined Jade, packing his few clothes and possessions into the same duffel bag. They walked silently to Gordon's hut in complete agreement on the decision they hadn't yet spoken aloud. There were three beds inside Gordon's hut, two of which were empty. The other was occupied by Lotus. Jade crept past her and rummaged quietly through Gordon's things. Trout watched as Jade pocketed all the cash he could find, then crept back out, pausing to look at Lotus for a few moments. He shook his head and rejoined Trout at the door. They went to one of the teepees next, where Boonray lay fast asleep next to a woman. Jade woke him up and explained what had happened.

"Are you shitting me?" he asked. He looked at Trout, who raised his chin so Boonray could see the line of blood.

"We're getting out of here," Jade said. "Will you drive us?"

"Where are you going?" Boonray asked as he dressed.

"Ruth and Mark's," Trout answered without thinking.

"Yeah," Jade agreed. "That's great."

Boonray stepped out of the teepee, and Jade assessed his empty hands.

"Are you coming back here?" Jade asked.

Boonray looked from one brother to the other. "Shit, not if you guys aren't here." He slipped back into the teepee and reemerged a few minutes later with an armload of clothes and his guitar. "I travel light," he said.

They set off toward the truck. Trout could hear Gordon's laugh booming toward them from the fire.

"You guys wanna say good-bye?" Boonray asked.

"I'm too tired," Trout replied.

"Me too," said Jade.

The truck started with a roar, and they backed out over the creek, turned around, and drove out of the driveway for the last time. The road that night was beautiful, like a long, dark river sliding underneath them as they sped through the starlit canyons. There was no one else on the road, and the bushes and stars looked like quiet spectators to their departure.

"Wait'll you see Heaven," Trout mumbled as he was falling asleep. "She's got such a pretty dress."

24

October 28, 1984

Sunday

"Things just don't feel settled," said Heaven. The three siblings sat around their living room with Michael, Laura, and Holly. "I keep thinking that once Gordon dies, everything will just ... resolve. But maybe it won't be that way."

"There's no making peace with him," said Trout.

"No ... But I can make peace in myself, right?"

Laura reached over and squeezed Heaven's hand. "I think that peace can take a long time to reach. And that's okay."

It was the day after the confrontation with Colin in Cielo. Trout lay on his back in the middle of the floor. Laura had placed several acupuncture needles in him to help with his injuries. After she placed the last needle, everybody else wanted some, so now they were all sitting and talking with needles protruding from their faces, hands, and feet.

"No offense," said Holly, "but Gordon is sort of a narcissist. I don't think you're going to get any resolution with him."

"I know," said Heaven.

"I get it, Hev," said Trout. "I've been feeling it, too. I haven't said everything I want to say. I have this letter I wrote to Gordon, and I can't bring myself to read it to him. I don't know why."

There was a series of quick raps on the front door, and then Boonray walked in. "Cool!" he said. "Pinhead party!"

"Hey Boonray!" called Trout and Jade. Trout couldn't turn his head for all the needles in it, but he felt a surge of warmth in his chest at the presence of his loyal friend.

"Guys, Gordon went into the hospital." Boonray plopped down next to Jade and started twisting the needles in Jade's arm.

"Ow! What do you mean?" said Jade, delivering a good wallop to Boonray with his free arm.

"Something happened. They freaked out. Winnie drove them down. They're here in Santa Fe."

One more chance to read his letter. It felt like fate. "Laura, can you take the needles out?" asked Trout. "I need to go do this."

Laura silently removed the needles, then helped him sit up.

"I'm coming with you," she said.

Trout nodded. Laura took the needles out of the others, but they didn't make a move to get up.

"Go ahead, Troutcito," said Jade. "You got this."

Laura drove them to St. Vincent's Hospital. They found Gordon in the Intensive Care Unit. Lotus sat in a chair nearby, her eyes closed. Trout and Laura walked up to his bed. Laura stared at Gordon's emaciated body, then into Trout's face.

"He's so tiny," she whispered.

Trout nodded. The letter in his pocket suddenly felt like an assault weapon. There was no way Gordon could handle anything more Trout had to say. He was dying. An oxygen mask covered his mouth, helping him breathe.

Laura glanced at Lotus. "Is that your mom?" she whispered to Trout.

Trout nodded again. He walked over to Lotus and shook her awake. She opened her eyes and stared at him dully. She was exhausted, Trout realized.

"Why did you guys come here?" Trout asked.

"He was in too much pain," said Lotus. "We needed more morphine."

That was when Trout saw the IV drip plugged into Lotus's arm. Bands of tape crossed Gordon's forearm where the needle had been placed for his pain medicine, then removed by Lotus. Laura squeezed Trout's arm. He turned back to his father.

"This isn't right," said Trout. "He doesn't want to die here. He always told me, told us, that he didn't want to die in a hospital."

Laura stared at Trout hard for a few seconds and then walked over to Gordon and gently removed the oxygen mask. "Where does he want to die?" she asked.

Trout smiled. He picked the phone up beside Gordon's bed and called Jade and Heaven to tell them the plan. While Laura finished removing the hospital supplies from Gordon's body, Trout tucked a blanket around Lotus and placed a pillow behind her head. She smiled. The clear fluid dripped slowly down its runway into her arm.

A few minutes later, Trout sat in the back seat of Laura's car, Gordon's head and shoulders lying across his lap. He cradled his father over the bumps and turns. Jade, Heaven, Holly, Michael, and Boonray followed behind. It was a short drive to the trailhead. They parked along the road, and Jade and Heaven came over to see Gordon.

"He hasn't opened his eyes at all," said Trout. "We don't have much time."

Gordon's breathing had become ragged and irregular. His mouth hung open on his slack face. Every once in a while, his face would contort in an expression of pain. Jade reached in the car and gently lifted Gordon into his arms.

"God, he weighs nothing."

Boonray set out on the path. The others followed silently. Trout knew Gordon would want to die in Cielo. Better yet on Truchas peak or in the middle of the forest somewhere. But Sun Mountain was the best they could do with the time they had. It was a large hill in Santa Fe that he and his siblings liked to climb. The path was steep and gravely. Scrubby piñon trees, chamisa, and sage bushes clung to the red sides. The late-afternoon light slowly changed from golden to pink. They climbed wordlessly. Trout and Jade took turns carrying Gordon. Heaven stayed close beside, one hand touching Gordon.

They reached the top before sunset, as Trout had hoped they would. The others stood nearby while the siblings settled onto the ridge, nestling Gordon between them so he could face the setting sun.

"Are you gonna read your letter?" asked Jade.

Trout pulled the letter from his pocket. He tore it into little pieces and tossed them down the hillside.

"No. I said everything I need to say. How about you two?"

Jade and Heaven looked at each other. "We're good," said Jade. Heaven smiled and nodded.

They each held a hand on Gordon and sat pressed together. The sun sank. The sky grew dark. The moon rose. And Gordon died.

That night, Trout held Laura in bed and cried. She stroked his hair and made shushing sounds. They said 'I love you,' to each other for the first time and made promises to be good to each other. In the morning, they all ate pancakes and cancelled work, school, and tests in order to tie up what they could. Gordon's body had been returned to the hospital. Lotus was back with Winnie, who wanted to arrange some sort of vaguely defined death-party for Gordon, which Trout didn't imagine any of them would attend.

Boonray and Jade pulled out their instruments and settled in the living room, playing goofy songs, trying to impress each other. Holly and Laura sat nearby, chatting and sewing. Heaven and Michael had their drawing supplies out and sketched the whole scene. Trout finished the breakfast dishes and leaned in the doorway, watching. There was something familiar about this. Like he had been in a place almost like it before. Laura patted the seat beside her on the couch, and he went over to sit down.

THE END